"Me" Time

Finding the Balance Between Taking Care of Others and Taking Care of Yourself

Jennifer Beall

"Me" Time
Finding the Balance Between Taking Care of Others and Taking Care of
Yourself

Copyright 2012 by Jennifer Beall

www.FindYourMeTime.com
Jennifer@FindYourMeTime.com

Published by
YourBalance Publishing
645 Baltimore-Annapolis Blvd., Suite 107
Severna Park, MD 21146

Because of the dynamic nature of the Internet, any Web addresses or links
contained in this book may have changed since publication and may no
longer be valid.

Book design by Rosamond Grupp

Printed in the United States of America.

1st Edition – August 2012

ISBN-13: 978-0615671741 (YourBalance Publications)
ISBN-10: 0615671748

To my daughter, April.

*I hope you never understand
what this book is about.*

Acknowledgements

I am grateful to the following people (and many more whom I have not named here) for making this book possible.

My parents, Jobie and June Riley, helped to make me the person I am today. My sister, Joelle Riley, has been a friend and someone who understands many of the struggles I have faced; she was also the first to suggest to me that our family operated like an alcoholic family.

My husband, Tim Beall, has loved and supported me even when that was not easy. Tim's family (now also mine) has made me feel like a part of the family from the first day I met them. My daughter, April, helps my inner child to come out and play and be spontaneous.

Kim McDowell, pastor of the University Park (Maryland) Church of the Brethren, has been the most long-standing and constant healing presence in my life, and is also a cherished friend. My acupuncturist, colleague, and friend Karen Moore has been my qi's best friend since 2004, and also edited my comments about acupuncture.

I have many friends who have supported and encouraged me, particularly Shelley Mowery, Gloria Kindy, Jenny Prince, Sharon Matthews, and the other members of the University Park Church of the Brethren. I have also gotten invaluable support from colleagues, particularly Donna Parker, Kathleen Horrigan, Rachel Strass, and Karlene Haines.

The faculty, staff, and students of Loyola University Maryland's Pastoral Counseling program gave me the best counseling training anyone could hope for, and are among the kindest, most thoughtful people I have ever met.

Mary Bieda, my first clinical supervisor at Chrysalis House, was the first to tell me that I had all the characteristics of an Adult Child of an Alcoholic; she guided me towards getting help with those issues.

All of my clinical supervisors have helped me through the very difficult process of becoming a therapist by both challenging and supporting me.

The staff and clients of Chrysalis House taught me much of what I know about alcoholism and addiction and tolerated my initial lack of knowledge.

I especially thank my private practice clients and others who have been courageous enough to engage in their own healing journeys and who have graciously allowed me to use some of their stories to bring this book to life.

And I thank you for deciding to take this journey, as well.

Note: many of the stories in this book are composites. In cases where examples refer to a specific person's experiences, names and details have been changed to respect confidentiality.

You will notice that the examples in this book are all about women. This does not mean that men don't struggle with these issues, as well, but in my personal and clinical experience it is more often women who feel an urgent need to address them.

Many of the examples relate to heterosexual women who are married and have at least one child. Again, it is not my intent to exclude people whose situations are different, such as those who are single, who don't have children, and/or who are in same-sex romantic relationships; the examples represent the women who most often come to me to address these issues.

Therefore, I invite you to change the examples as appropriate to fit your situation.

Contents

Introduction

Low self-esteem. Perfectionism. Wondering what "normal" is. Wondering who you are, and if you really matter. Feeling like an impostor who will be found out at any moment.

And spending significantly more time and energy taking care of other people than you do taking care of yourself.

Does any of this sound like you?

If the title and/or the questions on the back of this book caught your attention, I would guess that it's probably because, as one of my clients put it, you were "half raised." And if you were half raised you are probably an Adult Child (AC).

Adult Children had some of their most important needs (physical and/or emotional) go unmet when they were growing up. There are a variety of possible reasons for this, including having an alcoholic or chronically mentally or physically ill parent, a chronically ill sibling, parental divorce or separation, or a death in the family, among others. Having "half raised" parents is a common cause, because it's difficult for parents to give their children what they themselves were not given.

The term Adult Child fits well because, while you probably grew up very quickly in some ways, you most likely weren't given the tools and opportunity to grow up emotionally. Therefore you are an adult, but you have a hurt, confused child inside.

As you read this book it will be helpful to keep in mind a recommendation made in 12-step programs: to "compare in" rather than "compare out."

Comparing out means that you notice the differences between yourself and another person, such as, "I'm not as bad as she is!" or, "I didn't have nearly as difficult a childhood as she did!"

Comparing in, on the other hand, looks for commonalities. Think, "Did my experiences have a similar effect on me as hers did on her?" Your pain and struggles are your own, and they are always valid, whether or not you think you have the right to feel the way you do.

What Are the Goals of This Book?

I hope this book will help you to understand why you do, think, and feel some of the things you do. I hope that it will help you to choose new ways of thinking, feeling, and behaving that more closely match the life you would like to be living. And if you don't know what life you'd like to be living, I hope that the book will help you to figure that out, too.

My intention in writing this book is **not** to encourage you to hold resentments, or to blame yourself or other people for the way your life is or has been. That won't help you or anyone else.

My intention **is** to normalize your feelings and experiences, and also to teach you practical techniques that will help you to create the life you want and deserve.

Balance

As you read this book you will find that the idea of balance comes up again and again.

One of the most important types of balance is the one between being who you think you *should* be and who you actually *are*. Part of that is finding the balance between taking care of yourself and taking care of others.

There's no time like the present to start finding that balance. Otherwise you might find yourself going from an extreme caretaking role to the opposite extreme: caring mainly about what you want and need and ignoring others' needs and wants.

How Is the Book Set Up?

The book is divided into four sections with three chapters each.

Each chapter begins with a quiz. Not only will the quiz give you an idea of what the chapter is about; it can also help you to recognize ways in which the chapter might be relevant to you.

Each chapter ends with suggestions for "Putting It Into Action," including examples of how someone else has applied those suggestions. I hope that the examples will help you to find ways to apply them to your own life.

The first section of the book addresses the three issues that most often lead people to seek counseling with me. These include responsibilities, relationships, and setting and maintaining boundaries (such as being able to say no).

The second section looks at the source of these issues and suggests ways to begin to reverse their effects. This section addresses unmet needs, the nature of being an Adult Child, and getting in touch with the part of you that is still a child.

The third section explores physical and psychological results of growing up with family dysfunction, including feelings you might have about it and ways to work with those feelings.

The final section offers a variety of practical methods to change your thoughts, feelings and actions. This includes ways to challenge automatic negative thoughts, approaches that can be used to achieve and maintain balance, and guidance on balanced decision-making.

I invite you to read through the entire book, even parts that you think may not apply to you, because you never know where you might find new insights and new understanding. But you should also feel free to, as they say in 12-step programs, "Take what you like and leave the rest."

I will close this introduction with a story:

> *A man is walking on a beach that is strewn with starfish that have been stranded by the tide. He sees another man taking one starfish after another and throwing them back into the ocean. He questions the second man, saying, "There are so many starfish on the beach. You can't possibly get to them all. Do you really think you're making a difference?" To which the second man replies, as he throws another starfish into the ocean, "Makes a difference for this one!"*

Welcome to the book. May it make a difference for you.

Part I

Chapter 1

"Me" Time?
What's That?

1. Do you feel like you pretty much single-handedly hold your family together?

2. Are you generally in charge of making sure that things get done around the house?

3. If you have kids, are you usually the "taxi driver" who takes them to athletic practices, music lessons, etc.?

4. Do you feel like you're busy all of the time, but still can't get everything done?

5. Do you find yourself feeling resentful when someone else is relaxing while you're working?

If you said "yes" to any of these questions, you probably spend a lot of time taking care of other people and very little time taking care of yourself.

You have probably taken on a lot of responsibility at home, at work, and/or elsewhere. You probably feel overworked and under-appreciated. And I'll bet there are times you get *really* tired of it.

You may feel like Alicia, who finds herself resenting the fact that it seems she's always taking care of everyone else but doesn't get the same in return. It seems like every six months something happens to a member of her family. First, her daughter broke her foot playing field hockey and needed surgery. Then her husband had a heart attack and had to have triple bypass surgery. Then her brother, who worked as a roofer, fell off of a roof and was hospitalized, then in rehab, for months; when he got home he needed more help than his home healthcare worker could offer, and Alicia was usually the one who provided that help.

This reminds her of her childhood, when it seemed that her family wasn't very concerned about her well-being, in part because it seemed like some other member of the family was always having a crisis. Her parents always said that Alicia was "fine" and didn't need any help.

Even though there are often good reasons why others need her attention, Alicia often wonders, "When will it be my turn?"

If you're like Alicia, though, you might also be somewhat bothered by the concept of "me" time; that sounds so selfish!

Don't worry; I'm not suggesting that you become completely self-centered and only look out for number one. My intention (and the point of this book) is for you to find a balance between taking care of others and taking care of yourself. Neither extreme is a good idea; the goal is to find a healthy place in between the two.

Is Your Account Overdrawn?

You may have heard people say that you can't give someone else what you don't have. That seems obvious when you're talking about concrete objects; for instance, you can't give someone else a piece of cake if you don't have any cake.

But this principle also applies to intangible things like energy and time. Believe it or not, no matter how energetic you are, you can't keep giving more and more energy to meeting other people's needs without also replenishing that energy.

Think of it as an "energy bank." The bank won't let you take out more money than you have in your account, right? In fact, if you write checks for more than your checking account balance the bank charges you overdraft fees.

Some people bypass the bank account and use a credit card, sometimes to buy things they can't afford (or for emergency expenses that they can't cover); they may then find that their credit card bills become unmanageably high. Similarly, you might borrow against future energy and later find yourself with a big energy debt.

Only by doing things that replenish your energy (getting enough sleep, eating well, drinking enough water, exercising, and, yes, even taking the time to do things that you enjoy) will you have the energy available to give to work, family, and friends.

If you have a dog or a cat, take some time to observe him or her. Pets are great examples of living in the moment, not worrying about the future. Cats, in particular, tend to be very good at making sure they don't meet others' needs at their own expense. And they always make sure to get plenty of sleep!

Finding the Middle Ground

The name of the game here is finding balance instead of going to one extreme or the other. Unfortunately, the extremes are a lot easier to find than the middle ground. If you decide that you're only going to take care of other people and completely neglect yourself, that's pretty straightforward, although certainly not easy. If you go to the opposite extreme and worry only about yourself, that's also pretty easy to figure out, although (fortunately) it's difficult to sustain for most of us.

The challenge of the middle ground is that it involves constant decision-making. For instance, should I say yes in this case even when I want to say no, or is this a time that I should stand my ground and take care of myself? Can I find a compromise position that's good for both of us?

The balance of taking care of others and taking care of self is different for each person. Family members, friends, clergy, therapists, and others can offer feedback and suggestions, but only you can decide what the right balance is for you. If you're a perfectionist you might not enjoy the process of finding that balance, because it doesn't work perfectly at first; there's usually a lot of trial and error involved before a reasonable balance is achieved. And even then, there will be times that things will get out of balance and you'll need to make corrections.

What Makes You Worthwhile?

How do you define yourself? What do you think makes you worthwhile? Most of us, if we're honest, would admit that we determine our value by what we do, not who we are. And we have very high standards for ourselves where doing is concerned.

We look for external validation; if someone doesn't show us approval we're disappointed, because we don't feel like we did a good job unless someone else (preferably someone who has authority over us) tells us that we did.

If you believe in God (and maybe even if you don't), you probably at least say you believe that your very existence makes you valuable. But do you really believe that, deep down? If you don't believe it, how about trying it on for size?

Think about the fact that there are only so many varieties of facial features, complexions, hair, etc., and yet no two people (even identical twins) look exactly alike. No two people have the same personality. Might it be possible that your uniqueness gives you an important place in the world, no matter what you have or haven't accomplished?

I don't mean to imply that the things you do are unimportant; of course they're important. But they're not necessarily the most important things about you. If you suddenly became disabled and couldn't do the things you do now, you wouldn't be any less worthy a person than you were before.

Women as Caretakers

While there are exceptions to this, women on the whole tend to be caretakers. We take care of our partners, we take care of our kids, we take care of coworkers, and we often find other places that we can be caretakers, too: at church, in our children's schools, or in volunteer positions, for instance.

And if you grew up in a dysfunctional family, you learned to take even more responsibility for other people than you might otherwise have done. (More on that in chapter 2.)

Many women get a feeling of being worthwhile human beings from making themselves indispensable to others. In fact, many of us secretly (or not so secretly) believe that our families and possibly other things would completely fall apart if we weren't there to take care of them.

Let's start at home. How much do you do around the house? Do you do the laundry? Cook? Make sure the house is clean? Anything else? And how much do other family members do?

For many years most women stayed at home, and it was understood that wives took care of the cooking, cleaning, and other household tasks. Now that many women are in the workplace it can be hard to figure out how much, if at all, this should change. Should a woman who works 40 hours a week then come home and do all the cooking and cleaning?[1]

If you work outside of the home you may still try to single-handedly make sure the household runs smoothly. If you don't work outside of the home you may feel like you're not accomplishing as much as you could or should; if your "only" job is parenting and taking care of the house, shouldn't you expect to do it perfectly? (The answer, in case you're wondering, is no!)

Financial Responsibility

Some women who don't work outside of the home think they should have less influence over the ways the family's money is spent because they are not the ones who earn it. Or they might believe they have less of a say about finances if they work outside the home but earn less than their partners do.

More and more women are taking care of their families' finances, which can lead to taking more responsibility than belongs to them when it comes to making sure their families have enough money. This can be particularly difficult if their income is inconsistent.

This is true of Margaret, who is a self-employed massage therapist. Since Margaret pays the bills, and since she is the one who does not get a regular paycheck, she feels like it is her fault when her family has financial problems. She feels "less than" when she realizes that her credit score is lower than it once was because of this; it's as if people who check her credit will disapprove of her because she doesn't have perfect credit any more.

---

[1] For related articles, see Anne Glusker's "Go Ahead—Just Tell Me I Have It All" at http://anneglusker. com/HavingItAll.html and Anne-Marie Slaughter's "Why Women Still Can't Have It All" at http://www. theatlantic.com/magazine/archive/2012/07/why-women-still-can-8217-t-have-it-all/9020

Margaret feels fortunate, though, when she looks at what some of her friends are dealing with. For instance, Belinda is in a job she hates, but stays in it because of the benefits. She would really like to go back to school to become a teacher, but she doesn't feel like she can give up her current salary. She wishes things were more like they once were, when husbands were expected to earn enough money to support their families.

Responsibility for Children

No one in our families generates more responsibilities than our kids do.

If you have kids, chances are you've taken on more than your share of responsibility for meeting their needs. With the busy schedules that kids have today, that's quite a lot of needs! The long list of parental responsibilities includes making sure they get their homework done; getting them to sports practices, dance classes, and music lessons; keeping up with their medical and dental checkups; and more. All of this takes a lot of time and energy.

We also tend to take more than our share of responsibility for our children's behaviors. Amy has a 10-year-old daughter, Riley. Riley's teacher called Amy one day to tell her that Riley had been disrupting the class by talking too much. Amy's mother-in-law frequently suggested that Amy was solely responsible for Riley's behavior and that she didn't give Riley enough time and attention because she worked outside of the home. So Amy automatically assumed that Riley's misbehavior was all her fault.

She did not take into account Riley's natural talkativeness. She didn't think about the possibility that Riley might have been bored with the lesson that was being presented, or that Riley's friends might have had something to do with it, or that her husband and other authority figures also have an influence on Riley. Instead, she decided that she, as Riley's mother, was the sole determiner of her behavior.

Responsibility for Partners

It makes sense that we take a lot of responsibility for our kids; after all, parents have a great deal of influence in shaping their children. But many of us don't stop there; we also take responsibility for our husbands or partners and, by extension, our marriages.

Some women joke that their husbands are just big kids. They may treat their husbands as if they're not capable of taking care of themselves, and may do things for which their husbands could be responsible.

And, as they do with their kids, women might take more emotional responsibility for their husbands than necessary. They may take on their husbands' feelings and think it's their responsibility to fix them. And, if there are issues in their marriages, they may feel like it's their fault and, therefore, their responsibility to fix them.

Balancing Responsibilities

It's no wonder that we get resentful when it feels like we're responsible for everything and not getting any help, right?

I've got a question, though. Have you asked for help? Have you let other family members know what needs to be done so that they can do their share?

You may think, "No one tells me what needs to be done. I just figure it out and do it. Why can't anyone else do that?" That's a good point, but unfortunately it probably won't get you very far.

OK, so it would be nice if your husband already knew what needed to be done to help the kids with their homework, and if he knew their schedules without asking so he could get them from one activity to another on time. It would be great if the kids automatically cleaned their rooms or helped out with other household chores. But the fact is, whether you like it or not, the best way to make sure other family members do their share is to be proactive, show and/or explain to them what needs to be done, and then get their cooperation to help do it.

Letting Go

Do you have a hard time picturing yourself delegating some of the responsibilities you are currently taking on? I'm sure you can think of a lot of reasons why it wouldn't work.

It's very likely that other people will not joyfully accept new responsibilities. They will probably protest. They probably won't immediately take up those tasks.

Then there's the learning curve. They may not know how to do the tasks, or at least say they don't. It will be tempting for you to just take the jobs back: "If you want a job done right, do it yourself!"

The other person will probably not do the job exactly as you would have done it. It will be hard to watch that person doing it in a way that seems wrong to you. You will be tempted to just push the other person aside and take the job back.

Bonita found herself doing this shortly after she'd resolved to let others take on more responsibilities around the house. She asked her husband to help her put away the laundry, then immediately jumped in when he started to do it differently than she would have done it. She didn't allow for the possibility that his way of doing it might be as good as hers. She caught herself, though, and let him do it anyway, and it turned out fine.

What happens if someone else doesn't do a task as well as you would have done it? How big a problem is that, really? What's the worst-case scenario? Can you deal with it if it happens? It's unlikely that someone will die if the task is done imperfectly!

You may find that it's hard to let go of tasks, even when you've said that you're giving them to someone else. This is part of a need to control what goes on in your life.

It will feel strange to know that someone else is doing what you're used to doing. You'll probably feel at least somewhat lost without those tasks to define you. And you'll probably feel guilty for relaxing, especially if you're doing it while someone else in the family is working.

It will be tempting to take on new responsibilities to replace the ones you've let go. Can you resist that temptation and instead use your newfound time and freedom to take care of yourself?

You may be at a loss at first to figure out what to do with that time. You may no longer remember what you enjoy doing in your time off because it's been so long since you've had some. Here are some ideas to prompt your thinking:

- take a walk

- spend time in nature

- do yoga

- go running

- go to the gym

- watch a movie

- read a book

- take a nap

- call a friend

- go out with a friend

- work on a craft project

- play an instrument

- sing along with the radio

- draw or paint

- sculpt (such as with Sculpey® polymer clay)

- scrapbook

- take a bubble bath

- get a massage

- get a manicure/pedicure

- play with your dog

- pet your cat

- do a puzzle

- Knit, crochet, or do other needlework

etc.

Whatever you choose, make sure it's something you really enjoy and that rejuvenates you. Don't choose something because you think you "should" choose it. "Should" is one of those words that is rarely helpful and is often harmful.

And be gentle with yourself through this process. You may feel lost or adrift if you feel like you have to find a new way to define yourself. That makes sense. But give it time.

Many of us want instant gratification; we want things to work right away. But this is the sort of thing that will not happen immediately. Don't give up if it doesn't work the way you envisioned it, because it's uncomfortable, or because it isn't happening fast enough. It took a long time for the current patterns to be established, and it will take a while for new ones to take hold.

When you find yourself thinking that without you your family and/or workplace would not be able to go on, remind yourself that if you suddenly hopped a plane to another country and never came back they would manage to survive; they would figure out how to do what needed to be done. So why not give them the benefit of the doubt now and let them pitch in even though you haven't left?

Before you start trying new behaviors, though, let me say that I know we don't live in a perfect world. It's not possible to have things perfectly balanced and perfectly fair to everyone. There won't be a brief adjustment period after which everyone in the family cheerfully does all of their assigned tasks with everyone doing a fair share of the work all the time. There may be some tasks that continue to go undone; at that point you may need to decide if it's time to take those tasks back and do them yourself.

Again, I'm suggesting that you work towards a reasonable balance. The other part of the task, then, is making peace with the inequities that still exist, which is addressed later in the book, particularly in Chapter 12.

In the next couple of chapters we'll talk more about the reasons why it's not only better for you, but also for the people in your life, if you let them take on more responsibilities.

Putting It Into Action

What is a typical week like for your family? What activities go on, and who is responsible for what?

Rita: I have a husband (Fred), three kids (Bronwyn, age 17, Sam, age 14, and Jenna, age 6), a dog (Buster), and a cat (Allie).

I work 20 hours a week for the local newspaper as an editor and proofreader. Fred works at least 60 hours a week running an insurance agency.

I have arranged my work schedule so I can pick the kids up from school and shuttle them to their many after-school activities. Bronwyn has private violin lessons once a week and ballet two nights a week. She also has a part time job on the weekends. Sam is involved in sports year-round, including soccer, basketball, and lacrosse; he typically has practices two or three nights a week and games on Saturdays and/or Sundays. Jenna has ballet one day a week.

I arrange doctors' and dentist's appointments for the kids and vet visits for Buster and Allie; I also take them to the appointments.

When the kids and I get home on weekdays, I cook dinner and help them with homework. After dinner the kids finish their homework (and, in Bronywn's case, violin practicing) under my supervision, have some free time, then go to bed.

Fred never knows what time he'll get home from work. On rare days he may be home by 6:00 or 7:00; on some of those days he is able to have dinner with the family. Other days he doesn't come home until 9:00 or 10:00, so Jenna is often in bed when he gets home.

On weekends I take Sam to his games. Sometimes Fred is at home with Bronwyn and Jenna during this time, but he often works on the weekends, so I take Jenna with me on those days. All three kids have activities with friends throughout the weekend; I usually provide transportation for those, too. When Fred is home he mows the lawn and does yard work. He also takes care of the family finances.

On Saturdays, in between driving my kids around, I clean the house. Most Sundays I take the kids to church in the morning and then do laundry in the afternoon and evening. Fred occasionally goes to church with us. When he doesn't go to church he works around the house in the morning. In the afternoon he watches sports on TV because he's exhausted from all of the work he did during the week and wants time to relax.

Sunday nights are family nights, with family members taking turns choosing the activities. The kids always complain about family night and say they'd rather have the evening to themselves. I usually end up suggesting an activity and feeling like I need to make sure everyone is having a good time.

Bronwyn and I are the ones who walk Buster most of the time, although Sam was the one who had begged to get a dog. I clean Allie's litter box; for a time, I tried to rotate that duty, but no one else ever did it, so I took it over.

How do you feel about the current arrangement? Do you think your family's responsibilities are distributed fairly? Are you content to keep things as they are, or would you like things to change?

I am exhausted most of the time, and I resent the fact that my husband is rarely home, leaving most of the family responsibilities to me. I feel like I am reaching a breaking point. I am getting more and more irritable, and I feel like my husband and kids are avoiding me because of it. I've also been getting comments from coworkers about my temper being worse than usual.

I have been offered a promotion that would mean I would work full time instead of part time. I love my work and would like to feel like a "real" employee. I know that the kids will leave home eventually, and I want to have my career established before then. But I don't know how I can do it, particularly if nothing changes at home. If I'm exhausted now, what would happen if I worked more?

I have always prided myself on how smoothly I run the household with little or no help. Now I realize that a major change is needed; other family members will have to step up and start doing more or I will become more and more resentful and the whole family will suffer.

I have talked to Fred before about making changes, but I have never pushed the issue because I am used to the way things are and feel good about all of the things I am successfully juggling. Because of my ambivalence, Fred hasn't felt obligated to do anything about it. I now know it's time for the family to make major changes, though, and I am determined to make it happen.

I have never really assigned many chores to the kids and haven't been consistent about making sure that they do the jobs I have given them. Now I'm looking at things a bit differently. I realize that it can actually be helpful for the kids to learn to be responsible for some things, and so I decide to work with Fred to assign age-appropriate chores to them and make sure that they do them.

How might you go about making the needed changes?

I make a list of the main family responsibilities, including cleaning, homework (and homework supervision), laundry, mowing the lawn, transportation, etc. Next to each task, I write down who usually performs that task now, how often it is done, and the average amount of time it takes. I also list family members who are capable of doing each job.

The following Sunday I call a family meeting to look at redistribution of responsibilities.

Fred and the kids are skeptical, as expected. They're happy about the current arrangement. They do acknowledge that they would like me to be happier, though.

So, with some negotiations, the family agrees upon a plan. Fred agrees to delegate more work responsibility to the most experienced of his employees, which will free him up to get home earlier a couple of evenings a week and not work during the weekend. Then he will be able to help the kids with their homework and not have as many evenings when he doesn't see Jenna at all. He's also agreed to take the kids and pets to some of their appointments.

Fred agrees to take Sam to his games on the weekends, which helps him to be more involved in Sam's life. Because of his reduced work hours he will also be able to spend more time with his daughters, which they appreciate.

I have decided to accept the promotion. My boss has agreed to let me work 7:00-3:00. Bronwyn and Sam have to be at school early anyway, and Jenna likes getting up early and can go to a friend's house before school. With those work hours, I am available to get the kids from school and get them to their after-school activities.

Fred and I decide to pay half the cost of a used car for Bronwyn, with her paying the other half from money she has earned at her job. That way she can drive herself to her activities and free up some of my time. Bronwyn also agrees to watch her younger brother and sister once or twice a week so I can have more time to myself.

Fred and I ask each of the kids to be responsible for making their own beds, keeping their rooms clean, and cleaning up after themselves. All three of them are to help with doing their own laundry, including Jenna, who is to help fold clothes and put them away.

While I will still be the main person doing the cooking, Fred and Bronwyn will each make one dinner a week. No one in the family enjoys doing dishes, so we decide to rotate that job. Jenna isn't old enough to do the dishes by herself, but she can help load the dishwasher. The person who cooks the meal does not have to do the dishes afterwards.

There are other jobs that no one enjoys, like cleaning the bathroom or dusting, so we agree to rotate those, too.

Sam likes to vacuum, so that job is assigned to him. He is also assigned to do one dog walk a day. Jenna wants to help with pet care, too, so she agrees to help clean Allie's litter box.

Fred and I come up with age-appropriate rewards for the kids when they help around the house, and clearly spell out the consequences of not doing assigned tasks.

I agree that the family nights are not working, so we decide that family time will be more flexible and spontaneous, not like an assigned chore.

I sign up for a yoga class as part of getting back into an exercise routine. I also decide to return to some of the activities I enjoy, like reading and scrapbooking.

What are the biggest difficulties you have with making the changes?

Even though Fred and the kids agree to the changes, the transition doesn't go smoothly. Fred frequently allows himself to be caught up in his work, which means that he often doesn't get home when promised. He's not used to the family schedules, so I often end up reminding him about homework supervision, appointments, and practices. The kids aren't used to being responsible for chores, and they don't do them consistently at first.

Fred and the kids also don't do the chores to my satisfaction, and I find myself taking over tasks so they will be done to my standards.

I have problems taking time for myself. I'm not used to doing it, and my identity is very much wrapped up in being busy doing things for other people. It feels wrong to take care of myself, and I feel particularly guilty when I'm doing something for myself while someone else is working.

I decide to stick to it, though, and get used to not being quite so indispensable. When I find myself starting to take on the indispensable role at work, I remind myself to back off; I don't need to exchange one problem for another. I do get some resistance from coworkers, who are used to me working too hard and taking on their responsibilities as well as mine.

I work on relaxing my standards for how things should be done, and I try to be flexible when other family members do things in their own time rather than when I want them to be done.

The new plan is certainly not working perfectly, but it is better than before. I just hope that we'll be able to maintain this and maybe even improve it.

Chapter 2

Boundaries

1) Do others often make decisions for you without consulting you?

2) Are you unable to say no to requests, then feel resentful when you get overwhelmed?

3) Do you have difficulty trusting yourself or others?

4) When you were growing up, did you have a "best friends" relationship with one or both of your parents rather than a parent/child relationship?

5) Do you allow yourself to be hurt in relationships and accept behavior from your partner that you said you would not accept?

6) Do you find yourself feeling others' feelings as if they were your own?

7) Do you have problems with intimacy (emotional or physical)?

8) Do you tend to take responsibility for other people's feelings or actions?

9) Do other people often take advantage of your goodwill?

10) Do you have problems identifying feelings or find yourself trying to avoid feelings?

Picture these three scenarios:

1) You're at home and you hear a noise outside. When you investigate you discover that your house has no front door and your intrusive neighbor has just walked in and helped herself to something from your refrigerator.

2) Someone knocks on your door. You look through the peephole and you don't recognize the man outside. Instead of going away he knocks harder and then insists that you open the door. Even though you don't want to do so, you find yourself unlocking the door and letting him in.

3) A friend of yours comes over to visit. When she knocks on the door you try to open it, only to find that it is locked with a padlock to which you do not have the key.

These scenarios all sound ridiculous, don't they? If you look at them literally, yes, they do. They make sense, though, if you look at them as illustrations of problems with personal boundaries.

If you answered "yes" to any of the quiz questions above, you probably have some difficulties with boundaries. This chapter will help you to understand where you stand regarding boundaries and what you can do to establish and maintain firm but flexible boundaries for yourself. This is another important aspect of the balance between caring for others and caring for yourself.

The chapter will also explain what it means to be passive, passive-aggressive, assertive, or aggressive; you will be able to identify which style(s) you tend to adopt. If you're not satisfied with your current approach, you will learn ways to change.

Physical Boundaries

What are boundaries? They are the dividing lines between you and other people. For instance, there are physical boundaries including your personal space, which is an invisible line around you that dictates how close others can be to you without you becoming uncomfortable.

Personal space varies greatly from person to person. You might know one person who seems to have no personal space at all, and another who isn't comfortable with people being within five feet of her.

People also have different comfort levels regarding being touched. Some people don't like to be touched at all, even by people they know well. When possible, they avoid hugs and even handshakes. Others like to relate to people by making physical contact; they may hug people they barely know or just met.

Your clothes and your skin are physical boundaries, as well. If you feel uncomfortable in a situation you may leave your coat on indoors or hold it in front of you as a form of protection. You can use your body to establish a boundary by turning away from another person, crossing your arms in front of you, or avoiding direct eye contact.

An object placed between you and another person is a boundary that can create a feeling of safety. This is one reason why people who are making speeches, even memorized speeches for which they don't need notes, stand behind a lectern or podium. A closed bedroom or office door is a boundary that usually says you want to be by yourself.

Emotional Boundaries

There are emotional boundaries, too. These include, among other things, the information you're willing to share with others, the degree to which you're willing to be open to others, and your ability to say no to requests made of you. If you have healthy emotional boundaries you care about what others think of you but you don't let this have so much influence on you that you can't balance others' needs and your own.

If you have no emotional boundaries you have no sense of yourself apart from other people and you don't know how to keep others out (Scenario #1). If you have weak boundaries you don't know how to make sure your needs are met because you are putting everyone else's needs and demands first, whether you want to or not (Scenario #2). If you have rigid boundaries you don't (or can't) let anyone in (Scenario #3).

If you said yes to quiz questions 1, 4, and 6, you probably fit Scenario #1. Yes answers to questions 2, 5, 8, and 9 suggest that you should consider Scenario #2. And if you said yes to questions 3, 7, and 10, you can probably relate to Scenario #3.

Because people are complex, it's likely that more than one of these scenarios might fit you. How many of them, do you think, can be an issue for you? One? Two? All three?

As with many other things, we learn about boundaries (or lack thereof) while growing up, mostly from our families. You probably learned to imitate one or both parents' styles regarding boundaries. And even if you figure out that you'd like to do something different and put it into practice, it's likely that you'll have the hardest time sticking to the new behaviors when you're with your family.

Codependency and People Pleasing

Scenarios #1 and #2 are similar to each other and can both be put in the category of *codependency*. Codependency happens when you allow your happiness to depend too much upon other people; your life is intertwined with theirs to an unhealthy degree. You look to other people to complete you rather than being complete within yourself. Your boundaries are weak or nonexistent.

The Shel Silverstein books *The Missing Piece* and *The Missing Piece Meets the Big O* illustrate codependency. In *The Missing Piece*, a circular creature with a wedge-shaped hole is looking for its missing piece. It rolls slowly because of the missing piece. It has some pleasant experiences (like being a perch for a butterfly) as a result.

It meets various pieces, most of which don't fit. One piece looks like it would fit but doesn't want to be someone's missing piece. Eventually a willing piece of the correct size is found and they join together. Because they move quickly they miss out on the experiences the circle had before. And the circular creature can't sing any more. So it sets the piece down and moves on, singing happily (although still looking for its missing piece).

In *The Missing Piece Meets the Big O*, a missing piece is sitting and waiting, hoping that someone will come along that fits it and can give it a way to move. As in the other story, there are many that don't work for various reasons. Then along comes the big O, which is not missing any pieces. It encourages the piece to try to move on its own even though it is pointy and cannot move easily. The piece does; it finds that in time its pointy ends are worn off so that it's circular and can roll by itself. It catches up to the big O and they travel happily together.

Both stories show that there are disadvantages to depending upon someone else to complete you. The second story also points out that it really doesn't make sense to try to live your life completely independently of other people, either, or that you try not to allow other people's feelings to affect you. We are made to be social beings, so other people and their feelings do affect us.

As I emphasize in one way or another throughout the book, we need to find a balance, in this case between being too dependent and being too independent. We can look for *interdependence*, meaning that we are comfortable with ourselves as separate beings but are also able to share ourselves with others when we need or want to do so.

Revisiting the Three Scenarios

Scenario #1

Scenario #1 is an instance of no boundaries (in the example, no front door): an inability to separate yourself from others. If you fit Scenario #1, it is likely that you take a *passive* approach much of the time, meaning that you do not assert yourself and your own preferences. In general, you let life happen to you instead of shaping it into a life that fits you.

If you fit this scenario it is difficult for you to establish and honor your own identity. You're likely to let other people dictate what you do, how you think, and how you feel. You make yourself into a chameleon; rather than having your own opinions and preferences, you agree with the people around you. If you do this long enough you find that you can no longer identify your own thoughts, feelings, and preferences. If someone asks you what you like to do, you may give the person a blank look.

While dysfunctional families often have rigid boundaries that protect them from revealing their dysfunction to the outside world, the boundaries within the family tend to be weak or non-existent. For instance, children are not given privacy. Arianna's mother felt free to come into her room at any time without knocking and regularly read her journal without telling her about it until later.

A child in this situation may also find that she has nothing that is just hers. Fiona had one older sister and two younger ones. Her older sister regularly took her books and other possessions from her, and when one of her younger sisters wanted something of Fiona's her mother took it from Fiona and gave it to the sister.

In a healthy family there is a clear distinction between parents and kids. Parents do not share adult information with kids (such as concerns about family finances). They do not involve their kids in parental conflicts. While they have fun with their kids, they still have a parent/child relationship, not a best friend relationship. And they don't knowingly put their children in dangerous situations.

Dysfunctional families don't generally operate that way, though. Bridget's father told her and her sister that their mother had lost her job and that they were probably going to lose their house; Bridget, who was only eight years old at the time, decided that she needed to sell her most treasured possessions to supplement the family's income and save their home.

Angela's father told her that her mother was having an affair and made her follow her mother to confirm that it was true.

Cheyenne ended up acting as her mother's therapist, having to listen to her as she talked about her thoughts, feelings, and fears from having grown up with abusive parents. Ironically, this actually helped Cheyenne to see and understand the source and the wrongness of some of her mother's behaviors towards her.

Angelique, when she was graduating from high school, wanted to attend a conservatory and become a professional violinist. She was the oldest child in the family and wanted to make her parents happy, and her parents did not want her to take the risk of entering such a competitive field. Because she was young and suggestible, she abandoned her dream and followed her father's suggestion that she go to secretarial school; he said it was a more practical and appropriate thing for her to do.

It took years before she realized that just because her father thought it was the right thing for her to do didn't mean that it really was right for her. By that point, though, she felt trapped in a career she didn't like. In her late thirties she inherited a large sum of money that enabled her to quit her secretarial job and pursue her dream; she has yet to regret her choice!

If you, like these women, didn't learn to establish and maintain emotional boundaries, you may exhaust yourself by taking on the emotions of the people around you.

For instance, if your partner comes home from work and is angry, you may assume that he's angry with you or that, at the very least, it is your job to make him happy again. Only if he is happy can you be happy. This can also be applied to your kids, your friends, and your coworkers.

Unfortunately, trying to change others' feelings is generally a losing battle. You are responsible for your own feelings and no one else's. You can try to influence others' ways of thinking and feeling, but it is ultimately up to them to change. You can, however, change the way *you* feel by changing how you think. (More on that in Chapter 10.)

Scenario #2

In Scenario #2 you do have boundaries, but they're weak. To use my original analogy, you have a front door but you are unable to keep it closed even when you want or need to do so.

If you fit Scenario #2 you may be *passive-aggressive*. You are more aware of your wants and needs than you would be if you were passive, but you still don't have the tools to get those needs and desires met. You don't feel comfortable asking directly for what you want, so you may hint at it and hope that others will pick up on the hints. For instance, you might say, "A cup of coffee would taste really good right now" rather than directly asking someone to get you a cup of coffee.

Passive-aggressive people often, because they resent constantly doing things they don't want to do, attack others indirectly. You might agree to do a task and then just not do it, or do it but not to an acceptable standard. This happens when you don't feel like you can say no to someone's request but you really don't want to do whatever it is that was asked. You say yes, but your actions say no.

Eva's husband always expects her to do his laundry for him. Sometimes when she's mad at him she "forgets" to do it or leaves his clothes in the dryer so they'll get wrinkled and he won't have them when he needs them. If she felt like she could assert her own needs and wants she would be better able to tell him when she doesn't have time or doesn't want to do his laundry.

People Pleasing

When you have weak boundaries, you have difficulty saying no to others; you are a *people pleaser* who puts others' needs before your own more often than is good for you (or for them, for that matter).

People pleasers often hope that if they anticipate and meet other people's needs the other people will return the favor. That is rarely the case. In general, takers gravitate towards givers and vice versa. So if you are a people pleaser you are likely to find people who will take advantage of your kindness and generosity but give little or nothing back.

Alicia often listens to her siblings' and mother's problems, but they rarely listen to hers. Even when they do allow her to talk about what's going on with her they generally manage to turn it around to make it about them, or they give her the impression that there's something wrong with her for having the issues she's describing. These days she rarely calls them because she's tired of having one-sided conversations.

People pleasers often end up in the middle of conflicts between family members. For instance, Amber has long been the go-between for her mother and brother. Each will tell her things about the other; at that point, she often finds herself drawn to try to fix the relationship between the two. She is now working on setting and maintaining better boundaries with family members, making sure that she does not mediate between them.

Many women who are people pleasers have trouble telling men that they don't love them. They often don't realize that these men can't take hints and won't figure out what they mean unless they say something like, "I don't love you and I never will." Brenda has tried many times to communicate to her ex-boyfriends that she no longer has any interest in them. But because she doesn't want to hurt their feelings, she never says it in a way that they understand what she means.

Why is it that you might become a people pleaser? Because it feels a lot safer to do what everyone else wants you to do; hardly anyone will disagree if you go along with everything she says or does. Few would argue if someone said yes to every request made of her.

People pleasing, like other established life patterns, is learned in childhood. People pleasers learn while growing up that the only way to be safe is to do everything they can to make their parents and others happy.

People pleasers are good at taking care of other people but bad at taking care of themselves. Cassandra was very good at accounting, and she helped family members and friends with their taxes. When it came time to do her own taxes, though, Cassandra became paralyzed and unable to function. Every year she procrastinated and every year she had to ask for an extension because she somehow couldn't do for herself what she so easily did for everyone else.

Desiree was the one in her family who made a point of never arguing with her parents or siblings. She was the calm one, the one nobody had to worry about. Unfortunately, this led to a pattern of avoiding difficult situations. Because she avoided conflicts, she tended to leave (intellectually, emotionally, and/or physically) rather than try to work through the problems.

While you may feel responsible for another person's happiness, there is likely to be little or nothing you can do to change how that person feels. This can lead to a sense of powerlessness and a lack of safety, particularly with authority figures. It's truly frightening if someone has power over you and you can't do anything to make him happy, especially if that leads to abusive behavior towards you. So you may become a people pleaser because you're trying to gain some control of your situation by controlling his feelings.

Saying No to Everything

I find that when people pleasers first learn to say no they are often aggressive about it. They have decided to take control of their lives and are unwilling to give in to anyone else, even if it's something that they don't mind doing. You can tell that someone is in this phase when she automatically says "NO!" to any request, possibly even before the requester starts asking.

This is one example of flipping from one extreme to the other. While it is not good to be at the extreme of always doing everything others ask of you, it is also not good to refuse all requests and not cooperate with others at all. A better choice is to find a middle ground, which we'll talk about later in the chapter.

Cassandra was her mother's "yes woman," agreeing with everything she said and defending her in family arguments. One day, though, Cassandra decided she had had enough, and she blew up at her mother. All of the anger that she'd suppressed for years came out. The depth of her rage scared her. When she sought therapy she learned how to express her needs and feelings on a regular basis so they didn't build up and explode unexpectedly.

Scenario #3

If you fit Scenario #3 you have learned that the world is not safe and you have to protect yourself from it. You build a wall around yourself that no one can get through, including you. No one can get in, so no one can hurt you. Think of the Simon and Garfunkel song "I Am a Rock," ("I am a rock/I am an island/And a rock feels no pain/ And an island never cries") and you'll have a pretty good picture of this scenario.

The problem with living behind this wall is that you can't get out, and you can't let anyone else in even if you want to do so. You know that there are people outside of the wall and you'd like to be able to interact with them, but there is no way to escape. You are trapped in your self-made prison.

The Dar Williams song "What Do You Hear in These Sounds" talks about this problem. When she had her wall up she wasn't able to see other people's internal struggles, so she thought they were free and she wasn't. When she was no longer trapped behind the wall she realized that other people face the same struggles she does; she no longer felt so alone and afraid.

If you have a wall like this you may find that people (including your spouse or partner) say they don't really know you. If you are married, the marriage may feel more like you are roommates than spouses. You may lead parallel lives that don't often intersect.

This doesn't mean that you don't love or appreciate your partner; it means that you don't feel safe making yourself vulnerable, so you share little, if any, of your inner self. And chances are that, without trying to do so, you found a partner who has difficulty helping you feel safe enough to be open. Your partner probably also unconsciously feels safer with those walls in place even if he genuinely does want you to talk to him about these things.

Depending upon how you look at it, having a wall up can be seen as a sort of aggressiveness as well. You do not feel safe, so you vigorously defend your space and yourself. That doesn't necessarily mean that you attack others, but you are vigilant and wary of them, always ready to defend yourself. This may look like a retreat, but if someone pursues you, you may react like a cornered animal and strike out.

So What's Healthy, Then?

Twelve-step programs emphasize the importance of *acting* rather than *reacting*. Acting is assertive and self-assured. It comes from knowing who you are and what you want and need. Reacting, on the other hand, feels involuntary and/or out of control. You are more likely to regret what you do while reacting than while acting from a place of deliberation and thoughtfulness.

I've mentioned the unhealthiness of extremes and the desirability of finding a more balanced middle ground. Among other things, that means having firm but flexible boundaries. You have a clear sense of yourself as a separate being. You know how to keep people from intruding into your personal space. But you also know how to let others in when it's appropriate and safe. In this way you can let people get to know you and influence you, but you have some say about how this happens. This is the interdependence that I mentioned earlier.

If we use the example of the wall, you might picture making a door in the wall, making sure that you have a key to the lock, and keeping the lock well oiled so it works well.

That way you can get out and let others in, but if you need time to yourself or you're feeling unsafe you can go inside the wall and protect yourself.

Balancing Needs

When you have this sense of safety you can take an *assertive* approach. When you are assertive you are self-confident enough to ask for what you want or need but you don't go too far and aggressively insist upon it. You realize that the other person has a right to refuse your request, and if she does you can deal with it.

This brings me to a very important point that I often make to my clients: just because you don't get something doesn't mean that it's wrong to want it, or that it says something bad about you that you didn't get it. So try to find a balance between honoring your wanting while still accepting not always getting what you hoped for.

You may find that it's as the Rolling Stones' song says: "You can't always get what you want/But if you try sometimes/You just might find/You get what you need."

One of the difficult things about asserting your own needs is that, as reasonable as they might be, they might conflict with someone else's reasonable needs. This often happens in families. How do you balance your needs and your kids' and partner's needs? There is probably not enough of you to go around, but that doesn't mean you should ignore your own needs in favor of meeting as many of your family members' needs as possible.

And it is actually helpful to the rest of your family if you make sure to do things to take care of yourself. Self-care will enable you to be there for others more completely. And family members, in learning to meet some of their own needs, will be better prepared for dealing with life outside of the family because living in the world requires a degree of independence.

If one spouse, or even the kids, rule(s) the roost, it's easy to decide what to do; you do whatever that person wants or needs. But if you're trying to respect everyone's needs and desires it's harder to figure out what to do, because compromises will often be required.

How Much Is Too Much?

When I was a child I was introduced to Shel Silverstein's book *The Giving Tree*. It was presented as a wonderful story about giving, and that made sense to me. A few years ago, though, I read some reviews and realized that some people had a radically different reaction to the book.

The story is that there is a boy and there is a tree (referred to as "she") and they love each other. As the boy gets older he wants different things and the tree gives him part of herself (leaves, apples, branches, trunk) each time to fulfill those wishes. In the end the tree is reduced to a stump that the boy, now an old man, sits on.

So is this a heartwarming story about unconditional love and selflessness, or is it a cautionary tale that warns that there is such a thing as giving too much? I'd say it can be both.

It is good to give to others. But how do we know how much to give? When does it become too much? Did the tree only give what she could afford to give or did she give more? Did she give to the boy purely out of love for him, or because she wanted him to stay with her?

Marcus Pfister's book *Rainbow Fish* is another kids' book that can be controversial. The main character is a fish that thought he was too beautiful to play with the other fish. Another fish asked him for one of his scales and he said no, after which all of the other fish avoided him. He asked for help from a starfish and an octopus; the octopus advised him to give away his scales, even though it took away from his beauty. He did so (until he had only one scale left), and then had lots of friends.

So, again, giving to others is a good thing. And doing things to make others happy is good too. But how much is too much? Should the fish have given away fewer scales?

You could look at it as making things equal—each fish now had one beautiful scale. And there was an exchange involved that the rainbow fish was willing to make—lose scales, gain friends.

What kind of friendships do you think these were? Were they based only upon him giving and them taking? Once he had nothing left to give did they leave him, or were they still his friends?

Many times I have had a client in recovery from drug addiction tell me that the friends she had when she was using were only friends as long as she had drugs. Once the drugs were gone the friends were gone, too. That client was often also the person who said she'd give someone her last dollar or her last cigarette. Unfortunately, she then expected those people to return the favor and they rarely did.

You may not have a story like this one, but if you're someone who listens to everyone else's problems and/or someone who gives to others (including lending money), you've probably experienced a version of this yourself. Many times someone who is more than willing to let you listen to her problems day after day, or who is quick to ask you for a loan, will suddenly become unavailable when you have a problem that you need to talk about or when you need to borrow something.

Helping Yourself to Help Others?

One of the episodes on a "My Little Pony" video my daughter has gives a somewhat different perspective from those offered by *The Giving Tree* and *The Rainbow Fish*. In this story one of the ponies (who is a dress maker) creates beautiful gowns for all of the ponies. They don't think the gowns are good enough, though, so she makes new gowns that meet their exact specifications. In the end they realize that the gowns they asked for were a disaster and her original designs were perfect just the way they were.

One of the ponies explained what she learned from this: that if you try to please everyone, you're likely to end up pleasing no one, particularly yourself. It's not helpful to give away the essence of who you are; it makes more sense to use your gifts to benefit everyone, including yourself. Billy Joel expresses this idea in his song "James": "Do what's good for you, or you're not good for anybody."

Control Issues

Many of my clients are confused or insulted when I suggest that they have control issues. They think of the stereotypical idea of the "control freak": the person who always has to have things her way and who deliberately and unfeelingly manipulates others in the name of getting what she wants.

The control issues I point out to my clients often do involve manipulation, but in the name of safety. People pleasing is a control issue; we are trying to keep ourselves safe by trying to make sure everyone else is happy all the time.

But control like this is an illusion. The more you try to control all aspects of your life the more your life is likely to get out of control. Anxiety and frustration may lead you to try even harder to get a grip on things, likely leaving you with a feeling of powerlessness.

But even though we can't control or predict everything that happens to us, it's important to identify what we want and need so we can do our best to look out for ourselves while still respecting other people.

Once you've figured out what to ask for, practice asking and being OK with whatever responses you get.

Boundaries with Parents

Establishing, maintaining, and enforcing boundaries is a process that takes time. It is likely that if you have had no boundaries or weak boundaries you will meet with resistance when you begin setting limits and balancing taking care of yourself and others.

If you had weak or nonexistent boundaries in your family when you were growing up, that has probably continued into your adulthood. Now that you are making an effort to achieve balance in your life, how do you negotiate your adult relationship with your parents? Without a deliberate effort to establish your identity as an adult you will probably fall back into the relationship you had with them while growing up.

It can be hard to separate from parents and make it clear to them that you are now an adult with your own family with whom you do things, not necessarily including your parents. Grace's parents were angry when Grace and her husband decided to take their family to the performance of a musical that her parents would have enjoyed, but didn't invite them. For months after that her parents kept bringing it up, not understanding that they were not entitled to automatically be included in everything their daughter's family did.

Marissa's mother watches her three daughters after school some days. Because she is dependent upon her mother in this way it's harder to set boundaries regarding who is the girls' parent and who is not. How does she allow her mom to have authority over the kids when she's alone with them, but not when Marissa is there? And, of course, she doesn't have the opportunities to distance herself from her mother that she would have if they didn't have this arrangement.

It's difficult to know what to do when your parents embarrass you inappropriately in front of other family members, and particularly in front of your kids. For instance, when Denise said something to her daughter about cleaning her room her mother questioned her authority to do so, saying, "You might want to clean up the rest of the house before you tell your kids that they need to clean their rooms!"

It can be awkward to try to teach your kids appropriate behavior when their grandparents demonstrate inappropriate behavior. It's not helpful to tell your child, "Your grandmother doesn't know what she's talking about," but it's also not good to pretend it's OK. Where is that in-between place?

Boundaries with Siblings

If you grew up with little or no sense of healthy boundaries, the same is likely to be true of your siblings. What do you do if they make inappropriate requests or demands of you? And what will it be like for you if you look at the negative influences from your childhood and make changes but your siblings don't? What do you do if they claim that nothing was wrong with your family when you were growing up and that things are perfectly fine now?

If you are extremely responsible you are likely to have at least one sibling who is extremely irresponsible. She may come to you and ask for money or ask to live with you if she's lost her job and her house. You probably feel at least some sense of obligation to her because she's your sister. How much obligation do you have towards her, and what do you do about it?

If she asks you to lend her money, only give it to her if you will be OK if she never pays you back. And if you consider letting her move in with you, realize that it may be difficult to get her to move out again. Can you handle this if it happens? Do you set some ground rules or write up a contract that includes expectations of both of you as well as consequences for disregarding the terms of the agreement?

Being related to someone does confer some sense of loyalty and responsibility to that person. Remember the balance, though; how can you best balance your siblings' needs and your needs? What boundaries need to be set and maintained? What are the ways you are willing to help and the ways that you are not?

Parenting Boundaries

If you had very authoritative parents you may find yourself going to the opposite extreme, being a more permissive parent than you'd like to be. You might not have well-defined, firm boundaries with your kids. If you look at your parenting from the perspective of setting and maintaining boundaries you may realize that you would like to find ways to place more emphasis on your role as a parent, not letting your kids get away with things that they have gotten away with in the past.

If you decide to make changes it's important to make the transition as clear as you can, though. You need to let the kids know your plan and what the consequences will be for unacceptable actions. A sudden, unannounced change will be seen as unfair and arbitrary and will not help you to get your kids to cooperate with your efforts.

Remember as you do this that you will likely experience significant resistance from your kids if you're asking them to show you more respect than they've been showing you. And you have to look at what you're doing, or not doing, to earn their respect. The older your kids are the more likely they are to resist the new relationship you're trying to establish. It will take time and patience to set and maintain the new boundaries.

Boundaries Outside of the Family

It is also a good idea to look at your significant relationships, not just with your family, but with friends and coworkers, too. Are the people who are close to you respecting your boundaries? Are they willing to accept your changed behavior?

It makes sense to give other people some time to adjust to the new you. But at some point, if you can't negotiate a new, healthier relationship with someone in your life, you may need to limit or even end that relationship. We'll talk more about that in the next chapter.

I recommend that you continue to be aware of these issues so that you can set firm boundaries at the beginning of new relationships; this will make them much easier to maintain.

Putting It Into Action

1. Think of someone with whom you need to set and maintain firmer boundaries. Is there a family member, friend, or coworker who takes up more time than you have available? Is there anyone who frequently asks you to do favors for her without reciprocating? Are there people in your life who feel intrusive to you?

> *Bernadette: I work as a paralegal for a large law firm. It's a high stress job because the lawyers are very demanding and the workload is heavy. There's another paralegal in the office, Brandy, who comes to my desk several times a day to complain about the lawyers for whom we work. She sits down next to my desk without asking me if I have time to talk, and usually spends at least 15 minutes to half an hour complaining.*

> *I try to give Brandy hints that I'm not available to talk. I sit at my computer and type while she talks. I don't make eye contact. I say things about having a lot of work to do. But Brandy doesn't take the hint; she continues to distract me and make it difficult for me to get my work done. More than once I have had to stay late to catch up on work that Brandy has prevented me from doing during the day.*

> *When we happen to pass each other in the hall or go to the restroom at the same time, Brandy starts up the usual conversations. She follows me, which makes it hard for me to avoid conversation.*

> *As if that weren't enough, Brandy takes her lunch break at the same time as I do. I prefer to eat lunch alone and read a book because it gives me a break from the chaos of the office. But Brandy follows me and sits with me, talking incessantly.*

2. What can you do to set a boundary with this person?

I realize that I have to be more direct with Brandy if I want the constant interruptions and intrusions to stop. The next time Brandy comes to my desk I invite her to have a seat. I say that I understand Brandy's frustrations about work and admit that I'm frustrated, too. I tell Brandy that the conversations make me more frustrated, though, because they lead me to focus on the negative rather than the positive, and because it's harder for me to get my work done when so much of the day is devoted to talking. I also say that while I appreciate Brandy wanting to eat with me, I really need that time to be alone and decompress. Brandy looks confused and hurt and leaves without saying anything.

3. If you have set the boundary, how is your life different now that the boundary is in place?

Brandy leaves me alone for a couple of days. When we pass in the hall Brandy is polite but does not talk long. After a few days, though, Brandy starts going back to her old behaviors. I again have to talk to Brandy about what I need. We go back and forth in this way for several weeks before Brandy, who feels snubbed, withdraws from me completely. Brandy ends up latching on to Maria, who also works in the office. She does the same thing to her that she used to do to me, but also talks to Maria about what an unfeeling, unfriendly person I am.

At first I feel guilty for making Brandy feel bad. I try to keep in mind, though, that I have to take care of myself.

I also worry about the possibility that Brandy might turn everyone in the office against me. I acknowledge this fear when it comes up, but try to challenge it by telling myself that it's likely that at least some of the other people in the office feel the same way as I do about Brandy. If not, perhaps I'll just end up having civil, but not chummy, relationships with most of the others in the office. That would be uncomfortable, but not impossible to deal with. At least then I would get my work done!

And, in the meantime, I remind myself that I do have a close friend in the office who is unlikely to turn against me. I also make a point of being as friendly to everyone as I always have been. That way I won't let my anxiety about others' possible thoughts become a self-fulfilling prophecy.

Chapter 3

Relationships

1. Does your romantic partner ever remind you of one of your parents?

2. Were there any red flags at the beginning of your relationship that you ignored at the time, only to recognize them later?

3. Does it feel like you keep ending up in the same kinds of unhealthy relationships over and over?

4. Does it feel like you do more than your share of the work in your relationships?

5. Do you tend to engage in the same negative behaviors in relationships repeatedly and then get frustrated with yourself when you do?

Relationship Dysfunctions

We are often presented with the same life lessons repeatedly. This is nowhere truer than in our relationships with other people.

As we've already discussed, it can be difficult to maintain healthy boundaries with significant people in our lives. "Yes" answers to any of this chapter's quiz questions are indicators of some of those difficulties.

As children we were confronted with the insecurities and dysfunctions of our parents. At that point in our lives we were not mature enough to come up with good ways to deal with them, so we found whatever solutions we could. Often, without realizing it, we continue to use those solutions in adulthood even though the tools to find healthier solutions have become available to us.

As we go through life we find people who have similar dysfunctions to members of our family. Even hints of those dysfunctions can make us act the same way around those people as we do with our family members. And if we act the same way with them as we do with our family, we're encouraging those dysfunctions to come out even more.

For instance, Morgan's father favors his sons over his daughters and regularly makes insulting comments about women, so Morgan tends to assume that all men are that way. This is often true of the men that she meets, but not always, and probably not to the degree that she thinks.

This causes difficulties for Morgan because she works for a doctor who triggers all of her resentments about male chauvinism. Because she expects and notices his chauvinistic behaviors, she works hard to show him that women are just as good as men. Unfortunately, she does it in a way that triggers hostility in him, which reinforces her idea that he's a male chauvinist. And so the cycle continues.

How is a Boss Like a Parent?

Family-created relationship issues often show up with our supervisors or bosses. Your supervisor is an authority figure and, therefore, is in a position not entirely unlike that of a parent. She sets, or at least enforces, rules. She has power over you. If you defy her wishes there are consequences, often severe.

Many of my clients are skeptical when I suggest that we often end up working for people who remind us of our parents, but I have seen it happen again and again.

Maybe your boss gives you enough work for two people and expects you to get all of it done. Maybe she asks you for one thing but when you present it to her she claims that she asked for something entirely different. She may change the rules frequently so that you are in a no-win situation—if you follow yesterday's rules you end up getting in trouble because the rules are different today, and only she knows what they are. You may find yourself trying to read her mind. Or her mood may be unpredictable; you never know if she's going to praise you for all of your hard work or ask you why you haven't completed the one assignment you have not yet managed to finish.

Having a boss who does these things is familiar when you've had a parent or other family member who did similar things. People who grow up in dysfunctional families are used to no-win situations and arbitrary rule changes, so much so that they may not even realize that their version of normal is not the way things have to be.

I have a theory that people who grew up in dysfunctional families are more likely to be self-employed than are people who grew up in relatively functional homes. They tend to have difficulty with authority figures, including bosses, so it makes sense that they would be more likely to strike out on their own so they do not have someone telling them what to do all of the time. Of course they do have to pay attention to the needs and desires of their customers, but that is usually a more equal relationship than the one between an employer and an employee.

Did You Marry Your Parents?

The biggest, and in many ways most critical, situation where these relationship issues show up is generally with your partner or spouse. You've probably heard people say that most people marry their mothers, their fathers, or a combination of the two, and that is generally true.

When I'm working with a client who says, "My partner is nothing like either of my parents," I am skeptical. It's possible, but I've rarely known it to happen. Usually at some point the client recognizes the way(s) in which her partner is like one or both parents. Sometimes they're easier to identify than others.

Dating is like a job interview; you dress in your best clothes and are on your best behavior. Most people know not to go to a job interview and tell the interviewer that they're lazy and will spend most of their time at work surfing the internet; they will instead point out their positive qualities or lie about their work habits so they will get the job. Similarly, the guy you're starting to date is unlikely to tell you that after you've been together a while he'll spend most evenings in front of the TV with a beer in his hand.

I sometimes say to my clients that when we are getting into a new relationship there is often a huge red flag trying to alert us to the potential pitfalls. Rather than paying attention to it, though, we are likely to try to brush it aside: "Will someone get this flag out of my face so I can see this person I'm dating?"

Penelope has an alcoholic father and swears she will not become romantically involved with an alcoholic, only to find herself in relationships with one alcoholic after another. When she first starts dating them she does not realize they are alcoholics; either they manage to hide their drinking from her or she ignores the signs.

When Melinda was growing up her father was angry most of the time and was very violent. Melinda married a man who also had a bad temper. While he did not physically abuse her, he did express his anger in physical ways, including punching holes in walls.

Melinda, who did not realize how angry she still was at her father, found herself blowing up at her husband on a regular basis, arguing with the man who unconsciously reminded her of her father.

Sally, although she didn't recognize it at first, had abandonment issues because of having been ignored by her mother for long periods of time when she was growing up. The man she married, Spencer, also had abandonment issues; in his case it was because his father was away on business trips more than he was home when Spencer was growing up. Their mutual history of having been abandoned led them to emotionally abandon each other, thus recreating this feeling from their childhoods.

Athena, looking back on her childhood, has realized that her best friends were usually the misfits at her school. They were often much less intelligent or accomplished than she was. Whether she knew it or not, those friends felt safer. She didn't feel as insecure around them as she did with the kids who more closely matched her level of ability and intelligence. When she first started dating she chose guys who drank, used drugs, and dropped out of school and then were unemployed.

After she finished college she worked for an inner-city methadone clinic and ended up dating some of the men who were patients there. She eventually realized what she was doing and worked to improve her self-esteem so that she felt worthy of men who were a better match for her.

Bobbie's parents divorced when she was four years old. After the divorce she lived with her mother and her mother's new husband. Her stepfather made a lot of money and her mother bought her anything she wanted. But her mother never hugged her, never helped her with her homework, and did not appear to notice her most of the time.

Bobbie was confused. Her mother gave her all the material things she could possibly need or want, so it seemed clear that her mother loved her. She thought she should be happy, but she was lonely. She wanted her mother to pay attention to her. Later, she ended up marrying a man whose only way of showing love was by spending money, but who also used money to gain power in the relationship.

Attraction to "Bad Boys"

Some women are attracted to "bad boys." They can be friends with guys who are responsible, have good jobs, and don't party excessively on the weekends, but they find these guys romantically uninteresting—there's no spark there. Instead, they're attracted to the guys who feel somewhat dangerous. Unfortunately, these guys are generally not a good choice for a serious, long-term relationship. So what do you do if you're attracted to this kind of person?

Rachel Iverson, in her book *Don't Help a Man Be a Man: How to Avoid 12 Dating Time Bombs*, suggests that you find a man who has some of the dangerous qualities that attract you, but in tolerable amounts so that you can still have a healthy relationship with him. It's another one of those balance situations: can you find the balance between the qualities you consider safe but boring and the qualities you find dangerous but exciting?

The Rescue/Pity Partner

Most of my clients are used to taking care of others and not having anyone take care of them. Therefore many of them (again, without realizing it) find partners that help them maintain their caretaker and un-cared-for roles.

This can take a variety of forms. One of the most common is the partner who doesn't take his share of family responsibilities or who is emotionally unavailable. He may expect you to take care of him if he's sick, but then not reciprocate. He may be very focused on his own needs and seemingly incapable of recognizing your needs.

He may be someone whom you can rescue. For instance, he might be awkward, socially inept, and lonely, thus inspiring you to (unconsciously) choose him because you feel the need to make him feel better.

He may be a fixer-upper; you may unknowingly (or knowingly) see him and think, "He's a great guy, but he has a major flaw (alcoholism, for instance) that he needs me to fix." This effort will ultimately frustrate you because the only person who can fix your partner is your partner himself.

How and why do these things happen? Do you look for these people? Do they look for you? Is it a combination of the two? Is God/the Universe/a Higher Power making these relationships happen?

I don't have a definitive answer for that, although I suspect it might be a combination of all of these. And I do believe that we are presented with the same lesson over and over until we find a way to successfully negotiate it.

Why Do You Stay?

Believe it or not, if you find yourself in a dysfunctional relationship it is, in part, because it is doing something for you. It's like the person who grew up in a chaotic family and wants peace, yet keeps finding chaos.

Why is this? Because you are used to it. Until you become aware of the patterns that you learned as a child you will continue to find similar situations over and over, whether you want them or not.

Why do smart women stay in bad relationships? Why stay with an alcoholic partner or one who is physically, sexually, and/or emotionally abusive?

To people on the outside it may make no sense at all, especially if they have no personal experience with this. Friends may get exasperated and say, "Why don't you just leave? You know this relationship isn't good for you! You can do so much better!"

There are a variety of reasons why you might stay.

Sometimes women stay for very practical reasons. For instance, if you are financially dependent upon your partner you can find it difficult to leave because you don't know how you will support yourself if you do so. Or, if there are children involved, you may be worried about custody issues. If your partner treats the kids badly when you are there, how will he treat them if you're not there? What if they imitate characteristics of his that you don't like and you don't get the opportunity to guide them in a different direction?

Sometimes you may stay because you're afraid of what might happen if you don't. Maybe your partner has threatened to hurt himself, you, or your children if you leave, and you believe that he might do it. In that case, leaving feels dangerous.

Brianna has come close to leaving her partner, Alexandra, many times. Every time she does so, Alexandra declares herself to be a total screw-up, not deserving to live, and threatens to kill herself. Sometimes Alexandra, a recovering alcoholic, says that Brianna is going to drive her to drink. These threats serve to keep Brianna in the relationship because she does love Alexandra and doesn't want her to harm herself. She does not realize that she is not responsible for Alexandra's actions any more than Alexandra is responsible for her (Brianna's) actions.

If you have low self-esteem you may unknowingly find a relationship that reinforces your low opinion of yourself. If you were given negative messages when you were a child you may find a partner who gives you the same messages. Because you've been hearing them for years you probably aren't completely sure that they aren't true, which may keep you in the relationship.

Carrie's mother always used to tell her that she was worthless, wouldn't amount to anything, and wouldn't be able to find a decent man to marry. Carrie ended up with so little self-confidence that she didn't date until she was in her mid-twenties. When she did finally start dating she went out with unattractive guys who worked minimum wage jobs. All of them were verbally abusive to her. They, like her mother, told her that she was worthless and wouldn't amount to anything. Since she'd heard that message her whole life she wasn't able to shake it off as she might otherwise have done.

The abuse in a relationship that reinforces your worst fears about yourself is insidious. And it's not only your partner who may criticize you; other people, including friends, may blame you for what's happening, particularly if you're unwilling to leave the relationship when it's clear to them that you should do so.

Just as insidious as abuse that reinforces negative images of yourself is the fact that your partner is probably not all bad, and that he may really love you despite evidence to the contrary. One day you think, "I've had it! This is the last time I'll let him do that to me! I'm leaving!"

But then he apologizes, maybe gives you flowers, and treats you more like he did when you were in the honeymoon phase of your relationship. So you stay. But, gradually, things go back to the way they were before the apology and the cycle of abuse and/or negativity continues.

Like you did when you were a child, you may then turn things on yourself and take responsibility for his actions. "If I do X or don't do Y, maybe he will be more reasonable. It's probably my fault that he's acting this way." So you stay and, like you did with your parents, you try to accomplish the frustrating and generally impossible task of using your actions to change someone else's thoughts, feelings, or actions.

Cookie's husband, when she says that she wants a legal separation, tells her that she is the only woman he has ever loved. He tells her that they're soul mates and they're meant to be together. So she is torn, and she stays in the relationship because she hopes that what her husband says is true.

It doesn't help to tell someone in a dysfunctional relationship that she should leave. She is probably ambivalent about the relationship; there are reasons she wants to leave and reasons she wants to stay. It is human nature, when feeling torn about something, to argue one side when someone else argues the other.

So if you make arguments that support the side of her that wants to leave she will probably flip to the opposite position and be even more convinced that she should stay. In this way she maintains a kind of balance, although not the healthy kind of balance that this book is trying to help you achieve.

Unhealthy Loyalty

I had a conversation with my husband one morning about a pitcher who played for our favorite baseball team, and who was being traded to another team. My husband said that he couldn't blame him for wanting to leave because he was a really good pitcher and our team had been doing very badly for quite a while. I said, only half-jokingly, that that's not the way it's supposed to work; you're supposed to stay loyal to a team no matter how badly it's doing.

I realized a little while later that this is exactly what happens in many family or romantic relationships; you feel a sense of loyalty to the other person so you don't leave, no matter how dysfunctional the relationship is.

Repeating Patterns

It is not uncommon for a woman to be unable to clearly see unhealthy patterns in a romantic relationship until after the relationship is over. More distance can give more clarity. But it can still be hard not to get caught in the same patterns in the next relationship because the warning signs are subtle at first.

When you finally do leave a dysfunctional romantic relationship the lessons you learn from it may help you to make your next relationship healthier. Sometimes, though, the dysfunction and abuse are just less obvious.

For instance, Eleanor left a fiancé who was physically abusive and married a man who did not believe in physical violence. She thought she had found the man of her dreams but came to realize that while there was no physical abuse, her husband was emotionally abusive in subtle ways. His abuse was in the form of apparent concern for her well-being, but she found herself feeling stifled, unable to be herself.

When her husband was called up for jury duty and ended up on a sequestered jury he was gone until the trial was over six months later. During those six months Eleanor started to find herself again, doing the things she enjoyed and not having to worry about what her husband would think or say.

When he came back she found herself going back to her old self-denying way of being. She recognized it, though, and left the marriage two months later.

She realized, looking back on the relationship, that the fact that her husband was not physically abusive did not mean that she had been free of physical harm or danger. At a number of times during the marriage she found herself in places of such self-loathing that she punched walls, sometimes injuring herself. And her husband's lack of recognition of her as a person often led to suicidal feelings. Her husband's abuse, though not physical, could easily have led to her death.

With practice you can start to recognize from the beginning when, as one of my clients put it, "There's no prize at the bottom of that cereal box!"

The Runaway Girlfriend

Instead of staying too long in a relationship, you might go to the opposite extreme and leave at the first sign of trouble (or at the first sign that the relationship is becoming serious).

Mimi's mother, Martha, had a series of boyfriends when Mimi was growing up. Every time Martha and her latest boyfriend got into a big argument Martha broke up with him. Because of this Mimi didn't have a role model to teach her that all couples argue sometimes, but that it's possible to work through arguments and actually strengthen a relationship rather than break it up. So she did the same thing her mother did and broke up with her boyfriends when they had major arguments.

At some point Mimi realized that she wanted to do something different. She read some books and talked to friends who had successfully worked through problems in their relationships. When she and her boyfriend got into a big argument, she decided to try some of the skills she'd learned instead of just breaking up with him.

Tanya, whose mother seemed to have a new boyfriend every week, enjoyed the first month or so of a new romantic relationship, but once the initial excitement faded she got bored. At that point she just stopped calling the guy and didn't respond to his calls; she was already looking for the next guy. It wasn't until she got into her late thirties that she started to think it might be worth trying to find something deeper in a relationship than just the initial excitement.

Patrice didn't date casually; she only went out with guys with whom she had a lot in common and who were good prospects for long-term relationships. The relationships always started well. But when things started to get serious she would start flirting with other guys. Then she would start having one-night stands. Eventually her boyfriend would find out she was being unfaithful and break up with her.

It finally occurred to Patrice that she was afraid that her boyfriends would see through her and decide that she wasn't good enough for them. Rather than risk having her heart broken she did something to force them to break up with her. She realized that if she wanted to be able to sustain a long-term relationship she would need to work through the issues that were making her sabotage herself.

Summer was always attracted to guys who were like her father: charming, solicitous, and romantic. She knew, though, that her father was also unreliable and incapable of following through on commitments. The first time a boyfriend canceled a date or broke a promise to her she decided that he was just like her father and would break her heart, so she broke up with him. She eventually recognized her pattern and decided that it would make sense to give her boyfriends a second chance; just because they were somewhat like her father didn't mean they were necessarily exactly like her father.

How Long Should You Stay?

It's obviously a bad idea to stay in a relationship that is never going to get better. It's also a bad idea to give up on a relationship without giving it a chance to work. As with many other things, it's a lot easier to stick with one extreme or the other than it is to find a reasonable middle ground. How do you decide when it's a good idea to hang in there and try to work through problems and when it's a better idea to cut your losses and move on?

That's a very difficult balance question, and it's likely that there won't be a clear answer. If you find yourself in a situation like this, think about how well your needs are or aren't being met and how well you are or aren't meeting your partner's needs.

A healthy relationship is one in which the partners are generally on the same team. All relationships have conflict, but it makes a big difference whether there's mutual respect and caring or whether it's each person for him- or herself. If both partners want to work through conflicts and are willing to try to see and respect each other's perspectives, it's immensely helpful.

Another way of looking at this is the thoughts and feelings behind the things you do to hurt one another. Are you intentionally hurting each other? Are you unintentionally hurting each other? Or are you intentionally trying not to hurt each other?

A relationship often has a poor prognosis if the partners are intentionally hurting each other. If you're hurting each other unintentionally the prognosis is better because it suggests that you might change your behaviors once you understand what you're doing to hurt your partner. And if you're intentionally not hurting each other, each of you is conscious of your partner's needs and wants and is actively trying to support him or her. This type of relationship has the best prognosis.

Sometimes one partner starts to make changes, but the other partner already has one foot out the door. Maybe you've waited for years for things to change but now you're not willing to wait any more and you have emotionally disengaged. What do you do then? Do you try to get those feelings back? Do you stay in the relationship even though you don't think you will get the feelings back? Do you decide that your partner's changes are too little too late, and leave the relationship?

You can learn to take care of yourself without fleeing one relationship after another or staying in relationships too long. It takes practice. It can also help to get an outside perspective (from a friend, a therapist, or a religious/spiritual guide, for instance) although it's important to make sure that you're the one who makes the final decision about what's right for you.

How Do You Find a Relationship Balance?

For decades Josephine went along with everything her husband, Paul, wanted to do. When they were dating she told him she loved tennis because he had almost become a professional tennis player and it was his passion. She played tennis with him four or five times a week even though she secretly hated it.

Paul was an archaeologist, and before they had children Josephine went on many expeditions with him, usually having to live in primitive conditions at the site of the digs. She hated that, too; it reminded her of all the family camping trips that she'd had to endure when she was growing up.

Once they started their family Josephine no longer went on the archaeological expeditions because she was at home taking care of the children. Even when he was home Paul did little to help raise the children or even to show an interest in their activities.

Once the kids were out of the house Paul expected Josephine to resume going on expeditions with him and playing tennis four or five times a week. He was shocked when she told him she had decided that she was tired of accommodating him and was going to start doing what she wanted, not what he wanted.

It was understandable that Paul was surprised; after all, he and Josephine had always lived by the unspoken agreement that she would do whatever he wanted her to do, and Josephine was violating that agreement.

Eventually Paul and Josephine sought marriage counseling so they could find a middle ground. It wasn't easy, but they arrived at a compromise position where each person (more often than not) had an equal say in what they did or didn't do.

Making Personal Changes

If you grew up in a dysfunctional family there are likely to be things that you would like to change about yourself. It will feel strange and uncomfortable at first, but you can learn new ways to be in the world. Trying to find balance doesn't mean that you have to change everything; you just need to choose some new thoughts, feelings, and behaviors that counterbalance the others.

It does mean taking a serious look at your life and figuring out what to keep, what to change, and what to get rid of altogether. It's time to figure out what you want and need. Once you've done that you can figure out what might be realistically achievable, then begin to formulate a plan for how to do those things and bring more balance to your life.

And while you're doing this evaluation, remember that relationship issues are not caused by just one person; you have your role, as well. Changing your thoughts, feelings, and behaviors does not just mean protecting yourself against the other person's dysfunction. It also means that you need to identify the ways in which you also contribute to conflict and dysfunction.

Do you need to stop criticizing your partner's every move? Do you need to pay attention to ways you create drama, such as flipping from one extreme to the other, first blaming your partner, then declaring that everything is all your fault? If you, as they say in 12-step programs, "keep your side of the street clean," you'll find it much easier to negotiate and find healthier relationships.

Recognizing Relationship Patterns

A good first step when making changes in romantic relationships is to find the commonalities among your partners by doing a relationship history, starting with your father and, if you have them, brothers. What do the men in your life have in common? Which of these things do you like, and which ones would you like to avoid?

You can also look at the women who have been significant parts of your life: your mother, your sisters (if you have them), friends, teachers, etc.

You can do the same thing for employers and coworkers: what seems to be the common thread that runs through these relationships? How does that relate to your family of origin?

Take a close look at the characteristics that you don't want. Are you getting any benefits from them? These benefits probably won't be obvious. But, for instance, if you have a partner who always takes charge of situations you can avoid doing it yourself. That may feel easier to you, and if things go wrong you will not be responsible. Or the opposite: if you have a partner who tends to be lazy and irresponsible you may feel good about yourself because you're hard-working and responsible. If you have a friend who always talks about herself and never asks about you that means that you don't have to make yourself vulnerable by sharing things about yourself.

Now look at your own relationship thoughts and behaviors. Which of them might be contributing to your tendency to find the same kind of relationship over and over? Which of them might lead you to stay in unhealthy relationships or to accept normally unacceptable behaviors from others? Which of them might contribute to problems in your relationships?

For example, you may have low self-esteem and, therefore, choose partners who feel safe because they're less successful or good looking than you are. Low self-esteem can also lead you to stay in unhealthy relationships and accept unacceptable behaviors because you don't think you deserve better. But knowing that these people are not good matches for you may make you feel resentful and lead to hostile behaviors towards your partners. You may create conflict because you're used to chaos.

It's worth investing some time and energy to feel better about yourself so you can also feel better about your relationships.

When working on changes, remember to be gentle with yourself. Understand that there was a reason why you learned to be the way you are. Keep in mind that major changes take time and that you need to take things one step at a time rather than trying to change everything at once.

Is There Hope?

There is a type of couples counseling called Imago Relationship Therapy (see Chapter 11 for more information) that is built on the idea that we find romantic partners who, without us knowing it, trigger the issues we developed in childhood. It seems we are unconsciously trying to get a "do over." We were not able to successfully negotiate the relationship with one or both parents, so we find a similar relationship in which we can try again.

The hopeful part of Imago Relationship Therapy is the idea that partners, in working together on these issues, will find that in the end they are able to help each other heal their childhood wounds because of the very things that have been causing conflict.

Putting It Into Action

1. Do a relationship inventory as suggested earlier in the chapter. List the major characteristics of:

> a) your father
>
> b) your mother
>
> c) your siblings
>
> d) any other significant people in your life when you were growing up

Rianne:

Father: alcoholic; physically and verbally abusive when drunk; usually underemployed; sociable; played with the kids and showed a lot of affection when sober; loved going to the kids' games and other events but was unreliable because of his drinking; good at building and fixing things around the house, including cars

Mother: passive-aggressive; codependent; depressed; low self-esteem; emotionally distant from us kids and rarely found time to spend with us; worked a government job she hated so she could support the family; good cook; kept the house reasonably clean

Older brother, James: overachiever; perfectionist; anxiety problems; during high school was always busy with sports and student government

Little sister, Brandy: the "baby" of the family, so she expects other people to take care of her; more interested in clothes and makeup than in school or career; went to college but dropped out after her sophomore year to get married

Grandma: Took care of us while Mom and Dad were at work; spoiled us by buying us anything we wanted; didn't respect our parents' rules for us when we were staying with her; criticized Mom's housekeeping

Grandpa: Wasn't really involved with us; sat in a chair by the window all day watching the world go by; alcoholic, although he didn't drink in front of us.

2. Next think about other significant people in your life, past and present. (You don't have to include the people listed earlier.) What characteristics do they have in common with your family members? What patterns do you notice?

Include:

a) Your romantic partners

b) Your bosses

c) Your coworkers

d) Your friends

Romantic partners:

I have had only three romantic relationships in the past, each of which lasted a year or more. Now that I think about it, all of the guys had certain characteristics. All of them wined and dined me at the beginning but started doing it less and less as the relationships went on. After a while I never knew when they would treat me to dinner and when they would expect me to pay. All of them had major things that took precedence over me; one was an alcoholic, one played and coached soccer, and another one worked at least 50 hours a week. When they weren't doing those things they usually said they were too tired to go out or do anything with me. All three of them were good to me a lot of the time, but would unexpectedly turn on me and yell at me or even hit me. They always managed to turn it around and blame it on me and I usually believed them. Every one of the relationships ended with the guy breaking up with me, telling me I wasn't good enough (pretty enough, smart enough, rich enough, whatever) for him.

Just a couple of weeks ago I started going out with a new guy. This relationship seems to have started a lot like the other ones, so we'll see what happens.

Bosses:

During college I worked in one of the campus dining halls. We had two supervisors, one of whom was a total Type A personality; she made everyone nervous. The other supervisor was very friendly and laid back. Then one day the laid back supervisor totally lost it and started throwing things around her office. It reminded me of my usually good-natured dad and the total change in his behavior when he was drinking.

Immediately after college I worked for a small nonprofit agency. I really believed in the cause I was working for and I admired my boss, who was a petite, seemingly innocuous woman in her seventies. She used her grandmotherly look to her advantage when dealing with high-powered executives. She acted like she didn't know anything, but she was really sharp and always had something up her sleeve.

She was the same age as my mother and from a similar background, so it was like I was working for my mother. She was also passive aggressive, and negative in the sense that she frequently talked about what was wrong with the world that made it necessary for our foundation to exist.

My current boss is extremely success-oriented, which makes sense given the position he holds. I write and edit publications for the company and I don't feel like I fit into the corporate mindset. I have no interest whatsoever in climbing the corporate ladder and I do a completely different sort of work than my boss does, so he doesn't really know what to do with me!

I often feel left out, alone (there are no other writer/editors on staff and I'm the only woman in my office), and misunderstood. I feel inferior because, unlike the rest of the people in my office, I'm content to stay where I am and am not looking for promotions. It reminds me of all of the times I fell short of the standards set by my brother and was mocked by my mother because I wasn't as good as he was.

Coworkers:

My coworkers tend to be like my boyfriends; they only talk to me when they need something from me. They generally assume that I have nothing else to do but work for them, so they always bring me jobs at the last minute and expect me to complete them by the deadline. Then, if I can't get them done in time, they tell my boss that I'm a screw-up.

I know that's not true, but I haven't yet been able to assert my own needs and challenge them on this. Part of me is afraid that I'll be fired. Part of me believes I should be able to do the impossible things they're asking of me, so I'm obviously a loser if I can't! That reminds me of all the times, when I was a kid, that I tried and tried to keep my dad from drinking or to make my mother happy, or to do everything exactly the same way as James did. I was doomed to failure then just as I am now.

Friends:

I don't have many friends. I have a few friends from college, and that's it; I don't seem to be able to make new friends. My friends, like my dad and my boyfriends, are unreliable. For a while we'll talk every day and go out on the weekends, and then all of a sudden I won't hear from them for weeks on end. Our conversations and get-togethers always seem to be on their schedule. I always end up rearranging my life to fit theirs; it's never the other way around.

This is another effect of my low self-esteem; I think my friends are better than I am, so I don't feel like I have the right to ask them to accommodate me. I figure that if I rock the boat too much they'll just dump me and find another friend. All of them have borrowed money from me because I earn more than they do. They promise they'll pay it back but never do. I hint around about it but don't have the nerve to ask for it directly.

3. Now look at yourself. What characteristics do you have in common with the people described above that you would like to keep, and which would you like to change and/or eliminate?

I'm an intelligent, accomplished person. I graduated from college with honors and I have a high-paying job with a Fortune 500 company. But I grew up in my brother's shadow; no matter how well I did, I couldn't compete with him. My mother has always compared the two of us and made it clear that she loved and appreciated him much more than she did me. So even though there are many people who say positive things about me I still have extremely low self-esteem.

I inherited my mother's depression and, even though I try to avoid it, I find myself using some of the same passive-aggressive tactics my mother does. I care a lot about other people and will pretty much do anything for my family and friends; that feels a lot safer than asking other people to do things for me. Like my sister Brandy, I want nothing more than to have someone take care of me. But I don't have her sense of entitlement so I don't demand it the way she does.

I do like my conscientiousness and my dedication to doing my best; not only is that my nature, but being James' younger sister helped me to try even harder than I would have otherwise. My mother, as much as she complained, excelled at her job, so I learned the value of hard work.

I also like the fact that I have inherited some of my father's good nature and generosity.

The things I would like to change are pretty clear. I want to do something about my depression. I want to raise my self-esteem and see myself more realistically. I want to develop and maintain boundaries so I can say no to unreasonable requests. I want to be more assertive so that I can ask directly for what I need rather than being passive-aggressive.

4. Are there any deal breakers in your relationships? If so, what, if anything, do you think can be done about them? Are there any relationships that you think you might need to end?

Emotional and physical abuse from my boyfriends is a deal breaker. If my current boyfriend starts to do those things I will ask him to go to counseling and/or anger management classes. If he refuses to do so, or if he doesn't actively participate and improve his behavior, I need to leave.

Things need to change for me at work, too. I need to make it clear that I won't tolerate my coworkers' taking advantage of me. I do think that despite our differences my boss does respect and value me, so if I really push the issue I think he'll support me; I'm not really worried that I'll be fired.

My relationships, such as they are, with my siblings are fine. My relationship with Brandy is shallow and limited. We have no interests in common; we see each other on holidays and send each other birthday gifts.

My relationship with James is less superficial than the one with Brandy only because we have intellectual interests in common. He has never understood why I felt like I had to compete with him and he doesn't think that our mother treats me worse than she treats him.

My relationship with my parents is trickier. I usually just engage in friendly chitchat with my dad because he only wants to talk about happy things, nothing unpleasant or difficult. If he's been drinking he's angry and violent, so I avoid him. I might not have been able to get away when I was a kid, but now that I'm an adult I can.

I speak to my mother very little. Talking to her is a real downer; she's always negative and complaining and she often criticizes me. She rarely has anything good to say and her negativity drags me down. I've thought about cutting her out of my life entirely but I'm not prepared to do that right now.

5. Can you see any hidden benefits that dysfunction (yours and others') provides you?

I realize that I date emotionally unavailable men so I have an excuse not to trust them and open up to them. When I make disparaging comments about myself it's partly because I want other people to tell me that it's not true and that I'm really a good person. It's convenient, in a way, for me to have irresponsible and unreasonable people around me because I get to be righteously indignant about them. I get sympathy from others because of the people I have to put up with at work, in my family, and in my social life.

6. Which of your relationship behaviors would you like to change? What steps will you take to change them?

I would like to stop putting myself down around other people. It makes me feel worse about myself and I end up attracting people who take advantage of my low self-esteem. I tell myself that I don't deserve good things and I end up with friends and boyfriends who reinforce that belief.

When I'm feeling depressed I just hole up in my apartment and don't go anywhere or talk to anyone. I don't do anything to make myself feel better. I always say yes when people ask me to do things, but end up resentful if I didn't want to do them. I am afraid to ask people for what I want or need; I only hint about it and hope that someone else will pick up on the hint.

My mom has never acknowledged her depression or done anything about it. I have decided that I'm going to be more proactive. I've started going to counseling and am considering medication to help me overcome the effects of depression. I'm also learning to challenge my negative thoughts about myself. My therapist suggested that I treat myself the way I would treat a friend; would I talk to her the way I talk to myself? Of course not! So I'm practicing talking to myself as I would to a friend.

I'm also practicing saying no (for instance, saying no to my sister's request to borrow money) and asking for what I want or need (for instance, asking someone for directions). Because these are relatively new skills for me I'm starting with easy ones; I'll gradually work my way up to more difficult ones.

7. Do you find yourself staying too long in relationships or giving up on them too quickly? If so, how can you begin the process of finding the middle ground between the two?

Looking back, I realize that I've tended to stay in relationships way too long. It's part of my low self-esteem and my inability to say no. I don't want to hurt my boyfriend's feelings, so I don't tell him how I feel. I become passive-aggressive rather than telling him directly that the relationship isn't working for me. Because of what my mother told me when I was growing up, I constantly worry that I won't find another guy who's willing to go out with me.

Reading this book has made me much more aware of the signs of dysfunction in a relationship, which means that I'm now able to recognize the signs sooner, hopefully before I get too far into a bad relationship. The changes I'm trying to make in my thoughts and feelings should help me to value myself enough to leave the relationship if that seems like the right thing to do.

I know that being extremely alert to signs of relationship problems could easily lead to going to the opposite extreme and jumping out of relationships without giving them a chance. So I'll try to be alert for that, too, and talk to people I trust so I can benefit from their observations, as well.

Part II

Chapter 4

Needs

1. Did you experience or witness physical, sexual, and/or emotional abuse while you were growing up?

2. If you had siblings, did it feel like your parents treated all of you appropriately based upon your personalities?

3. Did your parents ignore your privacy, such as coming into your bedroom without warning?

4. Did your parents respect your likes, dislikes, and abilities, and did you have a voice in decisions about your extracurricular activities?

5. Do you find it difficult to ask other people for help?

6. Did it feel like your parents did well at helping you to feel safe while still allowing you to have appropriate freedoms?

So far we've talked about working towards a fairer distribution of responsibilities at home, at work, and elsewhere; setting and maintaining boundaries so you have a choice about how much time and energy you give to others and how much you use to support yourself; and becoming aware of and changing unhealthy patterns in relationships.

All of these topics have to do with needs. How can you try to find a balance between meeting others' needs and meeting your own needs? If you answered yes to questions 1, 3, and/or 5, or if you answered no to questions 2, 4 and/or 6, you probably had some problems getting your needs met in childhood. If you spend a lot more time taking care of others' needs than taking care of your own, this chapter will help you understand how this probably came about.

Childhood Needs

Young children are needy and self-centered by definition. It's their job. It's the job of the caretakers of those children to meet those needs as well as they can. No parent or other caregiver can do it perfectly. She can, however, do her best to help her child negotiate the stages of childhood, from the complete dependence of an infant to the increasing independence of an older child.

A parent can understand that there are times in a child's life when she needs the safety of a parent and times when she needs to be able to strike out on her own and assert her own identity. A healthy parent does her best not to be either under-protective or over-protective of her child. A healthy parent also knows that it is important that she take care of herself; her child is not responsible for taking care of her.

But if you have at least one parent who is unable to adequately take care of him- or herself, let alone a child, your needs will not be met satisfactorily. For example, Elaine's grandmothers both died when her parents were young. Neither of her parents had the nurturing presence of a mother in their lives so they were unable to give that to Elaine.

Children whose needs are not being met often conclude that they are wrong to have those needs, or at the very least that it's a problem to have them. Elaine gets confused because she can hardly blame her parents for having lost their parents, but she still needed more from them than she got; it's hard for her to accept the needs she had even though they were perfectly reasonable.

The Need for Guidance

Deirdre's parents expected her to do tasks like housecleaning and cooking but did not teach her how to do them. When Deirdre was six years old her mother, out of the blue, told her to do the family's laundry. She didn't tell Deirdre how to do it, and Deirdre was afraid to ask. So she tried to obey her mother. She had to stand on a chair because she wasn't tall enough to use the washer; when she put the clothes in she stuffed in as many as she could. The machine overflowed and flooded the basement. When her mother found out what had happened, she yelled at Deirdre and beat her for doing the job wrong.

Many women speak of not having had their mothers explain to them what happens when a girl enters puberty. The ones who had not been taught about the menstrual cycle panicked when they got their first periods. Because they didn't feel comfortable asking for help, they might have tried to figure things out on their own. Or, if their mothers did explain menstruation to them, they might have been reluctant to tell their mothers when they first got their periods, instead finding ways to get the necessary supplies on their own.

I've also heard from many clients that their mothers didn't teach them about other "girl things" like shaving their legs. Sophia's mother didn't buy her a bra or deodorant until after the need for them was so obvious that Sophia ended up being embarrassed by other kids making fun of her. This is yet another way that a girl might get the idea that she is unimportant to her parents and not worth noticing.

Sometimes a father is disappointed when he has a daughter instead of a son, so the daughter ends up becoming a tomboy, trying to be the boy that her father wanted her to be. Terri's father, Terence, had been in Little League when he was growing up, so he expected Terri to do the next best thing, as he saw it, and play softball.

Unfortunately, Terence was too busy with work to teach Terri how to pitch or catch. Most of the other girls on the team had parents who worked on skills with them, so they progressed a lot more quickly than Terri did. She was humiliated at every practice and spent most games sitting on the bench. She wondered why her father wouldn't help her; she eventually decided that she was a disappointment to him and just needed to figure things out on her own.

Physical Safety

One of the biggest needs a child has is for safety, which includes physical safety and well-being. No one would argue that a child does not need a home, clothes, and food to feel safe and secure. But a child also needs to feel physically safe, not living in fear of being beaten, sexually abused, or harmed in some other physical way.

Carolyn's father was very violent. Early in life Carolyn decided that it was her job to defend her mother and her younger brothers and sisters against him. She often physically came between her father and other members of the family so that he wouldn't hurt them.

Unfortunately that often meant that she was the one who was hurt. Even in adulthood she has found it hard to shake the idea that it's her job to defend everyone in her family. Only now, in therapy, is she getting in touch with the feelings of fear and helplessness that she tried so hard to deny when she was a child.

Sometimes one parent or child is singled out for physical abuse. This is obviously quite traumatic to the person who is being abused. But someone who witnesses this abuse, even if she is never physically abused herself, is also traumatized. Erin's father never hit her, but she saw him hit her brother many times. She didn't know until much later that witnessing those incidents was the cause of some of her fears about physical contact with others.

In the movie *Affliction* a man whose older brother was frequently beaten by their father said to his brother, "At least I was never afflicted by that man's violence." The older brother paused a moment, laughed, and said, "That's what you think!"

Emotional Safety

Emotional safety and stability are essential, too. A child needs to have adults show by their responses to and reflections of her actions and words that they have seen who she is; in this way they confirm that she exists. A child needs her parents and others to value who she is as a unique person so that she grows up knowing that she has a *right* to exist.

A child needs to learn about boundaries and personal space, including the dividing lines between her and other people as well as what her and others' rights are in relationships. For many people a major part of therapy is learning these things, because they were not taught them as children.

When a child is physically harmed she is also emotionally harmed. She is confused by the abuse, especially when it is perpetrated by a family member, a family friend, or someone else who seems trustworthy but is not.

The abuse is sometimes in the form of inappropriate sexual behavior. Unfortunately, the child is often reluctant to talk about it and parents, even if they know about it, may or may not admit that they know. Jillian and her sister have some vague, strange memories and wonder if their older brother abused them, but he and their parents deny that anything happened, so Jillian and her sister are left wondering.

Elise's older sister Moira was ten years older than she was, so when Moira was deemed old enough she became Elise's babysitter. Moira resented Elise and she terrified her younger sister, who was afraid that she would kill her. Moira threatened to really hurt Elise if she told their parents what was going on, so she never did. Elise dreaded being alone with her sister, even in public, even when it was for a very short time, such as when Moira took her to the restroom at restaurants.

One of Elise's worst memories was of a time that their parents had friends over for dinner; Moira and Elise were not allowed to be in the room with the adults, so they were sent down the hall and given dinner there. Even though Elise's parents were literally right down the hall, as far as she was concerned they might as well have been on Mars because she was still alone with Moira and at her mercy. Knowing that potential rescue was right down the hall but that it was unavailable to her actually felt worse than having her parents far away.

Predictability

A child needs predictability. When possible, if there is going to be a major change in her life such as a move or a new sibling, she needs to be prepared for it before it happens.

She also needs to understand and be able to count on cause and effect relationships. For instance, she needs, whenever possible, to know in advance what is acceptable behavior and what is not and what the consequences will be if she acts unacceptably. These rules need to be consistent from day to day and incident to incident. When discipline is delivered it needs to be delivered in a loving way, making it clear that the discipline does not mean that she is a bad person. She does not need to change herself to be OK; she just needs to change her behavior.

Unfortunately, one of the hallmarks of a dysfunctional family is its instability and unpredictability. You never know if Dad is going to be drunk or sober. Or you don't know if Mom is going to be happy or depressed. Your family may move frequently so that you aren't able to feel rooted in a community. Your parents may throw or give away your toys or other possessions without your knowledge, so you never know when something might disappear. Your parents may deprive you of any sense of privacy, feeling free to come into your bedroom without warning or to search your belongings when you're not present. The inconsistency prevents you from feeling safe.

There can seem to be no rhyme or reason to your parents' behavior and the mood or atmosphere can change in an instant. One time you walk past Mom and nothing happens, but the next time she yells at you to get out of her sight because you're bothering her. You didn't do anything different the second time and yet you got a drastically different reaction.

When Sophia was eight years old she and her family visited her mother's parents. One night she and her brother were awakened at 2:00 in the morning and told that they were leaving; their mother had gotten into a fight with their grandmother and did not want to stay another minute. Both kids, dazed and confused from the sudden awakening, were told that they had ten minutes to pack their things or their parents would leave without them. In her haste Sophia accidentally left her jewelry box behind; it was her favorite Christmas present from the previous year and it contained all of the costume jewelry she loved wearing. She never saw the box or the jewelry again.

After that incident Sophia's mom thought her whole family hated her, so they no longer attended family gatherings. Sophia wrote letters to her cousin and asked her mother to mail them for her; she didn't find out until years later that her mother destroyed the letters rather than sending them. She also intercepted the letters Sophia's cousin sent her. Her cousin, when she stopped hearing from Sophia, decided that Sophia didn't like her any more, so she stopped writing to her.

Sasha's father was in the military so they moved often. The children were never told about the moves until the day they were leaving; they never got a chance to say goodbye to their friends. They never knew how long they would stay in any given place and they were reluctant to make close friends that they knew they'd probably lose soon.

Ramona's father has schizophrenia, but he was not diagnosed until she was an adult. The entire family was terrified of him because they never knew when he would do something to them. One time he started bashing holes in the living room walls with a sledgehammer. Another time he sold Ramona's bed because he said he needed the money to pay bills.

Children who have parents or older siblings who are abusive cannot feel safe unless the abuser is not present. Penny loved when her father had evening meetings at work because that meant that she could actually be comfortable in her own home. She dreaded weekends and summer vacations because they meant more time spent with her father.

Unacknowledged Trauma

A child may be confused, angry or resentful if her parents allow her to be harmed emotionally, physically, or sexually at home, at school, or elsewhere.

Elise's parents never mentioned the emotional and physical abuse she got from her older sister Moira, so she didn't talk to them about it until she was an adult. They denied having known what was going on, but Elise wondered if they were just pretending it wasn't happening because it was more convenient to use Moira as a babysitter than to hire someone to do it.

Tasha, after an uncle made sexual advances towards her while he was visiting the family, wondered if he would not have done so had her parents not allowed him to sleep in her bedroom.

Lily remembers a time when her brother sexually abused her. She is ashamed of the memory even though she has learned that she did nothing wrong. She is still unwilling to speak of it with anyone other than one or two people whom she most trusts. She does not discuss it with her parents.

Lorraine went to a day care center from the time she was one year old until she went to kindergarten. One of the day care workers was angry most of the time and took it out on the kids, yelling at them and occasionally hitting one of them. Lorraine tried to tell her parents about it a couple of times but they thought she was just talking about normal disciplinary behavior, so they told her that it was fine. After a while Lorraine stopped trying to get them to understand.

Kendra was bullied at school. When she told her parents about it they said there was nothing they could do and that it was a sort of rite of passage, something that everyone had to deal with. The bullying kept escalating and Kendra was afraid that she was going to be seriously hurt, but she had concluded that her parents weren't going to help and she was on her own. This pattern followed her into adulthood; she never asked anyone for help because she thought it was her job to take care of herself and no one else's.

A child who experiences trauma often deliberately keeps this knowledge from her parents because of shame or because she doesn't want to hurt them. And in some cases she may not fully remember the events, wondering for years if they really happened. These experiences can lead her to question her own reality and her value as a person.

Unrecognized Needs

Sometimes parents don't recognize a child's needs.

Every year Serena asked to be allowed to invite a few friends over for a birthday party. Every year her mother told her no. Serena, her parents, her siblings, and sometimes her grandparents were the only ones who attended her birthday gatherings. Every one of her birthday pictures shows her, unsmiling, sitting at the kitchen table with her family. One year her mother, instead of a cake, bought some day-old cupcakes at the grocery store because they were half price. The cupcakes had strawberries in them. She had apparently forgotten that Serena was allergic to strawberries.

Madeline's siblings all had significant problems; one was physically disabled, another had a learning disability, and a third was prone to panic attacks. Madeline was the "good" child who didn't have any unusual conditions, so her parents decided they didn't have to worry about her.

This eventually triggered a deep depression during which Madeline tried to commit suicide by slitting her wrists. She was hospitalized and, for a little while, was the center of attention in the family. But then her physically disabled brother needed surgery, so things went back to the way they were before; Madeline was left to take care of herself.

Because Madeline's parents trusted her to be well-behaved they didn't give her a curfew or pay attention to what she did when she was not at school. During her senior year of high school she got pregnant. Her parents, without consulting her, decided that she would have the baby and put him up for adoption.

She was not given the opportunity to hold her son after he was born; she grieved for years, wishing she knew where he was and what he was doing. Her parents did not tell her that she could have had an open adoption so that she would have gotten photos and periodic updates on him.

She didn't meet her son until he was 19 and came looking for her. She found out that he'd been angry with her his whole life because he thought she had the option of seeing him and had chosen not to do so; they were both very glad, once he heard her side of the story, that he had looked for her despite his anger towards her.

Am I Important?

There are many times that a child in a dysfunctional household feels like she is an inconvenience to her parents and that they resent her being there and taking up their time. She doesn't feel like she's seen, respected, and loved for who she is.

In many cases this comes from having narcissistic parents. These parents did not get appropriate validation from their parents, so they have spent their lives trying to prove their own importance. This often happens at their children's expense. Dr. Karyl McBride's book *Will I Ever Be Good Enough?: Healing the Daughters of Narcissistic Mothers* and Eleanor D. Payson's *The Wizard of Oz and Other Narcissists: Coping with the One-way Relationship in Work, Love, and Family* are both valuable resources for understanding and dealing with narcissistic parents and others.

During the summer Sian and her siblings were told that they were not allowed to come into the house before dinnertime. When they needed to use the bathroom they asked friends if they could use theirs. Spending time with her friends' families (which Sian much preferred to being with her own family) showed her that there were parents who weren't drunk most of the time and who valued their children. She wished she could be one of those children.

Children in dysfunctional families often don't feel like they're important or special. They don't know if they're worthy of having their needs met. Evelyn feels greedy when she craves attention. Her sister, who is an award-winning artist, receives a lot of attention for her work. Evelyn resents this and avoids going to art shows where her sister's work is featured. Then she feels guilty for feeling that way.

People like Evelyn's sister often go to a lot of effort to make their parents proud of them, thinking that their accomplishments will earn the love from their parents that their mere existence has not gotten them. This usually doesn't work, but they keep trying, even into adulthood.

Validation of Feelings

Someone who grows up in a troubled household rarely has her reality validated because family members are usually too enmeshed in the dysfunction and people outside of the family are not allowed to see what goes on. In this kind of family kids are not only told that they're not allowed to express feelings; they're told that their feelings are wrong and they shouldn't (or even don't) have them. When these kids see something going on in the family that is not right they're told that they're mistaken.

Jeri, though, remembers a time that a friend was at her house when her parents didn't know about it. The friend was in the bathroom and heard an argument between Jeri and her father. Later the friend told her that she was shocked by what she heard.

Jeri tells this story to validate her perception that her family was dysfunctional. Unfortunately, the messages that she got from her parents usually overrule the saner response she got from her friend, so she is not completely able to believe what she is saying.

They Love Me, They Love Me Not

In most cases even the most dysfunctional parents do show love for their children at least sometimes. This is confusing to children, who see everything in black and white terms. Either my parents love me or they don't. Either they're good or they're bad. Either I'm good or I'm bad. There's no in between. If it's at least sometimes clear that their parents love them, children generally conclude that the parents' dysfunctional behaviors are the result of the children doing something wrong or being too needy.

Maeve's mother called Maeve her "shining star" when she was a child, but also put her down at every available opportunity. This confused Maeve, who didn't know which her mother believed: was she good or was she bad? She didn't understand that her mother could sometimes believe one, sometimes the other, or even that she could believe both at the same time.

Whose Life Is It?

"The greatest tragedy of the family is the unlived lives of the parents." –Carl Jung

Sometimes parents live vicariously through their kids. It's one thing to try to make sure that your kids have the opportunities you didn't have; it's entirely another to try to make your children into something they're not just so you can rewrite your own childhood.

Liza's parents didn't participate in sports when they were kids; her father was athletic but his parents either weren't able or weren't willing to take him to practices, so he never joined any teams. Liza's mother wasn't athletic at all. When Liza was a child her parents enrolled her in various sports: basketball, gymnastics, swimming, and soccer.

Liza, even though she wasn't athletic, did enjoy soccer. But she wasn't tall enough to be good at basketball, she was terrified of falling off of the gymnastics equipment, and she was afraid to dive into the water during swimming class. Her parents didn't listen to her when she asked them to let her stop. They didn't think about what was best for her; they were focused on making her into an athlete to make up for their lack of athletic opportunities.

Insecure Parents

Many dysfunctional parents try to help themselves feel better at their children's expense. Margot's mother was overweight and she usually prepared meals that were unhealthful and high in calories. Everyone in the family was trained to eat until they were stuffed, to belong to the "clean plate club," and to finish dishes that couldn't be saved for another meal. Margot, like the rest of the family, became overweight. Then her mother called her fat.

Louise's father often said to her, "We do everything for you and you don't appreciate it. You don't care about anybody but yourself!" Actually, the one who demonstrated the least care for others in the family was her father himself. Louise was a sensitive child and was deeply affected by her father's declaration.

Years later when she was working as a clinical social worker, part of Louise felt like her father was right even though her choice of career clearly suggested otherwise and no one other than her father had ever called her selfish.

Liesel was not allowed to spend much time alone with her father because her mother was jealous and thought her father liked Liesel more than he liked her mother. Liesel's mother allowed her jealousy to interfere with her daughter's ability to form a deep relationship with her father and, later, with other men.

Absent Parents

When a parent leaves it is very difficult for the children. That leaving can take many forms. A child will feel abandoned, for instance, if a parent dies. In this case the parent did nothing wrong, but the child was still deprived of an essential person in her life. In many cases a parent chooses to leave, which can lead the children to wonder what they did to cause the abandonment. And sometimes a parent who is physically present in the home is still absent in one way or another because of alcoholism, because of mental or chronic physical illness, or because he or she works long hours, for instance.

In Lauren's case it was a combination of two things. Her mother was bedridden and her father worked nights to support the family and was therefore usually not home when Lauren was awake. Lauren was an only child, so she was often lonely.

When parents are absent older children often take on their roles. Marina's oldest sister, Leah, essentially acted as Marina's father because their father left when Marina was two years old. Because Leah was taking on a male role in the family she rejected "girly" things like clothes and makeup. Marina, who admired her sister greatly, imitated her, but she really wanted to be able to act like a girl. Even as an adult she found herself torn between male and female roles.

When a parent leaves, a child may tell herself that she doesn't miss him and that it doesn't matter. Sometimes, though, she recognizes that there is a void in her life and that even if the parent were there he wouldn't fill that void. As Prue, one of three sisters in the TV series *Charmed* said of their father, "I miss who he should have been. I miss who he never was. I don't miss *him*."

Who is the Parent?

In some cases it seems that the parents' and children's roles in the family are reversed. The children may become what are called *parentified children* and may actually run the household (cooking, cleaning, etc.). They may also take care of their siblings and, if one of the parents is physically or mentally disabled, take care of the parent, as well.

For instance, Francesca was the oldest of four children. Her father worked long hours and was rarely home. Her mother, who was a stay at home mom, was severely depressed for most of Francesca's childhood. Many days she never got out of bed. Even when she did get out of bed she usually spent her days watching TV. She didn't have the energy to get the kids ready for school or to cook meals for the family, so Francesca took over those responsibilities.

It's also often the case that, emotionally, the parent becomes the child and the child becomes the parent. At a time when the child should be comfortable in the knowledge that her parents will meet her needs appropriately, she instead finds the tables turned; she ends up feeling responsible for meeting her parents' needs instead.

Faith's mother lost her own mother when she was five years old. Faith was born when her mother was fifteen and was given her maternal grandmother's name. There was nothing strange about that; after all, children are often given family names.

This seemed to go beyond that, though. Faith's mother, at fifteen, was clearly too young to be a mother. And it seemed that she had stopped growing emotionally when her mother died, so she acted like she was five years old. Without Faith's mom realizing it she put Faith in the role of the mother she had lost.

Sometimes parents are just plain childish. For instance, Gilda's father was a very bad sport. When the family played a new board game he would insist that other family members read the rules and explain them to him. If a situation then came up that was unfavorable to him he would claim he hadn't known that rule and the rule would be ignored. When he made a move that helped him at another player's expense it was just the way the game was played. If another player did the same, though, Gilda's father took it personally.

Eva's mother was often on a diet but she cheated a lot. She often sneaked a spoonful of peanut butter or a handful of crackers. More than once Eva came upon her mother munching on crackers, at which point her mother would stop chewing and pretend she had nothing in her mouth. She acted much like a child who has been caught with her hand in the cookie jar.

The Results of Abuse and Neglect

Self-Accusation

When you are a child you are dependent upon adults for your survival. You are pre-programmed to assume that your parents are perfect. It would be unthinkable that they might do something that was less than perfect or even wrong, so it is safer to conclude that you, the child, are inadequate or wrong in some way.

Believing that you are the cause of the problem is also, in a strange way, empowering. If you are the cause of the problem you can control the problem. If you think it's your fault it's possible to believe that you can somehow fix the problem and make the situation better.

But, as I've said in earlier chapters, this is a mistaken belief. Yes, it's possible that you did something wrong, as all children do. But it's also possible that, whatever you did wrong, your parent's reaction was out of proportion to the offense.

Even the best parents have times that they react in ways they later regret. The reaction may have been more about the parent and what was going on with him or her (including, among other things, being drunk, depressed, tired, or anxious) than it was about you. But you had no way of knowing that.

Denial of Physical Needs

Many children learn that expressing their needs does not necessarily lead to them being met. So they may try to deny that they have needs, a denial that generally continues into adulthood; they stop asking others for help or support.

This can include denial of both physical and emotional needs. When Harriet had an earache as a child she didn't tell either of her parents about it. A week later when she admitted to them that she was in pain they took her to the doctor. It turned out that she had a severe ear infection; the doctor asked them why they'd waited so long to get it treated. Harriet's parents punished her when they got home because she had unintentionally made them look bad.

Harriet carried this denial of her physical needs into adulthood. She was an elementary school teacher and was so dedicated to doing the best she could for her students that she never took a break, even to use the restroom or to eat. After a while she became unable even to recognize the signs that those needs were there.

Henrietta almost never asks anyone else for help. After she had an emergency appendectomy she called a cab to take her home because she didn't want to bother friends or relatives by asking them to come get her. She realizes that bad things have happened to her, but she beats herself up for being sad or angry about it; instead, she tells herself that she should just "get over it."

Denial of Emotional Needs

If you grow up in a troubled family you find yourself walking on eggshells, trying to get a sense of your parent's mood so that you know how to react, or deciding whether you need to go elsewhere until conditions are more favorable. This leads to chameleon-like behavior; you learn to adapt to whatever the person you are with is saying or doing in the hopes that you will avoid a negative reaction.

This adaptability can be a good thing; it can make you very responsive to others' needs. On the other hand, after a while you've changed yourself so many times for so many people that you no longer really know who you are, what you like, and what you need. And even if you do somehow know what you want or need you may be afraid to tell anyone about it or ask for it. If you do something to meet your own needs you might feel guilty about it. This also ties in to the lack of boundaries and the inability to say no that we've discussed earlier.

Carol Anne has a roommate, Cora, who has Huntington's disease. Carol Anne does her best to take care of Cora, but she is dealing with issues of her own and has a hard time finding a balance between taking care of Cora and helping Cora to remember the things she can still do for herself. As Cora loses more and more control of her body she understandably becomes angrier and angrier, and Carol Anne finds herself wanting to escape.

She feels guilty because she thinks she should be more selfless and do more for Cora, and because of her feelings of resentment. She is beginning to realize that she is doing the best she can for Cora; she is now trying to let go of the guilt and self-accusations.

Needlessness

Needlessness, not neediness, is romanticized in our culture. Think of all of those "hero single-handedly saving the helpless from a deadly threat" TV shows and movies that are out there. Certainly, heroic and dangerous acts like that are noble and require great courage.

But, looked at another way, if you are dealing with one crisis or physical danger after another you can avoid dealing with your feelings and your own vulnerabilities. The Swiss psychiatrist Carl Jung said, "Space flights are merely an escape, a fleeing away from oneself, because it is easier to go to Mars or to the moon than it is to penetrate one's own being."

Think about a movie in which the bad guy has killed one of the main character's loved ones and is threatening to kill others. The main character chases the bad guy so he can prevent more deaths from happening. While he is in pursuit he has one goal and one thought: catch the bad guy. There is no time for more than momentary feelings of grief and loss. Adrenaline keeps him going.

But what happens when the crisis is over? He is forced to face life without his loved one. He can no longer avoid grieving the loss.

It takes a great deal of courage (of a different kind) to be vulnerable and to ask for help. Being the person who offers or gives help can be seen as a power position, whereas asking for and/or getting help can be seen as weakness.

Can You Be Too Self-reliant?

The late author Shel Silverstein once said in an interview, "Don't be dependent on anyone else - man, woman, child or dog." This idea resonates with many people who grew up in dysfunctional families. They love the idea of being "fiercely independent."

They learned to be self-reliant because when they were growing up their caregivers neglected, abandoned, or abused them. During that early time in their lives when they were completely dependent upon adults who were supposed to take care of their needs, those adults let them down. They learned early on that they couldn't rely on anyone else, even in situations in which they should be able to do so. So, as they got older, instead of moving from completely dependent to interdependent (as is the ideal), they swung to the opposite extreme: doing their best not to need anyone for anything.

So, what's the problem with that? First, it's not possible. No person will ever be completely independent from others—we're made to be social beings, "pack animals," if you will. Second, the complete independence that many people seek also interferes with their ability to open up to other human beings, an essential part of significant relationships.

Sometimes Needy

Some people act very needy even if they are adults who are fully capable of taking care of themselves. You may sometimes act needy without even knowing it. If you have denied having needs for most of your life you may suddenly find yourself confronted and overwhelmed by those needs.

This can happen for many reasons, usually when the life that has seemed manageable to you has suddenly and clearly become unmanageable, possibly because of illness, injury, a life-changing event, or a family conflict (a blowup with a parent to whom you've always deferred in the past, for instance). At that point you may become uncomfortably (and often impractically) needy.

The Continuing Effects of Unfulfilled Emotional Needs

An emotional need starts in childhood and is a manageable size. But the longer the need isn't met, the bigger it gets, until it becomes extremely difficult to take care of it. I am reminded of a phrase someone used about one of my internship clients at a mental hospital. He referred to her as a "bottomless pit of need"—she would take all the attention that people were willing or able to give her, but it was never enough.

The last thing most of us want to be is a bottomless pit of need. Not only is that uncomfortable because there's a limit to what others can do for us, but it can make people feel inadequate because they can't offer the amount of help we're seeking; it may also be annoying and drive them away.

Big Kids Don't Cry

Most children in dysfunctional homes learn early that it's not acceptable to cry, so they rarely do, even when they're young. Brianne, as a teenager, loved the Melissa Manchester song in which she sang,

"Don't cry out loud, just keep it inside and learn how to hide your feelings." This was exactly what Brianne had learned to do, and what she continued to do until she was an adult and finally sought counseling for depression.

Many of my clients resist crying in session or apologize to me if they do cry even though they know that a therapy session is one situation in which crying is acceptable. Crying in front of other people is generally an uncomfortable thing for them, particularly if their parents discouraged it. That's a really hard lesson to unlearn.

It Must Be Out There Somewhere!

People who have had the experiences I've described have emotional needs, as everyone does, but they haven't acquired the inner resources that are needed to meet them.

So they may look outside of themselves to get their needs met. People-pleasers, as we discussed earlier, help others in the hope that they will be helped in return. Some people become alcoholics and drug addicts because they are looking for something to give them a quick fix. Some try to get answers from gurus or other authority figures, while others look to popular culture to try to find self-worth.

These attempts to get something or someone else to fulfill us will not work, though. And as much as we might want them, there are no quick fixes, either.

Relationship Challenges

It can often be hard to find a way to have your needs met while also respecting the needs of your partner. Some situations are particularly difficult to negotiate.

For instance, there are many romantic relationships in which partners' needs or desires for physical intimacy differ. What do you do then? Is there a way for each person to get at least some of his or her needs met without one or both partners feeling frustrated or coerced?

To give another example, what if one partner is offered a great job somewhere else in the country but the other is in a great job where you live now (or doesn't want to leave family, or whatever)? How do you decide on the best course of action?

What do you do if one partner wants children and the other doesn't? What if there's a conflict about whether to raise your children in one religion vs. another, or in no religion at all? What if your approaches to raising your children are radically different?

In these types of situations pros and cons need to be examined so that the most reasonable (even though imperfect) solution can be found. At that point it becomes a matter of adjusting to any unfairness to one or both partners that may result. How does each of you deal with your feelings about the compromises that are reached? How do you make the situation as positive as you can?

Parenting Challenges

Parenting can be a daunting task for people who grew up in unhealthy families, given that their parents were not positive role models. It is important for them to do their best to stop the cycle of unhealthy parenting, which often means being very conscious of their parenting styles.

Some, like Kat, choose not to have children at all. This is often a difficult choice because these women often do have at least some desire to be mothers. It becomes a matter of deciding whether to take the risk of perpetuating the parenting they received.

If you have children, how do you deal with their needs? How do you treat them when they need help or when they cry? Are you more understanding and gentle with them than your parents were with you, or than you are with yourself? Or do you treat them the same way you were treated?

I think it makes sense to adapt parenting styles to the personalities and needs of both parents and children. It is also worthwhile to think about how things were for you as a child and how it felt to you, and consider how your relationship with your kids is similar or different.

Many of my clients grew up with authoritative parents who never admitted having made mistakes and who said, "It's my way or the highway!" or, "When you're living in my house, you live by my rules!" My clients often react against this in their own parenting styles but have to be careful not to go too far the other way and be too permissive, letting the kids run the show.

Here's that problem of balance again. You can show your kids that you're human, admit (when appropriate) to having made mistakes, and treat your kids with respect. But you still need to make it clear that you're the parent and you're in charge, not them.

Justine's mother was an emotionally distant alcoholic. Justine constantly craved, but didn't get, her mother's love, attention, and approval. When she had a daughter of her own she decided that she would be emotionally involved with her child in the way that her mother was not. But she was acutely aware that she could easily go too far in that direction and become her daughter's friend instead of her parent, so she made a point of keeping their roles distinct.

Did your parents help you to feel good about yourself, even in the face of your needs (while still encouraging you to stand on your own when appropriate), or did their parenting feel over- or under-protective? If you put yourself in your child's shoes or imagine that you are an impartial adult watching your family from outside, what would you think and feel about the way you're parenting your children?

If you decide that there are things you want to change about your parenting style I encourage you to be gentle with yourself; there is a reason why you have acted the way you have, and even if you've decided that something else would be more appropriate there is no point to beating yourself up about it. Just make the changes you think are needed and move on.

Balancing Needs

Remember that taking care of yourself makes you better able to take care of your children. A concrete example is when you're on an airplane and they tell you what to do if the cabin loses pressure. Oxygen masks will drop down. If you have a small child with you, you should put on your own mask before putting a mask on her. If you've fainted from lack of oxygen you won't be able to help her. Help yourself first, and that will enable you to help your child.

So there are times when it makes sense to meet your own needs first so you are more available to meet your kids' needs. There are also times when it makes sense for a child to find a way to meet her own needs, which she might not do if you jump in and help her right away. Again, it's a matter of trying to find a healthy middle ground.

It's also a good idea to remain aware of the possibility that your kids may be meeting some of *your* needs that are more appropriately met by someone else. If you notice this happening, it's important to make changes so that your kids aren't taking responsibility for you.

Wishing for Acknowledgement

One of the challenges of being an Adult Child is coming to terms with the fact that you still want your parents to meet your needs despite logic that suggests it's unlikely that they will. Many people continue to seek their parents' approval even though they have gotten admiration and acceptance from many other significant people in their lives.

Cosette, for instance, painted her parents' house during her summer break from her high school teaching job. Her mother had complained for years that it needed to be done, so Cosette thought it would be a nice thing to do and would make her mother appreciate her. She was disappointed and hurt when her mother reacted to her gesture by criticizing her work even though Cosette had worked as a painter for several summers during college and had done an excellent job on the house.

You may find, as you discover what you needed from your parents but didn't get, that you would like to have them acknowledge the things that happened to stunt your emotional growth or the things that didn't happen that would have helped you to become emotionally healthy. Some parents, probably those who have done some personal growth work of their own, may admit to the family dysfunction. But many will continue to deny it and to throw your perceptions and memory into question.

Keep in mind that your healing work is about you, not about them. You cannot make them realize or see something if they're not ready or able to do so. You may, at some point, choose to confront them, but you need to realize that the purpose of that confrontation should mainly be about you asserting yourself and standing up for the vulnerable child that you were. If they understand and apologize, that's wonderful! But, although it's reasonable to hope for this reaction from them, it's not a good idea to get deeply invested in that hope. If you are not prepared for the possibility of your parents rejecting what you have to say it's best not to confront them at all.

If you're not sure whether confronting your parents would be helpful it would probably be a better idea to write them a letter that you never send or show to them. You can use the letter to say all the things you want to say and to vent all of your frustration, anger, and sadness without concern about backlash from them. After you've written the letter you can destroy it, or you can keep it so it's available to help you remember that stage of your healing journey.

As I've said in previous chapters, remember that the things we're talking about here take time and effort. If you are patient with yourself and your process you will find that it is possible to begin to achieve the balance you're looking for.

Putting It Into Action

Give an example of a time that your needs (physical and/or emotional) were not adequately met when you were growing up.

Laura: When I was growing up my parents and I spent at least one week every summer in Ocean City, NJ. I generally enjoyed those trips, but there was one thing I dreaded: my daily swims in the ocean.

My parents never went in the water but I was expected to go swimming every day. That was OK if the ocean was calm. Sometimes it wasn't, though; on those days, huge waves crashed over the other swimmers and me.

I was somewhat afraid of the water, and I was definitely afraid of the huge waves. I learned how to dive through them, which generally worked well, but sometimes a wave would knock me over and drag me along the sandy bottom. When I was underwater I lost my orientation; it would take a little while for me to figure out which way was up and manage to stand up. By then there was often another wave crashing over me and knocking me down again.

My parents decided how long I should swim and gave me a signal when it was time for me to come back; I had no say in it.

This continued until I left for college. Looking back, I wonder how many other teenagers would have tolerated the childish role that I was kept in—probably not many!

Decades later I still remember a day when a thunderstorm came up right at the time that I would usually be going into the water, so I didn't have to swim. I have never been so happy about a thunderstorm in my life!

What did you learn from that experience?

I learned that my parents did not think it was important to consult me when they made decisions about what I was going to do with my time, even on vacation. I learned that they had pretty much complete control over me even at a time when I was supposed to be increasingly independent. I learned that I couldn't count on them to respect my needs. I learned that they saw me as a child even when I was becoming an adult.

How has that experience affected how you feel and what you do about your needs or others' needs?

First, that experience and others like it have contributed to my continuing inability to feel grown up. My need to define myself during my teenage years was stifled, which probably had something to do with it.

Having my needs ignored by my parents taught me to ignore my needs, too; after a while I didn't even know what they were. I spend a lot of time trying to meet everyone else's needs in the hope that someone will return the favor. But no one does. I seem to keep finding people (friends, coworkers, partners) who aren't aware of anyone's needs but their own.

I have a 7-year-old daughter, and I occasionally notice feelings of resentment about being expected to meet her needs. My parents didn't really do that for me, so why should I have to do it for someone else? Mostly, though, I don't feel that way. I usually go too far in the other direction. I try to give my daughter everything she could possibly need or want. My husband says that I'm spoiling her and that it's not good for her. But it's so hard for me to say no to her!

Has reading this chapter changed your thoughts and feelings about needs? If it has, what will you do about that? How will you start?

Before reading this chapter I hadn't really thought of the ocean swimming sessions as a violation of my needs. I had always assumed that my parents knew about my fears and disregarded them. I'm sure they knew about some of my childhood fears about swimming. But I think that when they forced me to do things like swimming lessons they were probably trying to help me. Maybe that's what they were thinking about my swimming in the ocean. I think they probably believed it was good for me.

And now that I think about it, I'm not sure if I clearly communicated my feelings about swimming in the ocean to them. I do think that if they were at all tuned in to my needs, they should have figured it out, but they might not have. I wonder if they could have been tuned in but didn't try, or if they really couldn't do it.

If I had had experiences earlier in life that let me know that it was OK to express my needs and that they might be met, I might have been better able to tell my parents how much I didn't want to swim in the ocean.

I've realized from reading this chapter that it's important for me to learn to clearly express my needs to others. There aren't many people who are as sensitive to others' needs as I am. I've been assuming that everyone else can figure out what I need, but that might not be true. And, frankly, I get annoyed when people expect me to read their minds, so they probably feel the same way.

I know that it's best to start with small, relatively easy steps when I'm working on changing my thoughts, feelings, and behaviors. So first I'm just going to practice recognizing my needs. I'll record voice memos or keep a log or journal of some sort so I can get in the habit of noticing them.

Then I'll choose safe people and relatively easy requests to start. For instance, I can ask one of my friends to join me for coffee one morning after we drop our kids off at school. I often think about wanting to spend more time relaxing with friends but I usually tell myself that they're probably busy and don't have time for me.

When I really think about it, though, I realize that's probably not true. I know they enjoy spending time with me, so even if they don't have time to go for coffee I think I'll be able to convince myself that it's not because they don't want to do it.

When I get comfortable with easier requests, I'll try more difficult ones. I'll gradually work my way up to making requests that feel scary right now.

Chapter 5

Adult Children

1. When you were growing up was/were one or both of your parents an alcoholic or addict or have some other kind of compulsive behavior, such as being a workaholic?

2. Were there constant arguments at home when you were growing up?

3. Did you feel like you had to act like an adult even though you were a child?

4. Do you sometimes feel like a child in an adult's body?

5. When you visit your parents do you feel like you're treated as if you were still a child?

6. Do authority figures and angry people scare you?

7. Is it hard for you to accept compliments?

8. Do you take criticism, even constructive criticism, personally?

9. Do you wish you knew what "normal" was?

10. Do you ever make excuses or cover for your partner when he does something wrong? For instance, you might lie for him and tell his boss that there is a family emergency because he hasn't finished an important project on time.

11. When you were growing up did you feel like you needed to do exceptionally well in school to be acceptable and worthwhile?

12. Did you participate in a lot of extracurricular activities, at least partly because you wanted to be away from home as much as possible?

13. Were you the black sheep in your family, often in trouble, and blamed for family problems more than other members of the family?

14. When you were growing up did you try to ease the tension and distract from family arguments by saying or doing something to make others laugh?

15. Did you try to blend into the woodwork when you were growing up, particularly when your parents or other family members were arguing?

If your answer to at least two of these questions was "yes," it is likely that you could be considered an Adult Child of an Alcoholic whether or not you had an alcoholic parent. Being an Adult Child of an Alcoholic leads to the unbalanced behaviors we've been talking about, including taking care of everyone else but neglecting your own needs.

There is a 12-step group called Adult Children of Alcoholics (ACoA or ACA) that was founded in 1978 as an offshoot of 12-step groups for adults (Al-Anon) and teenagers (Alateen) who are affected by another person's drinking. This new group focused on the effects of having grown up in an alcoholic home.

At some point it became clear that many people who were attending ACoA meetings did not actually have an alcoholic parent. ACoA leaders realized that there are many kinds of family dysfunction that create the same results as having an alcoholic or addicted parent. The ACA handbook reflects this; it is titled *Adult Children: Alcoholic/Dysfunctional Families*.

The term Adult Children of Alcoholics is appropriate because people who grew up in alcoholic or otherwise dysfunctional families were not helped to grow up emotionally. While they are often outwardly very adult and successful, they have neglected and needy children inside. In the next chapter I will talk about how your inner child might show up and how you can help to meet her needs so she won't show up at inconvenient times or in inappropriate ways.

In this book I use the term "Adult Children" (AC) rather than "Adult Children of Alcoholics" (ACoA) to be more inclusive of readers without alcoholic parents.

What is an Adult Child?

What are the characteristics of an Adult Child? They include low self-esteem, perfectionism, people pleasing, control issues, codependency, and a fear of authority figures and angry people, among others. These characteristics can come from many things, including a parent (or sometimes a sibling) being mentally ill or having a chronic physical illness. Having one or both parents die or leave the family can also lead to these characteristics. The first nine quiz questions describe things that are common to many adult children.

The common denominator is that there is some situation in the family that leads to one or more of the children not getting the attention, care, and love that all children need to grow and thrive. In one way or another, the child ends up meeting the needs of the parents (and/or siblings) at the expense of having her needs met.

Family Roles

Whatever the reason(s) for family dysfunction, there are certain roles that routinely appear in such families. They are the *chief enabler*, the *family hero*, the *scapegoat*, the *mascot*, and the *lost child*. All of these roles relate to the neediness/needlessness dilemma in one way or another. And all of the role behaviors are cries for help, although those cries are often so disguised that they are not recognized.

The Chief Enabler

Question 10 of the quiz relates to the role of *chief enabler*. In an alcoholic family the chief enabler is usually the spouse of the alcoholic. This person could also be termed the *chief codependent*. She is the one who keeps an alcoholic husband from having to take responsibility for his actions. She calls his boss and tells him that her husband has the flu when he's really hung over. She makes excuses to friends about why she and her husband will not be at a social event because she's afraid that he'll get drunk and embarrass her.

She is also the one who tells him over and over that he needs to stop drinking; she probably tries to keep him from going to bars, and she looks for the places he has hidden his alcohol so she can pour it down the sink.

She tries to keep the family together and make sure things run relatively smoothly. As much as possible she keeps the outside world from knowing what's going on in the family; she does her best to save face. And she is secretly (or not so secretly) resentful of the things she has been "forced" to do. She is usually reluctant to look at her role in perpetuating the unhealthy family pattern. As far as she knows her husband has a problem; she does not.

An example is Jodi's mother, who looked like the perfect parent with the perfect family. She went to all the PTA meetings at Jodi's school and chaired a variety of committees. She organized a fundraiser to help the school buy musical instruments. She encouraged Jodi to participate in sports.

But she was much different at home. She was critical and angry most of the time. She yelled at her husband, who was a compulsive gambler. Although she told Jodi that she supported her athletic activities, she complained every time she had to drive Jodi to a practice or a game. The focus in the family was always on her and how much she suffered to keep her family going.

When an alcoholic parent gets into recovery the family realizes that his sobriety is not all that is required to make a harmonious family. The chief enabler, although she probably doesn't know it, has a part of her that doesn't want her spouse to get sober because then it will be harder to keep the focus on his bad behavior; she might be forced to become more aware of her own issues.

A mother who held her family together for years while her alcoholic husband lost one job after another and drank all of his paychecks away will probably be extremely resentful of the positive attention he gets once he is sober. Linda's mother seems to have decided that it is her mission to punish Linda's father for the rest of his life for the things he did while he was drinking, so she treats him abusively.

Rowena's mother resents all the kudos her husband is getting now that he is sober and doing volunteer work. Where were the kudos for her when she was holding the family together all of those years? Ironically, of course, she was part of the reason she didn't get those kudos, because she was the one who tried to convince everyone that nothing was wrong in the family.

Things also go the other way, of course, with the more dysfunctional parent attacking the relatively functional parent. Stella's abusive mother blamed Stella's father for ruining her arm because when Stella was ten years old her mother tripped over one of his shoes, fell, and broke several bones in her right hand and arm. She said that he had deliberately left the shoe out so she would trip over it. Even with multiple surgeries she never regained full use of her right hand, and she never stopped blaming her husband for what had happened.

The Family Hero

Questions 11 and 12 of the quiz describe the *family hero*. The family hero gets good grades and engages in multiple extracurricular activities. She is a leader. She is much admired. As far as anyone knows, she has it all together.

Whether she knows it or not, she, too, is trying to cover up the family dysfunction. After all, how could someone so successful and happy possibly come from a dysfunctional family? And all those extracurricular activities are also good ways to get away from the family for a while.

Deep down she feels inadequate. She does all of these things to try to win approval, particularly from her parents. She does not realize that their personal issues make it difficult or impossible for them to give her the approval she needs. So she looks for more and more successes, hoping that the next one will make her parent(s) proud of her. When she doesn't reach her goal she believes it's her fault even though it's not.

The Scapegoat

Question 13 of the quiz describes the *scapegoat* role. The scapegoat is the family member who draws attention away from the family dysfunction by taking it on herself. There are various ways she might do this: poor grades, skipping school, getting in trouble, drinking or using drugs, or defying parental and other authority. Unfortunately, by doing these things she's sabotaging herself.

Her defiance may not be this extreme, though. For instance, she may become the ultimate moody teenager or choose to dress and act in ways that let people know that she can't or doesn't want to relate to other people, but she may still get good grades and avoid drugs and alcohol.

Phoebe's rebellions were relatively minor. For instance, it was her job to dust the house on Saturday mornings and she hated doing it, so she skipped the parts of the house that she thought her father wouldn't check. Years later she could still remember her father running his finger along a dusty baseboard and shoving it in her face. Although she loved to practice the French horn she only did it when it was her decision; she refused to do it when her parents told her to practice.

Anything can be used to make a person a scapegoat. Phoebe spent most of her free time reading. This became something that her mother used to scapegoat her. While many kids who don't like to read are constantly urged by their parents to read more, Phoebe was criticized for how much time she spent reading. When her mother wanted to punish her she often threatened to take Phoebe's books away from her.

Sometimes children become scapegoats by being given responsibilities that are too much for them; when they fail at those responsibilities their parents blame them. When Sierra was eight her mother gave her a valuable necklace and let her wear it to school. When the chain broke and Sierra lost the necklace, her mother beat her. It seems unlikely that reasonable parents would put so much responsibility on young children, and they would be unlikely to blame the child if, having been given that responsibility, she failed at it.

Sometimes parents make a child's mistake seem more serious than it is. Many mothers, if their children accidentally spill their milk at dinner, will tell the children that it's not a big deal and will help them with the cleanup. Sidney's mother, on the other hand, acted as if Sydney had ruined the tablecloth when she spilled her milk.

Joy was the scapegoat in her family. Her father frequently came into her room while she was trying to do her homework, yelling at her about everything he thought she was doing wrong, including criticizing her choice of friends and the way she dressed. Her siblings heard the yelling through the walls and were scared that they might be next; they later felt guilty for not having defended their sister.

If any child in the family is sent to therapy it is likely to be the scapegoat. The parents may take her to a therapist and say, "Fix her," when what really needs to be fixed is the whole family system.

It is human nature to look for someone to blame for things. But it is damaging to a child to be labeled as the problem. She will begin to believe that she really is a problem, and possibly that she's completely bad or wrong.

This will be a tough pattern to break out of unless she gets some help from someone who recognizes what's going on and cares enough to do something about it.

The Mascot

Quiz question 14 relates to the role of the *mascot*. The mascot is often the youngest child in the family. She is the one who tries to distract from the family dysfunction by being light-hearted, maybe using humor. She might be the class clown at school. She is the one most likely to be asking people to take care of her—the baby of the family no matter what her age.

The mascot may be in denial about the family dysfunction. Years later when her siblings are talking about the bad things that happened when they were growing up she may make them question their reality by saying she doesn't remember any of those things happening. As far as she remembers, she had a happy childhood.

Quite a few of my clients have siblings who deny that anything was wrong in their family. They find it immensely helpful if they have at least one other person to confirm that those things really did happen.

The Lost Child

Question 15 of the quiz describes the *lost child*. The lost child is the one who doesn't make trouble and, therefore, is often not noticed, either in the home or outside of it. She may be an average student who doesn't have many characteristics that make her stand out, and she is likely very quiet.

It feels dangerous to her to be noticed but, like all children, she wants and needs nothing more than she needs positive attention. She really wants someone to come looking for her but it scares her if they do; she may withdraw even from positive attention because it may not feel safe to her.

If her parents insist on good grades and involvement in extracurricular activities the lost child may end up looking a lot like the family hero because, in this case, doing well is the way to avoid negative attention. If her parents reprimand her when she gets anything less than A's in school, it's likely that she'll make sure to do it so she won't be on the receiving end of their anger and disapproval. So questions 11 and 12 of the quiz can also describe the lost child, not just the family hero.

Kathy's parents got into loud, violent fights almost every day, screaming and throwing things at each other. Kathy hid in a small alcove under the basement stairs when her parents argued. She made it into a comfy little cave for herself. Her father found it one day and took all of her things out of it, telling Kathy she was not allowed to go in there any more. Years later, when her father asked her why she had done that and she told him, he said he didn't know what she was talking about because he and her mother had gotten along perfectly well when she was growing up!

Meanwhile, Kathy watched TV shows like *The Brady Bunch* and dreamed of living in a family where everyone got along.

When Mabel's father accused her of things she hadn't done and she tried to defend herself, he hit her. This taught her that it didn't matter what she thought or felt, and she was certainly not allowed to express herself or ask anyone to meet her needs.

Leigh felt responsible when something bad accidentally happened to her, so she never told adults about it. When she was in preschool she fell down a set of stairs on her way to the basement to take a nap. She got a lump on her forehead but didn't tell the teachers. When everyone went outside to play after naptime an adult noticed the lump and asked Leigh why she hadn't said something. Leigh, while glad that she was getting help, was embarrassed that she needed it and felt like the adult was accusing her of something when she asked why Leigh hadn't said anything.

Kristen was the fourth of seven children, so she was often overlooked. She found dramatic ways to force her parents to pay attention to her. Many times she just stopped eating; when she became dangerously thin they finally paid attention to her.

Phoebe played the French horn in high school. She was naturally gifted and practiced a great deal, so she was easily the best player at her school. She had been taught to question her own worth and abilities, though, and had learned not to stand out. She really wanted to earn the praise and attention that being the first chair player would have brought, but was also terrified of being the center of attention. So she became very nervous when she had an audition and, no matter how well she knew the music, made enough mistakes that she was second, third, or fourth chair every time, never first chair.

Role Combinations

These family roles are not cut and dried, distinct, or unchangeable, though. One person can take on a variety (or combination) of roles. Family members sometimes take turns playing the various roles depending upon circumstances. One of these is when one of the children goes to college. If she was the family hero or the scapegoat, one of the other children will likely take on that role when she is no longer there.

Sophia was an example of a combination—the lost child, the family hero, and the scapegoat. Like many lost children she tried to make peace among her siblings and her parents. She was also the family hero who played multiple sports as a way to escape what was going on in the family. She denied her feelings and focused on being rational and logical. She was emotionally divided from her siblings, who always saw her as the "good one." They often resented and blamed her for things, so she was a scapegoat as well.

The Effects of Labeling

Even though only one of the roles is labeled the "lost child," all the children in an alcoholic or otherwise dysfunctional family are, essentially, lost. They find themselves fitting into roles rather than being allowed to be themselves.

Dysfunctional families often label the kids: for instance, "the smart one," "the pretty one," "the stupid one," "the artistic one," etc. Children believe the labels that they are given and will do their best to live up (or down) to them. This can be a positive or a negative thing.

Natalie was reminded of this when her six-year-old son Aaron attended a day camp one summer. The camp leaders continually praised his artwork and often commented on the fact that he was an artist.

Not surprisingly, Aaron began to spend even more time drawing and painting than he had before, and he said that he wanted to be an artist when he grew up.

The label of artist certainly fit Aaron. He had always loved to draw and paint and he took pride in his creations. But being constantly described as an artist took this to a whole new level for him. It became a primary identity and a focus of his future plans in a way it had not done before.

While Natalie appreciated the fact that the camp leaders enjoyed Aaron's art, she found herself wondering if that label was keeping him from exploring other interests.

Labels can rob children of the chance to express their individuality. If you haven't been identified as the artistic one, for instance, any artistic interest or ability you demonstrate will likely be ignored, which means that you may forget about that part of yourself and never develop it.

Enmeshment

Enmeshment is another characteristic of dysfunctional families that keeps children from expressing their individuality. Enmeshment means that family members are connected to each other in an unhealthy way. The boundaries within the family are blurred so that it is difficult for individual family members to understand themselves as separate from the rest of the family.

Enmeshment between a parent and a child is particularly problematic. In a healthy family there are distinct layers. The parents are the top layer; they work together to support each other and the kids. The kids are the lower layer in the sense that they don't take responsibility for things that should be left to the adults. The kids are not put into adult roles and the parents don't act like children.

When a parent and child are enmeshed, *triangulation* can occur. Triangulation often happens among the chief enabler, her husband, and one of the children. For instance, the enabler may ally herself with her daughter, confiding in her regarding marital problems or other inappropriate matters.

When a parent confides in a child in this way it makes the child feel special. She feels like the parent likes and trusts her enough to treat her as a friend rather than a daughter. But on some level the daughter also knows that the friendship is inappropriate. She does not need a parent to be a friend; she needs a parent to be a parent. That boundary helps a child to feel safe and secure.

There are also times when a mother is enmeshed with a son. A mother like this will probably be jealous of the son's girlfriends and, eventually, his wife. After all, another woman is taking her son away from her! When this is the case, the son usually feels caught between his mother and his wife.

An Invalidating Environment

Psychologist Marsha Linehan uses the term *invalidating environment* to describe a family situation in which the parents suggest to a child that she does not see what she sees, feel what she feels, or think what she thinks. They question her perceptions so that she learns to question them, as well. When she expresses her thoughts and feelings they let her know that they disapprove of them, so she learns to hide them, even from herself.

Imagine you're eleven years old. You're eating lunch with your family and bite into the pear on your plate. It doesn't taste right, but you try another bite. That one doesn't taste right, either. You stop eating the pear and tell your parents that it's rotten. Your mother tells you you're wrong and insists that you keep eating it, and you do. A little while later your father tries the pear himself and confirms that it is, in fact, rotten, at which point you are allowed to stop eating it. As a result of this experience it is years before you're willing to eat another pear.

What do you think you would learn from this experience? Probably that what you thought or felt didn't matter. Or maybe that you couldn't count on adults listening to you and respecting your opinion—maybe they would (as your father did in this case), or maybe they wouldn't.

This was something that happened to Sheila. She remembered it decades after it happened because it was unusual. The thing that made this story stand out was not that her mother didn't respect her experience (because that happened often), but because, in this case, her father did.

Sometimes a child stands up for herself in the face of a parent attempting to deny her reality. Gillian, in the movie *Affliction*, responds to her father's excuses about why it's too late for her to go trick or treating by saying, "Whose fault is it then if it's not yours? You're the one in charge, Dad!"

Later in the movie Gillian again refuses to let him deny her reality. He attacks a man in a restaurant and, when he realizes what he's done in front of his daughter, says, "I'm sorry, I'm sorry...nothin' happened, nothin' happened!" He keeps repeating those phrases over and over as if they can change the reality of what has happened. She ignores him and says, "I want to go home!" (to her mother's house).

There are many things that your parents might do when you're growing up that make you feel like there's something wrong with you. For instance, if they laugh after you do something, then tell you, "We're not laughing at you, we're laughing with you," they're suggesting that you shouldn't be hurt by their laughter. If you are hurt by it you may start to wonder if you're too sensitive.

Or if you have a childhood fear of the dark they may tell you there's nothing to be afraid of. Even though that's true, most young children have fears, particularly of the dark; just being told there's nothing to fear without acknowledging your reality can make you question yourself.

A child who is upset about being bullied but whose parents tell her, "Sticks and stones may break my bones, but names will never hurt me" is also being invalidated. Being called names and treated as "less than" certainly does hurt.

Follow the Rules!

For a dysfunctional family, appearances are critical. It is necessary to show the world the picture of a happy family. The anger, fear, and sadness are not to be shown to anyone else. This means that even when there are people outside of the family who could help, it's not likely to happen because no one in the family lets it be known that help is needed.

The 12-step group Adult Children of Alcoholics sums up the rules of an alcoholic or otherwise dysfunctional family with the following: "Don't talk. Don't trust. Don't feel." The whole family lives by these rules, although they probably don't know that they are.

All three of these rules serve to perpetuate the family dysfunction and ensure that no one in the family escapes. Here's how.

Don't Talk

The "don't talk" rule applies both inside and outside of the family. Family members often don't talk to each other about what's going on. If Dad drinks too much one evening and ends up passed out on the couch, the rest of the family will probably go on as if nothing is wrong (and, by the family's standards of "normal," that's really true, because it's probably a regular occurrence). The next day no one will speak of it, most likely because they are feeling shame about it.

Have you heard someone talk about "the elephant in the room?" This clearly describes what goes on in a situation like the one above. The idea (figuratively speaking) is that there is a big elephant in the room but everyone is pretending not to see it. Imagine the elephant sitting on the couch with the family—family members are squashed and move aside because there isn't enough room for them. Maybe they are knocked off the couch entirely. But still no one talks about it.

Family members may very well see alcoholism as a moral failing or a sign that the alcoholic is "broken." Therefore the alcoholic will be ashamed of himself, and his wife and kids will feel shame by association. They don't really deserve to feel that shame, but they don't understand that. And it's because of that shame that they do their best to pretend that nothing is going on.

You know what it means when someone says that something has been swept under the rug. Imagine a member of a dysfunctional family sweeping the elephant under the rug and pretending there isn't a huge lump in the middle of it! Family members walk around it or run into it, but no one says anything about it.

On the other hand, someone in the family may call attention to the dysfunction, not in public, but within the family. It may be the chief enabler, who likely complains to the family about the alcoholic's behavior.

Members of a dysfunctional family don't talk to people outside of the family about what's going on, partly because of the shame and partly because it probably doesn't occur to them that they could get help. The chief enabler does her best to make the world think that their family is happy and functional; she often does a pretty good job of it. The children take their cue from her, learning that they are not allowed to talk about what's going on, either.

How might the "don't talk" rule apply to a dysfunctional family without an alcoholic parent? It's very similar—only the reasons for the denial change. Maybe a parent is depressed or suffers from another mental illness and is, therefore, emotionally abusive. Maybe there is physical abuse going on. Whatever the expression of the problem, family members are discouraged from talking to each other or anyone else about it.

Don't Trust

The second rule is "don't trust." The "don't talk" rule, not to mention denial from other family members, serves to make everyone in the family distrust both the rest of the family and their own perceptions.

The alcoholic parent doesn't trust anyone, partly because of the effects of alcohol, and partly because he knows that the family is opposed to his drinking. He feels accused by everyone. And it's likely that he had an alcoholic parent when he was growing up, so he learned early in life not to trust. That lack of trust probably contributed to the development of his alcoholism.

The chief enabler doesn't trust her husband not to drink, which is why she tries so hard to control his behavior. She probably also grew up in an alcoholic family and developed trust issues then. (Remember in

Chapter 3 when I mentioned that we unconsciously choose a partner who has similar characteristics to one or both of our parents?)

The children learn that they can't trust the two people in their lives who should be the most trustworthy: their parents. Therefore, they unconsciously decide that no one can be trusted. Whether they realize it or not, they learn early on that they are on their own. Their parents, for one reason or another, can't meet their needs, so it is up to them to find a way to survive.

And, unfortunately, because parents are the first authority figures in our lives, distrust of parents tends to lead to distrust of all authority. This shows up in different ways: sometimes outright defiance of authority, sometimes fear of authority that leads to compulsive obedience, and sometimes avoidance, whenever possible, of authority. (Remember my theory about Adult Children choosing self-employment so that there is no one in authority over them?)

This problem with trusting authority can also interfere with a person's spiritual life and/or religious faith. Many people (again, without realizing it) base their image of God on one or both of their parents, often their fathers. Therefore a person who might otherwise feel like she could turn to God when she needed help might instead feel like she needs to go it alone; she thinks that God will not, or cannot, help her. She may be so ashamed of herself that she doesn't feel worthy of asking for God's help.

This lack of ability and/or willingness to trust in a higher power is what makes the first three steps of any 12-step program so difficult, but so necessary. The twelve steps are essentially the same in every 12-step program; only the first step differs in its wording depending upon the issue that is being addressed. Step One of ACoA (Adult Children of Alcoholics) is: "We admitted we were powerless over the effects of alcoholism or other family dysfunction, that our lives had become unmanageable." Step Two: "Came to believe that a power greater than ourselves could restore us to sanity." Step Three: "Made a decision to turn our will and our lives over to the care of God as we understood God."

You could sum up these three steps as:

Step One: "I can't." Step Two: "God can." Step Three: "I think I'll let God."

Many people, even those who believe in God, have difficulty trusting that God will help them, but desperately wish they could find that trust. Consider, for instance, the popularity of the story "Footprints":

One night a man had a dream. He dreamed he was walking along the beach with God. Across the sky flashed scenes from his life. For each scene he noticed two sets of footprints in the sand, one belonging to him and the other to God. When the last scene of his life flashed before him, he looked back at the footprints in the sand. He noticed that many times along the path of his life there was only one set of footprints. He also noticed that it happened at the very lowest and saddest times of his life. This really bothered him and he questioned God about it. "God, you said you'd walk with me all the way. But I have noticed that during the most troublesome times in my life there is only one set of footprints. I don't understand why when I needed you most you would leave me." God replied, "My precious, precious child, I love you and I would never leave you! During your times of trial and suffering when you see only one set of footprints, it was then that I carried you."

(Carolyn Carty, 1963)

All of us have wounds from childhood. At one time or another all of us, whether we know it or not, wish that someone would take care of us and tell us that everything is going to be all right. Experience usually leads us to believe, though, that this is unlikely to happen and that we are on our own.

Don't Feel

The last of the three rules of dysfunctional families is "don't feel." Remember the dysfunctional family's emphasis on appearances? Everyone has to pretend that everything is fine. Happiness, even if it's fake, is OK, but "negative" emotions like sadness or anger are not tolerated.

When Michelle cried as a child her mother said, "Quit your brutzing!" ("Brutzing" is the Pennsylvania Dutch word for crying.) Then her father told her to wash her face so no one would know she'd been crying.

The "don't feel" rule is part of the invalidating environment kids in dysfunctional families experience. They don't get compassionate or understanding responses to their feelings of sadness, fear, or anger; instead, they are ignored or even punished when they express these feelings. Parents or other family members may take advantage of the vulnerability of a sad or fearful child, which also teaches her not to show these feelings.

As a result, children get to the point where they don't even know what they're feeling. I start the meetings of my counseling group for Adult Children with a feelings check because one of the goals of therapy is to begin to recognize feelings and then, for the first time, learn to honor and accept them.

What Happens When ACoAs Grow Up?

The Family Hero as an Adult

Children in dysfunctional families carry their family roles into adulthood. For instance Liesel, having been both mother and father to her siblings because her mother left and her father had no idea how to raise children, found herself in job after job where she ended up "parenting" most of the other employees and being frustrated by their incompetence.

Monique, playing the role of the family hero, went to law school and started working for the family's law firm after she passed the bar exam. She did extremely well and brought the firm a lot of new business. This came at a great personal cost, though, because she hated being a lawyer and only did it because it was the "right" thing to do.

She socialized with other lawyers in the firm because she knew it would be professionally beneficial. She believed that no one who didn't have an ulterior motive of some sort would want to be her friend.

In her early forties, though, she realized that life was too short to socialize with people she didn't like just so she could succeed professionally. At that point, although she continued to be friendly with the other lawyers, she stopped spending her free time with them. She consciously chose friends who had similar interests to hers and with whom she really enjoyed spending time. And she found that her earlier fears were unjustified; there were plenty of people who liked her for herself, not just as a tool to advance their careers.

The Scapegoat as an Adult

The scapegoat will continue to self-sabotage in adulthood unless she realizes what she's doing and finds a way to turn it around. Natasha, despite growing up in a family that seemed healthy, became a drug addict and was unable to keep a job, so she ended up broke and homeless. She found it hard to believe that she was worth anything, so she didn't know that it was possible to break that pattern.

Marlene was an interior designer for a large company. She had a supervisor, Lila, who liked to micromanage the designers even though she knew almost nothing about interior design. Lila felt insecure about her lack of knowledge, so she tried to compensate for it by abusing the authority she had over her supervisees.

Most of the designers who worked for Lila just gritted their teeth and vented to each other when Lila wasn't around. But Marlene wasn't like that. She had been the person in her family who stood up to her mother when she was being unfair to the kids. Marlene's mother was a single parent, and she took advantage of being the only authority figure in the family. She arbitrarily set and changed rules and punished the kids when she felt like it, whether or not they'd done anything to deserve punishment.

Marlene rebelled against Lila in somewhat subtle ways, like giving clients tips on how to save money by choosing different materials than those the company was pushing. Lila could never prove that Marlene was doing anything, but she suspected that she was, so she treated Marlene worse than she treated any of the other designers. Marlene helped the other designers by bringing more of Lila's negative attention on herself. This was similar to the way she had taken the brunt of her mother's anger, thus saving her siblings from some of their mother's punishments.

The Lost Child as an Adult

A quote from the movie *Affliction* shows that the lost child isn't found just because she becomes an adult. In the movie the younger brother, referring to the time he first heard about his father beating his older brother, said, "After I heard I became real careful around Pop. I was a careful child and I became a careful adult."

The adult lost child will continue to be the one who goes unnoticed. Even when she makes significant contributions at work or elsewhere she is less likely to get the credit than another person in the same situation might do.

Marian is an architect. She works overtime and does both her work and most of her coworker Mara's work. Mara is a much more aggressive person and speaks up so that she will be noticed. So when it comes time for one of the employees to get promoted, it will likely be Mara instead of Marian.

Nicola, who graduated near the top of her law school class, took a job as a paralegal after she completed her degree. She passed the bar exam and knew a great deal about the field of law in which she was working. She knew that she had many skills that were going unused, but she was afraid to say anything to the lawyers for whom she worked. She was afraid that they would reject her, so she decided not to take the chance. This was unfortunate, not only for her but also for the firm, which would have benefited greatly from her taking on increased responsibility.

Mary Beth is a talented artist and was told in high school that she was good enough to make a living at it. She didn't believe it, though, so she took an office job instead that made her miserable, but which gave her the opportunity to fade into the woodwork as she'd always done.

Adult lost children, as they did when they were growing up, try to figure things out on their own rather than asking for help. They do this even in relatively simple situations such as asking a store employee where to find a certain item. They may decline help even if the employee asks them if they need it.

They also beat themselves up for not knowing that a rule has changed even though they were not told that it was. For instance, Michelle returned some library books one day and put them on the counter as she always did. This time, though, there was a cart beside the desk and the librarian asked her to put the books there. Even though she had no way of knowing that, and even though it was not a big deal, Michelle mentally berated herself for not realizing that she was supposed to do something different.

Melinda, who grew up being told, "Children should be seen and not heard," walks very quietly and often startles people because they don't hear her coming. Even as an adult she obeys the things she was told as a child.

The Mascot as an Adult

The adult mascot still tries to get attention wherever she can. She might be the fun-loving person who continues to party like she's in college even into her forties and fifties. Adult mascots may do stand-up comedy as a way to be funny and to get attention. It's a way for them to express things they might not otherwise say.

One of my clients told me that she'd read the autobiography of a famous comedienne and was surprised to find that her childhood had been violent and abusive. When she thought about it, though, she realized that it made sense; the comedienne had learned to use comedy to safely express herself. Since standup comics often make light of bad things that have happened to them, it gave her the chance to voice at least some of the things that had gone on in her life without feeling as vulnerable as she would have if she'd directly expressed her true feelings.

Think of the character Hawkeye on the TV show M*A*S*H. He dealt with the terrible situation of being in a medical unit during the Korean War by acting like an irresponsible clown. When he found himself face-to-face with difficult emotions with no way to joke about them he almost literally went insane.

Multiple ACoA Roles in Adulthood

Sierra is an example of one who carried multiple childhood roles into adulthood. She was very intelligent and her parents always expressed high expectations for her success in life. Underneath the expressed expectations, though, was the message that she was not allowed to succeed and therefore make her parents, who had not distinguished themselves professionally, look bad.

So Sierra went to medical school and, because of her intelligence and her hard work, did very well. Her father began saying things to her about how he had wanted to go to medical school but wasn't smart enough. Sierra's grades started to drop and she eventually left school. She was perfectly acting out the message she was given: "Have high ambitions, but make sure you don't succeed!"

Adult Relationships with Parents

Dysfunctional parents usually assume that family relationships will stay the same no matter how old their children get. They will treat their children as if they were still kids, not adults. And they will often expect their children to continue to follow the rules of denial that were in place when they were growing up.

It can be very frustrating for an adult child who is trying to work through her childhood issues when she is repeatedly confronted with that unhealthy dynamic when she spends time with her family. And it's difficult when the adult child tries to work through or at least talk about the past with her parents.

Malika's father became defensive when Malika talked about the ways her mother was abusive, because he had not divorced her and had not intervened when she attacked Malika and her siblings.

Many adult children must decide whether to maintain an adult relationship with their parents and, if so, what kind of relationship it will be. Loreena severed all ties with her family. Jillian decided that she would relate to both of her parents, but only on a very superficial level. Janet, who lives in Baltimore and whose parents live in Arizona, uses distance as an excuse not to visit them on holidays.

When Liesel was 40 years old her mother decided to move from St. Louis to Annapolis to be closer to her. She moved in with Liesel, saying that the living arrangement would only last until she could find a house of her own. Many of Liesel's friends got to know her mother and found her friendly, warm, and generous, which was the opposite of Liesel's (and her family's) experience of her.

She lived with Liesel for two years before Liesel finally told her that she needed to move out. Her mother, hurt, moved to another community twenty miles away. For a long time after that Liesel's friends asked how her mother was doing and expressed regret that she no longer lived in their community. Liesel gave generic responses that did not express the true relationship she and her mother had.

A few months later Liesel developed a severe case of pneumonia. Her mother temporarily moved in with her again to help her during her illness. All of Liesel's friends were, again, impressed by the helpfulness of Liesel's mother. They didn't know that she was constantly reminding Liesel of how generous she was being by giving up so much of her personal time to help her daughter.

Lola is a recovering alcoholic with twenty years of sobriety. Her mother recently started attending Al-Anon meetings and told Lola that she was doing it as a favor to her, so that she could better understand her daughter's dysfunction. She did not realize that the main purpose of Al-Anon was to work on herself, not to talk about her daughter.

Lola was used to her mother making emotionally manipulative statements and later denying that she had any ulterior motives. She therefore had trouble trusting that her mother really was changing, even when it seemed like she had finally started to understand the point of Al-Anon and was working on herself.

To her credit, Lola was eventually able to begin to trust and adjust to her mother's new way of interacting with her, but it was a challenge to try to sort out the genuine from the untrustworthy and to envision and accept a new, less clear, version of the relationship.

When it was a black and white issue Lola didn't have to try to figure out whether her mother was being genuine. When Lola was young she always assumed her mother was genuine, and when she got older she always assumed her mother wasn't genuine.

Finding the middle ground between complete trust and complete lack of trust continues to be very difficult for Lola. Along with that goes the challenge of finding the balance between being there for her mother and being there for herself.

Adult Children learned to take care of themselves and their families, but not in healthy ways that allowed each person to be responsible for him- or herself while being in healthy relationship with others. Learning better ways of caring for self and others is an essential part of the task of healing childhood wounds.

Putting It Into Action

Did your family have the "don't talk, don't trust, don't feel" rules when you were growing up? How did they show up?

Adelaide: My parents argued a lot when I was a child, and they sometimes became physically violent with each other. I was once a talkative child with many friends, but I became silent and withdrawn. My teacher asked me what was wrong, but I was afraid to say anything because I didn't want my parents to get in trouble and I didn't want to be put into foster care. I also thought that I had probably done something wrong that caused my parents to fight, and I was ashamed. When my parents fought it frightened me so much that I made up fantasies about being somewhere else so that I didn't have to feel the fear.

Are you still following those rules in your life today? If so, how are they manifesting now?

Ariel: I was a fearful child and I have continued to be fearful as an adult. I am extremely sensitive to other people's anger and automatically assume that I've caused it somehow. I have ideas to contribute at work, but I am afraid to speak up. My husband is physically abusive to me. I blame myself for it and cover it up, not telling anyone what's going on. I still escape to fantasy worlds when I'm frightened or sad so I don't have to feel those things.

Which role(s) (chief enabler, family hero, scapegoat, mascot, lost child) do you think you have played in your family? How did you play out that/those role(s)?

Renata: I was the scapegoat in my family. I distracted from my father's alcoholism and my family's dysfunction by being arrested for selling drugs and getting pregnant when I was sixteen. My parents sent me to therapy and asked the therapist to fix me; their focus on my problems enabled them to deny their own.

How have you carried family role(s) into the rest of your life—for instance, into your career, your friendships, and your family life?

Ginger: I was the youngest child in my family and played the mascot role. Even in adulthood I tend to avoid serious subjects, making jokes to lighten the mood and create distractions. While I can be a lot of fun to be around I also make it difficult for people to get to know the real me because I generally stay on a superficial level when interacting with others.

Not all characteristics of these roles are bad or unhelpful; some are quite useful. What are the strengths of your role(s) that you would like to keep? How do they play out in your life today?

Jasmine: I was always the scapegoat in my family and I was never afraid to call things as I saw them. As an adult I have become an advocate for social change, confronting authority in a way many people rarely dare to do.

Raquel: I was the lost child in my family. I learned to empathize with the invisible people in our world. I am now a social worker who finds those people and helps them to get their needs met.

What are the things you'd like to change about your role(s)?

Hermione: I'm the family hero, a perfectionist who often tries to do the impossible, desperately trying to pound that square peg into a round hole. For the most part I do that by trying to change the thoughts and feelings of people in authority over me, as I did with my parents while growing up. For ten years I have worked for a woman who, because she has bipolar disorder and does not take her medication, is inconsistent and often impossible to please.

I started therapy six months ago and have begun to recognize the scenario I have acted out time after time. I am deliberately working to relax my perfectionism, reminding myself that it will not be the end of the world if I don't achieve perfection. I am also planning to find another job with a more reasonable and consistent boss.

What is the first change you would like to make? How will you begin?

Hermione: I started small in my attempts to let go of perfectionism because I knew that starting with a relatively easy change would make it more likely that I would feel empowered to build up to bigger changes. So my first step was to go easier on myself while cooking. I love to try new recipes, but I have always beaten myself up if I tried a recipe and it didn't work the first time.

I am now making a deliberate effort to give myself a break and remind myself of my real purpose for trying new recipes—the adventure of trying something I haven't done before and the discovery, at least sometimes, of a delicious new dish that I can add to my repertoire. I also remind myself that some things take practice and that when I retry something that didn't work the first time, it usually tastes much better the second time because I have learned from the earlier experience. I remind myself that some recipes are just better than others, and that all cooks have their own tastes; maybe the recipe tastes good to the person who wrote the cookbook but doesn't taste good to me. I try to keep in mind that there's nothing wrong with having a different opinion than someone else does.

In what way(s) have you used your role(s) to sustain the image that your family tries to portray? Is there anything that you could change that would contribute to better self-care? How might change(s) help, rather than harm, you and the other members of your family?

Joan: I was the family hero; I always got straight A's and participated in multiple extracurricular activities when I was in high school, even though it meant that I often had to stay up until 2:00 in the morning to finish my homework.

Other people often said things to my parents about how successful I was; they thought it was a result of their great parenting. They didn't know that I was working so hard because I was trying to get my parents' approval, and because I was trying to escape my family dysfunction.

As an adult I have continued to be an overachiever. I am a registered nurse and work in a hospital emergency room. I have often worked extra shifts, usually clocking 60 hours per week. I've also worked out daily and run in marathons.

I have started therapy because I am getting panic attacks. I have come to realize that my lifestyle is self-destructive, so I have cut back on my work hours and lessened the intensity of my workouts.

My younger siblings are benefiting from the changes because they no longer feel so strongly pressured to measure up to nearly impossible standards.

My parents see that I am much happier after making the changes. While they still tend to define success in terms of overachievement, they have relaxed some of the pressure they put on me to do more than I can reasonably be expected to do.

Chapter 6

Inner Child Work

1. Have you ever felt like you were a child among adults?

2. Have you ever been intimidated by a child or teenager and wondered why?

3. Have you ever felt like you were an impostor, pretending to be competent when you really weren't, and that someday you would be found out?

4. Do you ever find yourself reacting to a situation in what feels like a very childish way?

5. Do you feel like everyone else got an instruction book for life that you never got?

In this chapter we'll talk about how to take care of a part of you that you may not even have known existed: your inner child. She is another essential piece of the balance puzzle.

To Believe or Not to Believe

If you answered yes to at least one of the questions above, you have been in touch with your inner child.

Are you rolling your eyes? Are you thinking, "I have an inner child? That's ridiculous!"

That was my first reaction, and the thought still comes up sometimes. I often have new clients who are skeptical about inner child work, too, but they usually decide at some point that it is valid and useful.

You don't have to believe that you have an inner child for it to be true. And if you did roll your eyes, bear with me—later in the chapter I'll propose an alternate perspective that may work better for you.

You've probably seen nesting dolls—a large doll contains a smaller doll, which contains an even smaller doll, etc. You can look at yourself in a similar way. Every age you've been is contained within you, from the baby, to the toddler, to the preschooler, to the schoolchild, to the teenager, to the young adult, and so on.

Dr. Ihaleakala Hew Len, who teaches a version of an ancient Hawaiian practice of forgiveness and reconciliation called ho'oponopono, says that the inner child is our subconscious mind. He refers to the conscious and subconscious minds as "mother and child," and says, "This is the most important relationship in creation, more important than any physical relationship you have."

What Does My Inner Child Need?

According to psychologist and psychoanalyst Erik Erikson, some of the most important tasks of childhood include developing trust, autonomy, and a sense of self worth. These tasks are accomplished in stages. If you do not successfully complete the task of one stage, it will be difficult to complete the tasks of later stages. It's like mathematics, in which new skills build upon old ones; for instance, if you can't do algebra you won't have the tools you need to learn calculus.

Your ability to complete these tasks is largely dependent upon the parenting you received while growing up. Remember that your parents, who were responsible for meeting many of your needs, would have found it difficult to give you what they had not themselves been given. Therefore it is likely that you were not able to successfully complete at least some of the tasks listed above.

When I say that your parents did not meet all of your needs I am not suggesting that you blame them, though, although you may still choose to do so. I'm only saying that you still have those needs today because your parents did not meet them then.

Can you go back to your parents now and demand that they meet those needs? No, you can't. It's too late for that. So who is responsible for meeting them?

You are.

Actually, that's not entirely true. You are responsible for making sure that those needs are met. In many cases that means that you will have to re-parent yourself. But in some cases it means seeking help and support from others who can give it to you—your spouse, a friend, or a therapist, for instance.

Whose Problems Are They?

I used to earn my living as a private flute teacher, and I still have a few students. One of the things that I teach my students is how to deal with the innate flaws in the instrument. Every instrument has these flaws; it is up to the person playing it to compensate for them.

When I talk to my students about these flaws, I tell them, "It's not your fault, but it is your responsibility." Is it a flutist's fault that some notes tend to be sharp, while others tend to be flat? Is it her fault that it is very difficult to play low notes loudly or high notes softly? No, of course not! She didn't design the instrument, so it is not her fault that it is not perfect.

It is, however, her responsibility. As a flutist she is expected to learn how to deal with the quirks of the instrument so that she can create as good a sound as possible—it is her job to do so.

Alcoholics and addicts in recovery have their own version of this. Yes, alcoholism and addiction are diseases, not moral failings. Yes, their family histories and their genes predispose them to alcoholism and addiction. But only they can decide to put alcohol and drugs into their bodies. The alcohol and drugs don't jump into them on their own. And (with a few possible exceptions) other people don't put the drugs and alcohol in the addicts' and alcoholics' bodies, either.

You can apply this idea to issues that you have developed as a result of growing up in a dysfunctional family. You were not the one who caused those issues; the adults (or others) in your life caused them because they had their own problems. But it is now your problem to solve; it is no longer up to them to fix the problem because it is past the time in your life when they can.

You can spend your life bemoaning your fate or pretending that everything is OK when it isn't. But in the end, it comes down to this: you are responsible for playing the hand that you have been dealt. Now it is up to you to rewrite your story. (More on this in Chapter 11.)

If They Knew the Real Me...

Do you remember *parentified children*, discussed in Chapter 4? Having to take on adult responsibilities as children is the source of Adult Children's fears that they are impostors who will be found out and recognized as incompetent. The child who knew that she was in over her head is still present in the adult who thinks she's not up to the tasks she's performing, even when the adult is fully qualified and is not an impostor.

The Inner Child Who Can't Say No

Your inner child is the part of you who can't say no, even when that is a perfectly reasonable thing to do. After all, it was reasonable to say no to taking on adult responsibilities as a child, but you did not really have the option to do so. Because you didn't learn to say no as a child you probably don't know how to say it now, either.

When you were growing up, saying no to your parents may have had negative results. It can be very difficult for a parent to react calmly and reasonably to a child who is defying the parent's wishes. Relatively well-adjusted parents can remind themselves that it's the child's job to assert herself (although that doesn't mean that she has to get her way). But insecure parents are likely to take the child's defiance as a threat to their authority and discourage or punish a child when she says no. If this happened to you, you probably learned to give in rather than to assert your needs and wants.

What About Feelings?

Parents who were never taught what to do with their feelings don't teach their children those skills, either. Their children lose touch with their feelings and can no longer identify them. But they probably don't realize that anything is missing.

These feelings are part of their inner children; by burying their emotions, they're also burying the children inside, teaching them that they're not valuable and that they shouldn't exist.

How Does My Inner Child Show Up Now?

When situations come up that inspire uncomfortable feelings an Adult Child may regress to childhood. You can recognize that this is happening to you if you find yourself reacting emotionally in a way (or to a degree) that you would not normally do. This generally indicates that you either have not learned adult coping strategies to deal with that sort of situation or you have temporarily forgotten them, particularly if the current situation has triggered something from the past.

For instance, there may have been a time in childhood when you proudly presented your straight-A report card to your father, only to be crushed when you were ignored instead of praised. As an adult you may present a successfully completed assignment to your supervisor, hoping for praise, only to be dismissed. The similarity between the two situations may bring back those childhood feelings.

When Sierra was in tenth grade she wrote a play and showed it to her mother, who was a screenplay writer. Her mother didn't consider her daughter's age or the fact that she had never written a play before. She critiqued it as she would critique the work of an experienced author. Not surprisingly, Sierra's effort didn't measure up. Her mother called it garbage and threw it into the trash. Sierra was ashamed, saddened, and angry; she never wrote another play. And from that point on she was cautious about sharing her work with her parents or other adults.

When you're an adult and your work is rejected by an authority figure you may be transported back to your childhood. Instead of having an adult reaction to the situation, you may be devastated and go back to your desk and cry. You probably feel ridiculous for having reacted this way because you don't know why you went to such an extreme.

But if you realize that the current situation has triggered memories of childhood experiences you can be more understanding of yourself. You now know why you unexpectedly felt and acted like a child.

Having realized this, you can begin to notice times that you regress to childhood. Eventually you will learn to catch yourself before you act like you're the age you're feeling. As I tell my clients, it's appropriate to be understanding and sympathetic with your inner five-year-old, but that doesn't mean that it's OK to give her the car keys!

Patience often encounters her inner teenager, who tries to keep her from fulfilling adult responsibilities such as getting up early enough to get to work on time. She is learning to negotiate with that inner teenager much as she does with her teenage sons. And she knows when to take the car keys.

This Inner Child is Embarrassing!

Your inner child is the part of you that can seem ridiculously optimistic. She has what is called *magical thinking*, so she believes things are possible that are not; for example, she still believes that it's possible to go back in time and change things that happened years ago.

When you were a child you may have maintained optimism despite repeated evidence that it wasn't warranted. For instance, Lee was convinced throughout her childhood that her parents were going to get her a dog, although her mother repeatedly said that they weren't going to get one. Lee visited pet stores and imagined the day that her parents would bring the dog home. Every time there was a hint that her parents might have a surprise or might be giving her something unexpected, she assumed she was getting a dog. But she never did.

Even today Lee's inner child is unrealistically optimistic. When she watches TV shows that she's seen before she truly believes it is possible for the characters to do something different, thus saving themselves from the embarrassing or dangerous situation they found themselves in the first time she watched the show. She forgets that the outcome will be the same every time no matter how many times she watches it.

Am I an Adult or Am I a Child?

You can look at your inner child in any way that makes sense to you. You can picture an actual child within you who is looking for your help, or you can just accept that you have childish thoughts and feelings that need to be dealt with. Either way, it's good to be aware that there is still a part of you that isn't grown up. And, while you do want to do your best to have the adult part of you be in charge, I hope that you will be understanding of yourself when you regress to childlike thoughts, feelings, and behaviors.

You have probably learned to see this childlike part of yourself as nothing but trouble. She doesn't understand why life feels so unfair and she wants someone to take care of her. She's very impractical and she comes out at inconvenient times.

Sometimes she's embarrassing. For instance, Molly was embarrassed when she realized that her inner child was in love with her daughter's preschool teacher in the way that 5-year-olds often are. She came to realize that it was OK for her inner child to feel that way, but that she needed to make sure that her adult self was in charge of what she did and said around that teacher.

I hope that, with practice, you will also start to recognize what is going on, realize where those feelings are coming from, and not beat yourself (or your inner child) up for it. This kind of understanding is often all that is needed to satisfy your inner child's needs.

As we've discussed before, having feelings and being vulnerable (both part of your inner child) did not work for you when you were growing up. Instead of strengths they were seen as weaknesses, things that could be used against you. And what point was there to needing someone to take care of you when that clearly was not going to happen?

It's not surprising if you feel that way. But your inner child is not only about needs and vulnerability; she is also about joy, spontaneity, and fun. Without her you not only won't be acknowledging your pain and your needs; you will also be shutting off these positive, enjoyable qualities.

Attention, Attention!

If you pretend the child inside you (or the childlike part of you) doesn't exist, she might cause trouble to get your attention. It's like the child who acts out and does things she knows she's not supposed to do because she's not getting any positive attention; she figures that negative attention is better than no attention.

The inner child is impulsive. She doesn't know about the future; all she knows is now. If you let her be in charge you might end up doing things you'll regret. For instance, let's say your boss makes your life difficult day after day. The adult part of you knows that it's best to try to work through the situation or find another job that works better for you. The inner child, however, might just get fed up one day, storm into your boss's office, and shout "I quit!" without considering what will happen next.

Carl Jung proposed the idea of the *shadow*. Your shadow consists of all of your personal qualities that were discouraged when you were a child. Because your parents told you or showed you in some way that they didn't approve of those qualities, you buried them and pretended, to yourself and everyone else, that they didn't exist. The inner child's qualities became part of your shadow.

Burying them didn't make them go away, though; instead, they went underground. Now, because you've turned your back on them instead of using them positively, they're likely to bite you in the you-know-what. So it's better to look for them and find ways to honor them and incorporate them into your life.

Any negative quality can be turned into a positive quality (or vice versa). For instance, I had a client at Chrysalis House, a residential treatment center for women with addictions, who was better than anyone else I've ever known at thinking on her feet, a necessary skill when you're a drug addict who lives in a rough part of town. Every time I had a session with her I thought about how much good she could do if she used those skills to support her sobriety rather than her drug habit.

So What Do I Do With Her?

It may sound exhausting to take care of your inner child. After all, it's hard enough taking care of your adult self and all of your responsibilities, including those to your own children, if you have them. But your inner child's needs are not always difficult to meet.

For instance, Molly got to her yoga class a little early one day because she wanted to greet the teacher and talk to her a bit before class started. When she got there she discovered that another student was already talking to the teacher. She waited for a little while, saw that their conversation was not likely to end soon, and then just went upstairs to prepare for class.

She noticed, while sitting on her mat and trying to center herself, that she was feeling sad, which puzzled her at first because she hadn't been sad earlier. Then she realized where the sadness was coming from—the little girl inside her was hurt that she hadn't gotten a chance to talk to (and, therefore, be noticed by) the teacher. When she realized that and mentally acknowledged and sympathized with her inner child's feelings, the sadness went away.

With practice, Molly has been doing better with this. She's working harder to get in there and talk to the yoga teacher even if others try to take over, but it's a challenge. She's not used to being assertive; it's so much easier to ignore her wants or needs and give in to others.

It's not easy to overcome these tendencies to hang back rather than approach people in authority, particularly ones you admire and from whom you want attention. The little girl in you was probably given the impression that her parents didn't have time for her and that she was bothering them when she asked for their attention. She's likely to believe this is true of people she admires, as well. So she may be afraid that she's bothering them or is too needy for them and that they'll be annoyed by her.

What Do You Do When She Asks for More Than Others Can Give?

Just as your inner child is often inconvenient for you, she can also, unfortunately, be inconvenient for the people she wants to love her, including those authority figures mentioned earlier. As was true of your parents, there will be times that those people are not available to her. There will be times that her needs will be greater than their ability to meet them. And there will probably be times that she will bother them and/or make them angry.

This will probably make her feel shame again. She's too much for these people. She's taking up too much space. She's asking for too much. She's not worthy of getting what she needs.

You can help her in these times. You're the only adult who will always be with her. You're the adult who's most likely to be able to meet her needs. And, at the very least, you can help her to understand that even when she doesn't get the attention and love she wants it's not because she doesn't deserve it or that people don't want to give it to her. It's that the practicalities of life don't always allow it to happen. Even though she is sometimes unreasonable, that doesn't mean she's bad or wrong. All of us are unreasonable sometimes, but we're still worthwhile.

Just as you need to try to find a balance between taking care of other people and taking care of yourself, you need to find a balance between taking care of your inner child and taking care of your adult self.

It's like the challenge parents face: how much of my time and energy should I dedicate to taking care of my child's needs, and how much should I use to recharge and meet my own needs so I can be more fully present for my child? How much should I encourage my child to learn to help herself so that she'll be prepared for living in the world, and how much is too much to expect or demand of her?

It's often not easy to take care of your inner child, but the more you are able to let her be herself and express herself the happier she (and you) will be.

Have Patience

If you're willing to try talking to your inner child, remember that it will take some time for you and for her to become comfortable with it. Don't give up right away if you try to talk to her and don't get a response.

Imagine a small child being locked in a closet for years without interactions with a caring adult. If you were to unlock the closet and rescue the child, how likely is it that she would immediately open up and be talkative? Most likely she'd be withdrawn and afraid; you'd need to be patient and encouraging, allowing her to communicate in her own time.

Remember the self-blame and the shame that you learned as a child. Your inner child may be afraid to be seen for fear that she'll be rejected as she was before. She may feel like she is permanently broken, so she doesn't want to show herself and let others know just how broken and unworthy she is.

This is particularly challenging in therapy, as the inner child may be afraid to trust the therapist and the defensive parts of the client are usually unwilling to let the inner child speak for fear she'll get in trouble.

There's also a good chance that your inner child feels resentment towards you. After all, you were there all of that time and could have helped her, but you didn't even know she existed!

Cassandra, as many of my clients are at first, was skeptical when I suggested that she talk to her inner child. The session after I made the suggestion she announced that she'd tried it, but she hadn't gotten any response. I told her what I just told you, that maybe it would take a while for the child to feel safe enough to speak. So Cassandra persisted, and now her inner child has a lot to say! While the child still feels very unsafe much of the time, she is vibrant and enthusiastic when she does feel safe to come out. Her joyful energy is an essential part of Cassandra's presence in the world.

The "Putting It Into Action" section of this chapter contains some exercises you can use to become more familiar with your inner child and to help her to get what she wants and needs. You don't have to try all of them if you don't want to; you can pick one or two that seem reasonable or doable to you. Again, try to be patient; it takes some time to get in touch with that part of you enough to see some benefit from it.

And remember, it's OK to feel silly doing this or to wonder if there's a point to it. Understand and respect that, but don't let it stop you from trying. You might be surprised with the results.

Be alert for times when your inner child shows up. If you have children, think about how (as your ideal parenting self) you react to them when they are feeling the way your inner child is. Then do the same for your inner child. If you don't have children, try to remember what it was like when you were a child and imagine how you would have wanted to be treated in the situation.

When your inner critical voice says something about your inner child, picture yourself standing between your critical self and your inner child. Tell the critical self that you will not let her hurt the child any more.

If you're not comfortable picturing an actual little-girl (or teenage, or whatever) version of yourself inside your head, just think of her as a part of you that acts and reacts the way a child (or teenager) would. Whichever image you choose, I encourage you to maintain awareness of that part of yourself and see what you can do to stay in touch with her.

Putting It Into Action

1. Find a photograph of yourself as a child. Picture yourself with her in a safe place. Talk to her and tell her that you've come to help her. Ask her what she needs from you.

Lindsay: I don't have any childhood photos of myself so I ask my mother for some. She asks why I want them, and I tell her that I'm in counseling and trying to remember my childhood. She thinks that's pretty weird, but she gives me a few photos anyway. She doesn't have many. I choose one that was taken when I was six years old. As I look at the photograph I picture my adult self in my childhood bedroom, sitting next to the six-year-old me on the bed. I imagine putting my arm around her. She leans into me. I apologize to her and tell her that I didn't know she was there, but now that I know, I want to take care of her. I ask her what she needs. She doesn't say anything; she just looks sad, like she does in the photo.

2. Have a written conversation with your inner child. Write questions to her using your dominant hand. Use your non-dominant hand to write down whatever responses come to you.

It has taken a while, but I've finally gotten young Lindsay (nickname Linnie) to talk to me. Here's our conversation (M=my adult self, L=Linnie; Jill is my older sister):

M: Hi, Linnie. It's Lindsay again.

L: Hi.

M: How are you?

L: OK.

M: Really?

L: I guess.

M: Anything you want to talk about?

L: Not really.

M: Do you mind if I ask you some things?

L: No.

M: Do you cry a lot?

L: Yes.

M: What does Mom say?

L: She tells me to stop.

M: Can you?

L: Sometimes.

M: How do you feel about crying?

L: I don't know. I try not to let people make me sad.

M: What if they do?

L: I try not to cry.

M: Is it because of Mom?

L: I don't know.

M: Do you wish you could cry?

L: Yes.

M: What happens when Mom and Dad go away?

L: I cry.

M: Do you get sick?

L: Yes.

M: Why?

L: I want them to stay.

M: Does it happen?

L: No.

M: How do you feel being small?

L: Sad and scared. Nobody listens to me.

M: *What is it that animals like about you?*

L: *I'm gentle.*

M: *What did Jill say to you when you were alone?*

L: *She hated me.*

M: *How did that feel?*

L: *Scary.*

M: *Why do you want to be like her?*

L: *She's my big sister. I need her.*

M: *Why?*

L: *To know what to be like.*

M: *Are you like her?*

L: *No.*

M: *Not at all?*

L: *A little. I'm good at school. I like animals. I wish she liked me.*

M: *She will.*

L: *Really?*

M: *Yes, really. Actually, she will not just like you, she'll love you. And I love you, too. You're a very sweet girl* [hug]. *I'll talk to you again soon.*

L: *OK.*

3. Remember a difficult situation that you experienced as a child. Picture yourself, as an adult, being with your inner child in that situation and intervening to protect her and help her to feel safe in a way that no one did for you when you were growing up.

I remember a time when Jill was babysitting me and she threatened to hurt me. When I started to run away she stuck out her foot and tripped me. I fell and twisted my ankle. Jill got scared because she knew I had probably sprained my ankle and she didn't know what to do. She didn't know how to get in touch with Mom and Dad so she waited for them to get home. When they got home Jill said that I tripped over an electrical cord, fell, and hurt my ankle. They took me to the doctor, who told them that my ankle was sprained. It took a couple of months for it to heal; I had to sit inside while my friends were outside playing. My parents never knew what happened that day.

Here's the new version in which my adult self is able to protect Linnie:

Jill gets mad at Linnie the way she did when this really happened. This time, though, my adult self is there to help Linnie. Linnie is beginning to realize that she can trust me and that I'll keep her safe. Jill starts to threaten Linnie and I intervene. I tell Jill that I will be with Linnie from now on, so she will no longer be able to abuse her emotionally or physically. Now Linnie has an adult who knows what Jill has done in the past; she finally has an adult who will listen to her.

4. Imagine your inner child trapped inside a high wall with no means of escape. Picture yourself using a ladder to climb over the wall or making a door in the wall so you can let her out.

"The Wall"

Once upon a time there was a small village. Near the village there were beautiful trees that people could sit under and that children could climb, and open spaces where they could have picnics. A little farther into the trees, though, it was not so open.

The trees were closer together and there was a lot of underbrush that was difficult to get through. Very few people ventured this far in.

One day a woman decided that she would get past these trees and find out what was on the other side. With a lot of patience and persistence she made her way through, only to find that there was a thick stone wall behind the trees. She realized that the wall had been there for a long time, but that few had known about it because it had been hidden. There was a house behind the wall.

She called out, "Is anyone there?" A young female voice responded, "Yes." They introduced themselves to each other and got into a long conversation. After a while the woman began to feel that the wall was interfering with their process of getting to know one another, so she asked if she could come inside. The girl could tell that the woman sincerely cared about her; she had come to trust her even though they had not known each other for very long. She wanted to let her in, but, unfortunately, this was not easy.

The girl explained that the wall had been built years ago to keep her safe. Eventually, though, she had forgotten where the gate was. "Now people can't get in even if I want them to, and I can't get out. Can you help me?" Because the woman wanted to get to know the girl better, she agreed.

Together, one on each side, they explored the wall. They found the gate, but the lock was rusted shut. They managed to loosen it. Finally, the gate could move freely and the woman was able to get in.

After they had spent some time together, the woman and the girl worked on clearing out some of the underbrush and pruning the trees outside of the wall. This made it possible for the girl to be part of the nearby community when she wanted to be, but to have privacy when she needed it.

The villagers helped to maintain the newly cleared area so that everyone could enjoy it. Kids played near the wall and birds made nests in it because it seemed much less threatening and insurmountable than before.

5. Watch a small child for a while. Remember what it was like to be that age. When you find yourself being self-critical because you "should" have been able to defend yourself as a child, ask yourself if you would expect that child to defend herself from the things you went through.

I go to the mall and spend some time in the play area observing the kids. There are some teenagers there who take over the play area, knocking over some smaller kids in the process. The small children's parents don't notice because they're busy with their cell phones—talking, texting, or playing games. One child falls down and bruises his knee. He runs to his mother, who tells him he's not really hurt; she sends him back out to play. Another parent has trouble getting her child to put her shoes on and leave the play area, so she says, "Goodbye" and walks away. The little girl, panicked, shouts "Mommy!" and runs after her, carrying her shoes. Looking at the small children, I realize that the things that adults think are no big deal can be really traumatic for the kids. I want to yell at the parents and tell them to respect their children's needs.

6. Ask your inner child what she would like to do for fun—go to an amusement park, go to the zoo, or maybe go to a toy store and buy a toy that she would like to have. Choose one of the activities, and then do it! And make sure to do things like this periodically so you and your inner child can count on having some fun, non-adult times.

When I ask Linnie what she wants to do, she doesn't hesitate: she wants to go to the zoo. So on Saturday we make a trip to the zoo. I make sure not to have any particular agenda. We go to see all the animals Linnie wants to see and skip the ones she doesn't. We take our time and enjoy the sunshine. We get ice cream. Linnie wants to skip rather than walk, but I draw the line there—maybe next time. I'm amazed at how much fun it is!

7. Get some kids' art supplies and some play-doh. Allow your inner child to draw, paint, or whatever art she would like to do. Play with the play-doh. Have fun!

The next day we go to a really cool toy store. Linnie wants to buy almost everything in the store, of course, but I'm the adult and I set a spending limit. I promise Linnie that this will not be our last trip to the toy store. She chooses a stuffed animal and then we head for the art supplies. We buy paper, watercolor paints, colored markers, a big box of crayons, glitter glue, and some Play-Doh. When we get home it's hard to decide what to use first! Most days we find at least some time to do art projects or play with Play Doh. Linnie is finally getting a chance to be a kid, and it's great for both of us. There are still many challenges, of course, but now at least I know she's there and can listen to her when she has something to say.

Part III

Chapter 7

Life Should Be Fair

1. When you were a kid, did you ever wish that you were adopted and that your real parents would come looking for you so your life would get better? Or if you were adopted, did you wish that your real parents would come and rescue you?

2. Do you ever wish you had a time machine so that you could go back and change your childhood?

3. Do you ever find yourself thinking that your life should be exactly the way you want it to be, then criticizing yourself for wishing for something that's not possible?

4. Do you pretend that everything's OK with you even when it's not?

5. When something bad happens to you, do you ever find yourself saying, "This is not what I expected! How can this be happening to me?"

If your answer to any of the above questions was yes, you're familiar with the childlike wish that life should be fair. But as you know, it isn't; if life were fair I wouldn't have written this book and you wouldn't be reading it. If life were fair you wouldn't need to work towards a balance between taking care of others and taking care of yourself; you'd live in an ideal universe in which everyone gave and received equally so everyone's needs were met without even having to ask. There would be no such thing as a people pleaser, because no one would have to worry about constantly giving to others, hoping to get something in return.

Although it makes sense to wish for fairness, in the end it's our job to find and maintain balance as well as we can.

Do You Believe in Magic?

You would think that growing up in a dysfunctional household would lead you to expect the worst most of the time. And that is often true. But having a child inside you who never grew up also leads to the magical thinking I mentioned in Chapter 6.

This child is the part of you that believes in unicorns and the pot of gold at the end of the rainbow, the part that believes you will win $300 million in the lottery, the part that believes that one of these days you will find the time machine that will help you go back and make everything better.

It's good to have this childlike idealism, but it can become inconvenient and embarrassing when the child's expectations are not met. What do you do if a friend tells you she got a raise and your inner child stomps her foot and shouts, "It's not fair! Why did SHE get a raise and I didn't?"

It's one thing if your inner child just says it inside your head, but quite another if she triggers you to say it out loud or to act on that feeling. Your friend won't appreciate it if you respond to her good news by saying, "You're no better than I am! How come you got a raise? I haven't gotten a raise in forever!" It's also not cool to storm into your boss's office and angrily demand to know why you haven't gotten a raise in three years when everyone else you know has gotten annual raises.

If you buy self-help books expecting a quick fix and not doing the work that's required for change to happen, you are practicing magical thinking. It's as if you hope that the mere act of having bought the book will transform your life. If that was your (unconscious) expectation, you might forget about the book entirely, say it didn't work for you, say it was too hard or didn't fit your lifestyle, or something else that explains why you haven't changed as a result of buying the book, rather than admitting to yourself that you were engaged in magical thinking.

Magical thinking can also come into play when you start the latest fad diet. Maybe *this* one will miraculously take the pounds off and keep them off without too much effort on your part. Or maybe *this* exercise equipment will transform you into one of those sexy people in the TV commercials. Unfortunately, that's not usually how it works. Have you ever read the fine print in those commercials, like "results not typical" or, in the case of the exercise machine, "along with a healthy diet?"

The *geographical cure* is another type of magical thinking. Some people believe that moving to another part of the country or of the world will make their lives better. I'm reminded of women at Chrysalis House who said they were having conflicts with other women in the house. They thought that if they left the house their issues would be solved. But, as I pointed out to them, at least part of the problem was in their own heads, and those would go with them if they left!

Reality is Overrated

Work can be one place where wishes and reality may clash. There are many people who entered a work field because their parents told them to do it or it seemed to be the most practical idea at the time. Years later they may find themselves resenting the years they've spent in a job they hate, feeling helpless to change things and being afraid to try. Their idealistic sides don't see why they can't do what they want to do; they're not concerned with practicality or the need to pay the mortgage.

Paige still struggles with this. She has an office job and knows that the practical thing would be to get a certification that supports her office work and expands her job possibilities in the field. But her inner child wants to be a professional singer; she still hopes she'll be discovered one day and will leave her life of drudgery for a life of fame, fortune, and glamour.

Longing for Rescue?

When Rose was growing up her main leisure activities were ones that helped her to temporarily escape her reality. She went on long bike rides to get away from her house and dreamed of just continuing to ride, never to return. She played the violin to express feelings for which she could find no words. She drew pictures of her life as it was and how she wished it could be. She read fantasy and science fiction novels; she loved the fact that they were about different worlds than the one she lived in.

In middle school she loved books written by Anne McCaffrey. Her favorites were about young women whose musical abilities weren't respected where they were, but who were discovered by someone to have extraordinary talent. They were whisked away from their mundane realities where they were unappreciated and were taken to places where they were honored and rewarded for doing what they did best.

Rose dreamed of this happening to her. When was someone going to notice her and take her out of the life she was living into one that she could love?

She watched the TV show *Fame* and was angry that some kids got to go to a school for the arts and she didn't. The fact that she was made aware of the existence of a school like that made her hate her own high school even more than she had before.

There's a part of Rose that's still looking for that rescue. She's still waiting for someone to come and find her and take her to a magical place where everything is OK. She doesn't want to believe that happiness is more likely to be achieved than bestowed.

Yes, there are times when someone is discovered and suddenly finds herself living a new life of performing and being admired, particularly now that there are TV shows that catapult previously unknown singers, dancers, and others into stardom, but it doesn't happen to most of us. It probably just points out to us how different our lives are from what we wish they could be. And when we're feeling jealous we probably forget that it wasn't just luck that got those people where they were; persistence, determination, skill, and hard work were also needed.

Rose has enjoyed the *Harry Potter* books as an adult; she knows she would have loved them and found them very helpful if they'd been written when she was growing up.

Harry Potter is a somewhat more realistic fantasy series than the ones Rose read as a child. The title character is clearly human and gets in trouble fairly often. He has to face the internal struggle between choosing good or evil. And, unlike the heroines in the Anne McCaffrey novels, despite his having been discovered and taken to a place where his talents were appreciated, there were times that he had to return to his former life. Knowing that his new life was waiting for his return, though, made it more bearable.

Like Rose, many of us would like to be magically transported to somewhere like the bar in the TV show *Cheers*—"where everybody knows your name, and they're always glad you came."

Where's the "Happily Ever After?"

Many of us dreamed of a better life when we were kids. And many of us wish that we could go back and change our childhoods so that our present realities could be better, too. We might also want to go back and change things that we regret having done (or not done).

There are many fairy tales we heard and read as children that did not serve us well. I'm sure you remember the ones that essentially boiled down to, "They met, they fell in love, they overcame a challenge of some sort, and then they lived happily ever after."

I don't remember any of those stories mentioning that it takes work to create that "happily ever after," though. And they certainly didn't give any pointers on how to make that happen! So here many of us are, thinking that we're supposed to have the "happily ever after," but having little or no idea of how to get there.

The reality is that you don't need a fairy tale life to be happy, happiness does not come automatically (or even easily), and you can't expect others to bestow happiness upon you.

As 12-step programs say, "Expectations are premeditated resentments." You need to be willing to do the work to make happiness happen, and you need to be aware that things will not always go the way you'd like them to go. If you expect them to automatically work out you're likely to end up angry and bitter when they don't.

"Poor Me"

Some people who have had difficult lives develop a sense of entitlement. They may assume that because their lives have been hard the world owes them something. Instead of doing what they can to improve their own lives they play the "poor me" card and hope that it will make others take care of them. Some do this without even realizing it.

Shana had a sponsor in Narcotics Anonymous who said that Shana needed to work on adult child issues because she often portrayed herself as a victim of her childhood. Her sponsor hoped that adult child work would help Shana to realize that she needed to take responsibility for her own well-being, not try to get others take responsibility for her because they felt sorry for her. Shana had never thought of herself as a victim, so it took a while for her to internalize the message she'd gotten from her sponsor.

Years later, Shana was struck by an illustration a speaker gave at a retreat she attended; it reminded her of the way she'd been before she'd followed her sponsor's recommendation. The speaker asked what people would do if they found a pile of horse manure in the middle of their living room.

One person might scoop it up, take it outside, and clean the floor to remove any trace of manure.

Another person might put a rug over the manure. She might pretend the manure isn't there, even after maggots start appearing in it and flies start buzzing around the house.

Then there's the person (with whom Shana was once able to identify) who puts the rug over the manure but lifts the rug periodically, looks at the manure, and comments on it, noting the maggots and the flies, but not doing anything about it.

That's the type of person who can talk, day after day, week after week, month after month, year after year, about the things that are going wrong in her life without doing the work needed to fix it. This is a sort of victim mentality. That person is saying, "Look, there's something wrong here, but I (can't/won't) fix it. I (need/want) someone else to take care of it!"

But I Don't Play the Victim!

Many of my clients can't imagine how they might be playing a victim role. After all, they have spent their lives relying on themselves and not asking anyone for help. Shana, for instance, is someone who is really good at advocating for herself and others. Once she even sued a large corporation and won. How could she be a victim?

You, like Shana once did, are playing the victim if you say you'd like to help the child inside you but you can't. You think that her needs are impossible to meet, or at least that you can't meet them. Maybe someone else can be a parental figure for her, but not you. If you're really honest with yourself you'll probably realize that you are either afraid or unwilling to try to help her.

Life Is Good But I'm Still Not Happy

What would happen if you suddenly found yourself in what you've always imagined would be your ideal situation? What happens, for instance, if you have lots of money, everyone likes you, you have the perfect, fulfilling job, you're able to give generously to others, and your life is generally beautiful, but you find that you're still not happy? Then you're really in trouble!

That is, I think, one reason why so many celebrities become alcoholics and drug addicts. You would think someone who has it all wouldn't need something like that, right? But think about it. Celebrities know that, for many Americans, the dream is to be rich and famous. They have gotten the fame and fortune but they're still not happy. Now what? If fame and fortune won't buy happiness, what will?

Try to find happiness and fulfillment where and when you are rather than hoping for some mythical other place and time that will magically grant you happiness. This is part of the idea of *mindfulness*, which comes from Eastern religions but is increasingly being used by psychotherapists (see Chapter 11 for more information on mindfulness). And be willing to do the work necessary to achieve your goals.

No, Really, I Am Happy!

Most of us don't usually tell people that we wish for happily ever after, a life where everything we want and need magically comes to us. First, we know logically that it's not going to happen. And we realize that others might look down on us for being so childish and unrealistic. Plus, having grown up in dysfunctional families, we learned to pretend we were happy even when we weren't; we certainly don't want to admit to others how we really feel.

When you were a child you probably were not allowed to tell your parents or anyone else that you were unhappy, or if you did, nothing changed anyway, so you probably gave up. Maybe one or both of your parents didn't want to know that bad things were happening to you so they ignored those things, or maybe they got upset. While they might have genuinely wished that things were going better for you, you probably would have thought that you were somehow at fault and that they were blaming you.

In any case, you probably learned to put a brave face on things and pretend that everything was fine when it wasn't. And you probably still do that today, including possibly telling yourself that you have gotten over the things that happened to you in the past.

The problem is that it's not true, and on one level or another you know that. The unhappiness is there and it will come out one way or the other. This is the source of resentments, of passive-aggressive behavior, and of acting happy most of the time, but having periodic outbursts of extreme anger.

It can also be a contributor to some of the issues I'll discuss in Chapter 8, including depression and anxiety.

How Should I Feel About My Childhood?

Many of my clients don't want to be angry about their childhoods because their parents did the best they could. Why blame them for what happened when they couldn't do anything about it?

If you feel this way I invite you to take a slightly different perspective. You can acknowledge that your parents did the best they could but also be aware that you did not get what you needed from them.

You have probably tended towards one side of the "taking care" idea or the other. One side is taking care of your parents and their feelings by telling yourself that they did the best they could and you have no right to be angry. The other side is trying to take care of yourself by shutting them out of your life and your consciousness so they can't hurt you further.

The situation doesn't have to be black and white, though, and the two scenarios I described may or may not truly take care of anyone. It is not a choice between two options, with option one being that your parents did the best they could and, therefore, it is your obligation to not be angry about your childhood; or option two, that you need to blame your parents for everything bad that has ever happened to you. Instead of either/or, it can be both/and. You can acknowledge feelings of sadness and anger about what you needed and didn't get while still respecting your parents for having done the best they could.

And if you find a way to balance those two things you might find a new, more helpful, way of taking care of both yourself and them.

Balancing Wants and Needs with Acceptance

Just because you didn't get something doesn't mean it was wrong to want it. That applied when you were a child and it still applies today. It's OK to want life to be fair. It's OK to wish for a time machine so you could go back and fix your childhood. But you have to be OK with wanting those things while simultaneously knowing you're not going to get them.

We got the message in childhood that we were wrong for wanting and needing things that our parents were unwilling or unable to give us. But it wasn't true, even if our parents let us believe it.

It's difficult, though, to hold those two ideas simultaneously, especially in current situations. Can you accept and hold the feeling of wanting something while still accepting the reality that you might not get it? Can you resist criticizing yourself for wanting it?

You may have heard of the book *When Bad Things Happen to Good People*. That book tells us that we shouldn't assume that bad things come to us as punishment for things we've done wrong, or because of our character flaws. Sometimes bad things happen even if we don't deserve them.

Remember what I said before about "It's not your fault, but it is your responsibility"? This is where it comes into play. You did not deserve the neglect and/or abuse that you suffered as a child, and therefore it's not your fault that you developed the issues you're facing today. But it is your responsibility, and no one else's, to do what you can to heal from those childhood wounds and to choose different ways of being in the world. You can also find or create meaning in the things that happened to you, if you choose to do so.

Why Did This Happen?

We all know that terrible things happen in the world. Natural disasters destroy property and take lives. People die young from diseases, suffer from chronic illnesses, are murdered, or are injured mentally, emotionally, or physically. We hurt each other on a regular basis, often without meaning to do so. One bad thing after another happens for no apparent reason. Life is full of inequities and tragedies. Now that technology enables us to find out about events across the world almost instantaneously, it can seem overwhelming.

Many people want to know why these bad things happen. Did people do something wrong to deserve them? Are these experiences meant to happen so that we can learn from them? If you believe in God, could God have prevented them, and if so, why didn't God do so?

People have come up with a variety of theories to answer this question. Maybe it's the presence of evil in the world that creates these things. Maybe God allows bad things to happen because we were made with free will, and part of free will is the opportunity to make mistakes or to hurt ourselves or someone else. Maybe it's like a "choose your own adventure" book; we make a choice, and that choice leads to a certain path that offers new choices and consequences, etc.

Maybe there is a master plan and bad experiences will, down the road, lead to positive results. Søren Kierkegaard said, "Life can only be lived forwards, but it can only be understood backwards." There can be times that you find yourself in a difficult situation and don't understood why you're there, only to figure out later that it was a stepping stone to something better. Some people use the example of taking a journey in a thick fog with only a flashlight to guide you; the flashlight shows you the part of the path that's immediately in front of you, but it won't show you what's coming farther down the road. But does that mean that everything is meant to be and will lead to something good?

Or you might believe it's just chance that makes bad things happen. Statistically, a certain number of people will have certain bad things happen to them, and you just happened to be one of those people.

Whatever you believe, it can be hard to accept pain and trauma in your life. If you try, though, you may be able to find benefits that come out of them. Do the benefits justify what happened? Only you can decide that for yourself.

Forgiveness

Forgiveness is a tricky thing. Many people think that forgiving means saying that what someone else did was OK. But as Dr. Fred Luskin points out in his book *Forgive for Good*, forgiveness does not have to mean condoning the other person's actions. Instead it can be an exercise in healing yourself and moving on with your life, free of the effects of the wrong that was done to you.

There is a saying, "Holding a resentment is like drinking poison and waiting for the other person to die." People also speak of "letting someone live in your head rent free."

Both of these are so true. If someone has wronged you and you continue to hold onto anger and resentment about it, you are hurting yourself; you are not hurting the person who hurt you. It's possible, in fact, that the other person has completely forgotten about the wrong done to you or if she does remember, doesn't feel guilty about it.

So what is the benefit in your holding on to resentment about it? That will negatively affect you while doing nothing whatsoever to right the wrong that was done to you. One speaker at a seminar I attended pointed out that if you break your leg in a car accident that was another driver's fault, it doesn't make sense not to go to the hospital and get it fixed just because the other person caused the injury, not you. It won't hurt the other person, but it will certainly hurt you if you don't get the injury treated.

The English clergyman and poet George Herbert wrote in his book *Jacula Prudentum: Or Outlandish Proverbs, Sentences, Etc.,* "Living well is the best revenge." Wouldn't it be great if you let that other person see that his or her treatment of you has not kept you from living a happy, fulfilling life?

Gotta Go Through It

Do you know the children's song/story "Going on a bear hunt" (which, when I was a kid, was "Going on a squeegee hunt")? One obstacle after another comes up, and the response every time is, "Can't go over it. Can't go under it. Can't go around it. Gotta go through it."

Just as the story goes, if you want to be healthy and happy and move forward in your life you can't pretend that you're over things that you haven't really worked through. You need to go through feeling the feelings so you can let go of them.

And you have to recognize the things you're still doing that hurt you.

One of the most frustrating things about the results of childhood abuse and neglect is that in the beginning, our parents (or others) are the ones inflicting harm on us, but after a while we take over for them and start doing the same things to ourselves by treating ourselves badly and committing acts of self-sabotage.

Changing Your Patterns

In twelve-step programs the fourth step is to "make a searching and fearless moral inventory" of yourself. What would happen if you did this?

It's worth taking some time to look at unhelpful patterns you are repeating from the past, adaptations you made or things that you learned from your parents. What messages did you get in childhood (and that you still live by) that aren't true? What have your relationships looked like? How has your self-image been? What parts of your life would you like to change?

When you figure out what it is you don't want, it's easier to clarify what you do want. And once you know what you want it becomes possible to figure out steps you can take to make it happen.

Let's face it, it's unlikely that you'll be magically whisked away to an ideal existence. Finding real happiness is going to take some work. But you can succeed if you put forth the effort and are willing to believe that you can change your life for the better.

You can decide what you need to do to find the balance between wishful thinking and realistic thinking. You can also look at the ways in which you hope for or even expect to be rescued. Are you secretly waiting for your knight in shining armor to come and sweep you off your feet? Or are you giving too much to others in the hopes that they'll do the same for you? How can you respect and even work with the idealistic part of yourself to begin to find the balance you need?

Putting It Into Action

1. What types of magical thinking do you engage in? When you notice you're doing it, do you automatically have a self-critical thought? If so, what more positive statement can you substitute for it?

Monique: I have not heard from my brother, Jack, in ten years. I don't understand this because we had always had a close relationship until Jack seemingly dropped off the face of the earth. Every year I send Jack birthday and Christmas presents, and every year I hope that he will reciprocate or at least thank me for the gifts. When I get no response at all I beat myself up for being so naïve as to think that he would suddenly reappear in my life.

This year, though, I am telling myself something different. Instead of calling myself stupid and foolish I tell myself that it's OK to want my brother in my life, and sending him gifts is a way to acknowledge the possibility that he may come back into my life at some point. It's OK to believe in the possibility of a response even when it's unlikely, as long as I'm prepared to deal with it if it doesn't come.

2. Think about what living happily ever after would mean for you. Create a mental picture of what your life would be like if you had everything you most wanted.

Vivian: I have always wanted to own a stable and make my living boarding, training, and showing horses. I have always felt more comfortable around animals than people. I would like to have a small house on the same property as the stable and live alone with my cats and dog.

Right now I am working as a customer service representative for an appliance company, and I hate it. Not only do I have to talk to people for a living, but the people I talk to are usually angry and take it out on me.

How much of your dream is already true for you?

When I look at my present situation I realize that I have already achieved a small part of my dream. On weekends I go to a local stable and ride horses in exchange for grooming them, cleaning the stable, etc. I do live in an apartment by myself, and I am allowed to have one dog and one cat there; it's not as many as I'd like, but it's something.

What changes can you realistically make to get closer to that "happily ever after?"

More than once I have been offered a job at the stable I go to on weekends. I haven't accepted the offer for a couple of reasons. First, I don't like some of the people I'd be working with because they don't treat the horses as well as I think they should. And second, I am afraid that the stable owner will find out that I'm not as competent as he thinks I am. I think that if he finds out what I'm really like, he'll fire me and I'll be out of a job.

I decide to look at the situation differently. Maybe if I'm working at the stable I can influence other people's behavior and get them to treat the horses better. I also decide to talk to some people who work at the stable and others who can look at my performance more objectively than I can so that I can get their opinions about my competence.

What changes could you make to the way you look at your life that would help you to better appreciate what you have now?

When I think about it, I realize that I probably wouldn't like to own and operate a stable; I've never been the type to enjoy being in charge. That feels like too much responsibility, and I would probably have to relate to a lot of people in ways that I wouldn't find comfortable.

I'm also glad that my current job has hours that allow me to go to the stable on weekends. Now that I'm thinking of leaving I realize that I don't hate everything about my job; for instance, I do like some of my coworkers. I'm happy that I am getting some time with horses. I have decided that the next time I'm offered a job at the stable I will take it, but in the meantime I will make a point to notice the good things about where I am right now.

3. Describe a resentment you still hold from your past.

Adele: I grew up in an alcoholic family. I felt like Cinderella. I was expected to keep the house clean and to cook meals. My mother criticized me if I got anything less than straight A's in school. I worked part time so I could earn money to buy the things I wanted and needed, including clothes and a car.

Meanwhile, according to my mother, my brother Chris could do no wrong. She never criticized his grades. He didn't have to do any chores at all. And not only did our parents buy him a car; they bought him a second one when he totaled the first one, and then a third when he totaled the second one.

I had to work to put myself through college; our parents paid the entire cost of Chris's education, including graduate school. I lived in an apartment because I couldn't afford a house; our parents bought a house for Chris.

How is that resentment affecting you today?

I don't have a relationship with Chris because of my resentments about the inequities of our childhoods. I don't have any other siblings and I don't get along with my parents, so it essentially feels like I have no family at all.

I have become a very independent person, not looking to anyone else for anything. This has had its good points, but it also leads to loneliness and the inability to trust other people to have my best interests at heart.

Has the resentment been keeping you trapped in unhealthy patterns? If so, what are those patterns?

I have never dated and I don't have any close friends. I have never trusted people enough to let them in. I have never asked anyone for help and I have tried to ignore problems that I couldn't fix myself.

What can you do to change them?

Having had my independence thrown into question by a serious illness for which I was hospitalized, I have come to realize that complete independence is not realistic. I've had more time to think about my life and to realize how lonely I am. I am considering contacting Chris, and I am going to try to socialize more and maybe even find someone to date. I have decided to proceed with caution rather than throw myself headfirst into a relationship in which I make myself completely vulnerable.

Find a way to get those resentments out; many of my clients journal about them, but you could also use other things like visual art, music, and dance. It helps to use something that you enjoy and are likely to actually do.

I have chosen to do a couple of things to get the resentments out. I am writing about them in my journal. I also play the violin, so when I want to release feelings of sadness and anger I play my favorite piece of music, Mendelssohn's violin concerto in e minor.

4. Have you ever been told (by yourself and/or others) that you need to forgive someone who has been or is in your life? If so, who is it, and what is/are the reason(s) why forgiveness has been recommended?

Sandy: When I was fourteen years old my father, who is an alcoholic, drank and drove and caused a serious accident when I was in the car with him. My injuries were so severe that I have walked with a limp ever since. I had been on my school's field hockey team and loved to play; because of my injury I had to stop playing.

I go to church regularly. I have been struggling with the church's directive to forgive those who have harmed me. I've tried to remind myself that my father had not intended to cause the accident; he was under the influence of alcohol so he wasn't in control of his actions. I have tried to excuse him on that basis, but I just can't.

The car accident is still a huge factor in my life. I sometimes have panic attacks when I'm riding in a car. My limp makes me feel self-conscious, so I am often unwilling to go out in public. I would like to teach my kids by example how to be self-confident, but I don't feel confident myself. And the damage to my leg prevents me from playing with my kids the way I would like to do.

I'm now reading Dr. Fred Luskin's book Forgive for Good. *I am starting to apply his techniques for letting go of the fear and*

*anger I experience on a daily basis. I am realizing that I don't
have to say it was OK that my father did what he did; I am
just taking steps to end the suffering that I have experienced
because of it.*

**You probably don't think that you are waiting for someone to
rescue you and take care of you. But if someone told you that you
were waiting for rescue in some way and asked you to figure out
what it was, what answer could you come up with?**

*Adele: I have always lived a very independent life because I
learned early that no one else was going to take care of me; I
had to take care of myself. I didn't realize until my time in the
hospital that the young girl inside me was still waiting for the
care and attention I never got from my parents. Now I know
that even though I have made a point of not needing anyone,
it's only because I assumed my needs would not be met. I have
been unwilling to make myself vulnerable because I don't want
to be hurt.*

*Having recognized that young girl inside me, I am now taking
time to talk to her and reassure her. I am finding ways to reach
out to other people for friendship and care. For instance, I have
neighbors who have reached out to me and invited me to go
to dinner; while I had always declined in the past, I am now
accepting those invitations and developing some friendships in
my neighborhood and at work.*

*I am going to therapy and learning more about the hurt child
inside me. I reassure the child, telling her that I, the adult, will
help her to survive if something bad happens as the result of
making herself vulnerable.*

Chapter 8

Coping with Illness

1. When you were growing up did anyone in your family have a chronic mental or physical illness?

2. Did you ever wish that you had a major illness so that someone would pay attention to you?

3. When you got sick as a child, how did your parents react?

    (a) Made you go to school anyway.

    (b) Let you stay home, but didn't give you much attention.

    (c) Let you stay home and took care of you.

    (d) Let you stay home and paid more attention than usual to you, making you feel special.

4. When you get sick now, do you:

    (a) Try to ignore it and go on as usual.

(b) Feel uncomfortable with being sick and getting attention.

(c) Stay in bed and feel sorry for yourself.

(d) Take care of yourself but don't overdramatize your illness.

(e) Feel more important and worthy of attention because you're sick.

5. What do your family members do when you get sick?

(a) Tell you to "get over it."

(b) Leave you to take care of yourself.

(c) Gladly take care of you.

(d) Resentfully take care of you.

(e) Treat you like you're more important than usual because you're sick.

6. When other people are sick, do you:

(a) Gladly take care of them.

(b) Resentfully take care of them.

(c) Tell them to "get over it."

(d) Offer some help but encourage them to take care of themselves, too.

7. Do you have any chronic physical or mental illnesses?

In this chapter we will not only look at the balance between taking care of others and taking care of yourself; we'll also look at the balance between taking care of yourself and getting help from others.

We'll explore possible links between a difficult childhood and mental or physical illnesses and self-sabotaging behaviors that develop later in life. We'll also look at possible relationships between codependency and physical health.

Adult Children and Illness

Mental and physical illnesses and injuries are difficult for anyone to deal with. But Adult Children face particular challenges in this area.

If your answer to question 4 of the quiz was "a," it's not surprising. As we discussed in Chapter 4, Adult Children are not used to having their needs met and they generally have no idea how to ask for help. Many Adult Children will deny illnesses and injuries as long as they can to other people and even to themselves.

They're ashamed of showing a flaw or a weakness and they're terrified of needing help because the message they got early in life was that no one will help them—they're on their own (question 3). They're used to being self-sufficient, so when something happens that makes them dependent (temporarily or permanently) on someone else they can have a very difficult time adjusting.

This is a situation that can force Adult Children to look at how much they take care of others and how little they take care of themselves (or allow others to take care of them).

They usually try to avoid being a burden on other people even if those people really do want to help. Low self-esteem can interfere with an Adult Child's ability to ask for or accept help; she may feel like she is unworthy and doesn't deserve other people's time, attention, and effort.

If you're an Adult Child you probably don't want to feel like you owe something to someone else. You may have learned from your family that there is a sort of accounting system that tracks everything everyone has done for others and that any debts incurred must be repaid as soon as possible. You might have gotten the impression that you owe a debt to your parents that you will never be able to repay because that gives your parents power over you. So now you don't want to allow someone to do something for you and therefore put yourself in the "one down" position of being a debtor.

How Do You Feel When Others Get Sick?

Adult Children who don't take care of themselves often end up in relationships with people who go to the opposite extreme by complaining about every ache, pain, and sniffle they experience. Just as a busy person often resents people who sit around and do nothing, someone who ignores her own illnesses generally resents those who make a big deal of theirs. If she isn't allowed to seek attention when she's not feeling well, why should someone else be allowed to do it?

Geraldine has fibromyalgia. She rarely takes her medication because it makes her dizzy, nauseous, and fatigued, so she is in constant pain. She doesn't complain, she doesn't ask anyone for help, and she hasn't made any changes to her busy daily schedule.

Geraldine's husband, Adam, was spoiled by his parents, who gave him anything he wanted. They didn't ask him to do anything around the house when he was growing up or to get a job when he was old enough. They paid his way through college and continued to support him financially even after he left college.

Adam was used to being waited on hand and foot and he thought Geraldine would do it, too. When he got a cold he stayed in bed for days and expected her to stop whatever she was doing so she could nurse him back to health.

This became a huge source of conflict for Geraldine and Adam. The conflict got worse and worse, so they went to marriage counseling. During the counseling both of them learned more about why Geraldine ignored her illnesses and Adam exaggerated his. Over time they began to understand each other's points of view and to try to change their own thinking and behaviors.

It's still a struggle, but Geraldine is doing better at taking care of herself and asking for help, and Adam is doing better at putting things into perspective and not expecting so much from Geraldine. Because she is no longer ignoring her own needs Geraldine is finding it a bit easier to be willing to take care of Adam when he really needs it. Because he is taking more responsibility for himself, Adam asks for less from Geraldine and is willing to give her some help when she needs it.

What Does it Mean if Part of Me Wants to Be Sick?

Just as the "lost child" in a dysfunctional family is both afraid to be noticed and desperate to be noticed at the same time, an Adult Child, despite her independent functioning, still has that small child inside who wants someone to take care of her. This child may appreciate illnesses and injuries as possibilities for that wish to be fulfilled (question 2).

Elise (whom we met in Chapter 4) was terrified of being alone with her older sister Moira; she often became physically ill and vomited when their parents were going to go out for the evening, thus preventing them from going.

When Elise was in middle school she fantasized about breaking her leg and having her favorite teacher pick her up and carry her. She also fantasized about getting cancer and being in the hospital so she would finally be important and people would have to pay attention to her.

As an adult, when threatened with the possibility of a lung disease that could diminish her ability to live her usual active lifestyle, Elise was torn. The independent, "I need to take care of myself" part was horrified at the prospect of having limitations that might force her to ask for help in new ways. And she didn't want to face the possibility that she wouldn't be able to play with her kids as she was used to doing.

The small child inside her, on the other hand, felt differently. She may or may not have wanted to lose lung function, but she did want the threat of it to remain so that doctors (and others) would have to pay more attention to her. She thought she could be special only by being damaged (questions 3, 4, and 5).

Why Would This Happen?

This sort of situation is particularly likely if you grew up in a family in which someone was seriously ill (question 1). You would have seen how specially that person was treated and how much more attention she got than you did; you would probably have envied her that attention despite the difficult circumstances that led to it.

Or you might have been the one who had the serious illness and you remember how much more attention and care you got then than you did when you were healthy.

Even with a serious physical or mental illness it's often not easy for a child in a dysfunctional family to be noticed, though. Janet's depression started in her teens, and she asked her father repeatedly to take her to therapy. He kept ignoring her, so eventually she called him when he was at work, told him she was going to slit her wrists, then hung up. He called 911, she ended up in the emergency room, and she was finally the center of attention, at least for a little while.

Am I Being Overdramatic?

Sometimes you may feel like you are using illness to get attention that you don't deserve. You may feel guilty about this and wonder if you're driving others away with your neediness (question 4).

Like many other things, this doesn't have to be all or nothing. It's possible that you may be using illness to try to get attention but that doesn't mean you don't deserve the attention, too. And others may sometimes be annoyed by your neediness, but at the same time they may understand it, sympathize with you, and genuinely want to help you. We're all human, so sometimes people get tired or busy and react in ways that they didn't intend or later regret; that doesn't necessarily mean that they don't want to help.

Natalia had multiple times in her life that she felt suicidal. One time she came close enough to attempting suicide that she was almost hospitalized. She didn't believe she really would commit suicide, though, so she wondered how legitimate her suicide threats were. Was she just trying to get attention or was she really in danger of harming herself? Now she is trying to find that middle ground, accepting that her suicidal thoughts were real but that she was also trying to get attention because she was in a great deal of emotional pain.

Could My Childhood Make Me Sick?

Many of my clients can directly trace mental and physical health issues to childhood events and/or to learned ways of coping. Sarah, for instance, grew up with a mother who used food to self-soothe, so Sarah learned to do that, as well. It was not until recently that she recognized the pattern and realized what was underneath her impulsive eating.

Zoe drank to excess in college and later realized that she very nearly became an alcoholic as her mother had been; upon realizing this she became very aware of and cautious about her drinking and her motivations for it.

Adele learned from her father that it was important to be busy, preferably busier than she could reasonably handle. Unless she was exhausted she probably wasn't doing enough. Through therapy she began to understand the compulsive nature of her workaholism. After developing understanding she began the hard work of letting go of her need to be constantly busy. She is learning to act on the knowledge that it is just as important to take care of herself as it is for her to accomplish tasks and help other people.

Anne was raped in high school. Now, as an adult, she has difficulties with physical intimacy; she attributes this to her teenage experience. Having realized that, she has begun the challenging process of developing trust and a feeling of safety that will enable her to partner with her husband emotionally and physically in ways that were not possible before.

Adele has major depression that started in her late teens. When she was 30 years old she was diagnosed with rheumatoid arthritis, an autoimmune disease that causes inflammation in the joints. She has now identified both depression and rheumatoid arthritis as ways that she attacks herself, mentally and physically, which is consistent with the self-criticism she learned as a child growing up in a dysfunctional family.

While the specific nature of these women's issues varies, some of the underlying questions are the same. What can they do to support rather than attack themselves? And while they are doing that, how can they make peace with the knowledge that they have unintentionally become their own worst enemies? How can they accept the fact that it isn't their fault that they have these issues while still taking the responsibility to do what they can to recover?

The Adverse Childhood Experiences (ACE) Study

A study conducted by the Centers for Disease Control and Prevention and Kaiser Permanente called the Adverse Childhood Experiences (ACE) Study demonstrates that people who experience physical, emotional, or sexual abuse and/or family dysfunction before age 18 are at greater risk than others for certain physical, mental, and emotional conditions in adulthood (question 7). The study links these issues to long-term elevated levels of cortisol, a hormone that is produced when under stress; the issues include depression, obesity, alcoholism, drug addiction, suicide attempts, and autoimmune disorders, among others.

To get more information on the ACE study or to calculate your own ACE score, see http://www.acestudy.org.

Type C Personality

You have probably heard of Type A and possibly Type B personalities, but did you know that there's also a Type C personality? The "C" stands for cancer. Researchers have noticed that many people who develop cancer are people pleasers who repress their feelings and deny their own needs in favor of taking care of others. They have difficulty setting and maintaining boundaries and have trouble saying no to requests. Sound familiar? These are the characteristics of codependency, which we explored in Chapter 2.

This does not mean that everyone who gets cancer is codependent or that everyone who is codependent will develop cancer. But it is an example of the power of your thoughts to influence your health.

Physical Illnesses

For a child in a dysfunctional family a physical illness can be a source of shame, as if it is the person's fault that she has it. This has some commonalities with the (unmerited) shame that victims of rape or sexual abuse often feel, as though they did something wrong that brought it on. And some people may be raised to believe that illnesses are punishments for sin.

Although most physical illnesses don't carry the stigma that is generally attached to mental illness, there are physical issues with psychological components that are stigmatized by our society, such as obesity or smoking, to which Adult Children are more prone than is the general population (remember the ACE study).

And if you grew up in a family that led you to believe you were not worthy of someone taking care of you, even a non-stigmatized illness can be a source of shame.

The "don't talk, don't trust, don't feel" and "elephant in the room" issues contribute to the shame; dysfunctional families will often avoid discussing serious illnesses in public, and quite possibly in private, as well.

For instance, Brianne's mother stopped attending church after developing severe chronic pain. When she later developed ALS (Lou Gehrig's Disease), no one at the church was told about it. When she finally died of ALS, church members who had been close to her in the past were shocked; they had only known about her chronic pain, not the life-threatening disease.

Psychological Disorders

As you read the rest of this chapter please keep in mind that I am not saying you should blame yourself if you have any of these disorders. I am just trying to help you to recognize possible contributing factors to and results of these disorders so that you are better able to understand and cope with them.

Difficulties and Misunderstandings Related to Mental Illness

Despite advances in understanding psychological disorders, many people with mental illnesses continue to be misunderstood and stigmatized. And many people with these illnesses don't realize that they have treatable disorders or are reluctant to seek help.

If you have depression, particularly dysthymia (a type of low-grade chronic depression), you may just think you're an unhappy person. Or if you have anxiety, particularly Generalized Anxiety Disorder (fears about a variety of things), you may just think you're a worrier. In both cases treatment can improve your quality of life, but you may not seek treatment because you don't realize that something better is possible for you.

While I hope that most people are educated enough about mental illnesses, particularly mood and anxiety disorders, to realize that they are not moral failings, even people who know that may find themselves feeling like they are.

Many people think that mental illnesses are easier to overcome than they are; they may say that someone who is depressed should just "pull herself up by her bootstraps" or tell someone with anxiety to quit worrying.

It makes sense that someone who has not experienced clinical depression or anxiety might have this misunderstanding. After all, who hasn't felt sad or worried at some point in her life? The difference, though, is the degree and the duration of the depression or anxiety, and whether the depression or anxiety interferes significantly with the person's life.

And unfortunately, it's not just other people who may dismiss depression and anxiety and tell sufferers to get over it. Many of the people who have the disorders feel the same way; they criticize themselves for being the way they are and for not changing, as if they are weak or have chosen to become and remain ill.

You may believe that taking medications for mood disorders or anxiety is a sign that a person is crazy. If you believe this and have been prescribed these medications you may be unwilling to take them long-term, or possibly at all.

There are quite a few books that can help you manage depression, bipolar disorder, and anxiety. They include Dennis Greenberger and Christine A. Padesky's *Mind Over Mood: Change How You Feel by Changing the Way You Think*, David J. Miklowitz's *The Bipolar Disorder Survival Guide: What You and Your Family Need to Know*, 2nd *Edition* and Dr. Edmund J. Bourne's *Anxiety and Phobia Workbook, 5th Edition.*

It can also be helpful to read people's stories about their own experiences. Among these are Sharon O'Brien's *The Family Silver: A Memoir of Depression and Inheritance*, Dr. Kay Redfield Jamison's *An Unquiet Mind* (bipolar disorder) and L.A. Nicholson's *What Doesn't Kill Us: My Battle with Anxiety.*

Other Repercussions

In addition to the stigma of having a mental illness there can be financial and other repercussions. Someone who has been diagnosed with major depressive disorder and/or has been hospitalized because of a suicide attempt or another issue related to mental illness, for instance, will likely pay higher life insurance premiums and may be denied individual health insurance coverage. I live in an area where many people are required to have security clearances for their jobs; these people often do not feel free to seek mental health counseling because it could jeopardize their careers.

Having any psychological or physical disorder can cause isolation, particularly if it is a rare disorder or one that may make it difficult to go places and/or engage in activity. This is unfortunate, because community support is helpful.

Shame and the message that children in dysfunctional families frequently get that they should just ignore problems or "get over them" also make Adult Children less likely to seek support.

Happily, the internet has changed this somewhat. It is possible to go online and find information about any illness or disorder that exists. And there are online support groups, including Facebook groups, which can provide invaluable support and information. The fact that the internet is relatively anonymous makes it particularly useful to someone who is ambivalent about seeking help or support.

If you have a mental illness and are ashamed of it, remember that there is a reason why insurance companies are willing to pay for mental health counseling. They recognize that mental illnesses are medical conditions and have biological components. This is also why 12-step programs use a disease model to explain alcoholism and other addictions. They are not moral failings; they are treatable medical conditions.

Suicide

As misunderstood as depression and anxiety are, suicide is even harder for most people to understand. When someone has attempted or committed suicide many people, even those who did not grow up in a dysfunctional family, are likely to invoke the "don't talk" rule. They are uncomfortable with the idea of suicide and don't know whether to talk about what happened. This can make funerals tricky as people struggle to decide how much, if at all, the cause of death should be discussed.

Some people look down on those who consider, attempt, or succeed at committing suicide. They may be eager to convince themselves and others that they would never consider such a thing. In Dar Williams' "The Mark Rothko Song" one woman refers to Rothko's suicide and says, "'Some folks were born with a foot in the grave, but not me, of course!"

A suicidal person's loved ones are likely to be scared and angry. Will she kill herself or not? What, if anything, can they do to prevent it? Why is she even considering it?

Because suicide is a selfish act, loved ones may question how much a person who has committed suicide really cared about them—if she really cared, would she have abandoned them?

I believe the selfishness often comes, not from a lack of caring for other people, but from a desperate need to escape what feels like an unbearable situation. Or, as a character in Elizabeth George's novel *Careless in Red* said of suicide, it's "not a choice. That's a decision based upon the belief that there are no choices."

Why Do Some People Become Suicidal?

I also believe some form of chemical imbalance in the brain is almost, if not always, present when someone attempts or commits suicide. And remember the findings of the ACE study that suggest that childhood trauma increases the likelihood of suicide.

For those who suffer from severe depression the feelings and the despair can be overwhelming and feel intolerable. They might believe that things will never get better and will, understandably, look for any escape that is possible. Sometimes it can feel like ceasing to exist is the only way to escape.

But, as is often said, suicide is a "permanent solution to a temporary problem," something that almost everyone who has been suicidal learns after the episode has passed, assuming that they don't follow through on their feelings.

If you have never experienced these feelings, though, consider being open to the possibility that, at the time, suicide not only seems reasonable, but necessary. That is not to say, of course, that it is OK for someone to attempt or commit suicide!

I think sometimes about paramedics, nurses, and doctors who do everything they can to save the life of someone they've never met before. Why would they do that? Because they know that every human life has value; even if they don't know who you are they know that you have a valuable place in the world and are worth saving.

Adult Children and Suicide

Believe it or not, people sometimes become suicidal because they are (unconsciously) trying to meet a parent's expectations. Roberta's mother made it clear that she only wanted boys. Olive's mother said that if she had had the choice to have children or not she would have chosen not to do so. Then, completely confusing Olive and her siblings, she said that she loved them dearly and she wouldn't give them up for anything!

Natalie's mother resented being pregnant with her. She never said anything to Natalie, but it seems that Natalie somehow sensed it anyway, feeling like she didn't have the right to exist even though the words had never been spoken to her.

Some mothers tell their kids flat out that not only did they never want to have kids, but that they never loved or liked them. How could such a child not get the message that she didn't have the right to exist? And, having gotten that message, does it not make sense that she might unknowingly try to give her parents what they wanted by trying to kill herself?

Elise realized as an adult that the issues she developed from having grown up with a sister who threatened to kill her had almost led her to kill herself. She determined that she would not give in to this, and she decided to do everything she could to live.

Self-Sabotaging Behaviors

Addiction is a common self-sabotaging behavior for Adult Children. Addictive behaviors include alcoholism, drug addiction (including to prescription medications), pornography addiction, workaholism, perfectionism, and eating disorders, among others. These often seem to be passed down from generation to generation, although it can be hard to tell how much of it is genetic and how much is created by witnessing family members' behaviors and consciously or unconsciously copying them.

Many self-sabotaging behaviors such as binge eating or excessive drinking start as coping mechanisms. When you were growing up you had limited resources to deal with the challenges you faced, so you turned to whatever behavior you could find to help you survive.

The problem is that you have continued to use that behavior even after it has stopped being helpful to you, and even when other resources have become available to you. You may not have even been aware that you were engaging in self-sabotage, so you have had no reason to consider other ways of coping.

Once you become aware of these behaviors you can gently thank that part of yourself for helping you to get through some very difficult times, then begin to choose new, more effective coping mechanisms that are available to your adult self. But you can feel free to keep those old coping mechanisms in a mental closet so that the fearful part of you doesn't have to panic about losing the safety of those long-familiar strategies.

One of the benefits of looking at self-destructive behaviors in this way is that it can de-stigmatize them. If you can see someone as a person with a problem, if you can get to know her real self that is separate from the behavior, you can find compassion that you won't have if you label her.

Working at Chrysalis House taught me that it's possible for me to really like drug dealers and prostitutes. In the four years I worked there I only had one or two clients whom I had difficulty liking.

Sitting with those women and hearing their stories, really getting to know them, made me realize that their addictions and other undesirable behaviors developed because they needed to survive. Most of them had suffered great traumas, including witnessing or being the victim of violence or rape.

More than once a client told me that her mother's boyfriend had raped her; when she told her mother what had happened her mother chose to believe the boyfriend over her daughter. In many cases the mother kicked her daughter out of the house.

Many of the women in Chrysalis House were first introduced to drugs like crack and heroin by their parents. Or, as children, they sampled the adults' alcoholic beverages after all the adults had passed out following a party.

If I had gone through those experiences I might very well have turned to drugs or alcohol to cope, too.

But there are many kinds of traumas that can trigger alcoholism, addiction, and other self-sabotaging behaviors, and you don't have to have grown up in the poorest section of Baltimore to have experienced them. These include traumas that I've mentioned previously: neglect; emotional, physical, or sexual abuse; parental alcoholism or addiction; a parent being unavailable because of illness, work schedule, divorce or death; and others.

How Much Do You Identify With Your Illness or Your Self-Sabotage?

Here's one of those balance issues again. If you have a chronic mental or physical illness or a self-sabotaging behavior, how much do you identify with it? Is it such an integral part of your self-image that you're not sure who you would be without it? Or do you try to ignore it and deny its existence? Can you find a middle ground between the two?

How does the illness or behavior make you feel? Ashamed? Embarrassed? Weak? Needy? Important? Worthy of attention?

Does it feel like it limits you, or not? If there are limits, how do they feel to you? It may seem obvious that limits would feel confining, but that's not necessarily the case. Sometimes those limitations feel safe.

You may have had an illness or behavior for years and identify with it so much that it's frightening to think of your life without it. Who would you be if you didn't have depression, anxiety, rheumatoid arthritis, perfectionism, or whatever else you're dealing with?

It's like the people who don't want chaos but who continually create it because it's familiar to them. It's "Better the devil you know than the devil you don't know," even if the unknown devil might be positive change. If you find yourself in this situation it can help to explore the "you" that is separate from your illness or self-sabotage so you can begin to create a vision of a future without it.

Your feelings about your illness or behavior have a big influence on what you do or don't do to cope with it. If you are ashamed of it or think it makes you weak you're likely to try to ignore it; this may or may not work, and may make it worse.

But if the illness or behavior makes you feel special or worthy of attention you may be torn. Logically, it doesn't make sense to want to be sick or to self-sabotage, and yet the emotionally needy part of you doesn't recognize that logic.

Acceptance of Chronic Illness

Another question is that of acceptance. If you have a chronic illness, do you assume that your situation is unchangeable or not? If you do think it's unchangeable, what do you do to accept that fact? Can you balance that acceptance with optimism about your future? Or, as Michelle's doctor told her, can you work on accepting the limitations of your illness while still hoping for a miraculous cure? Is a physical cure the goal, or could healing mean something different for you?

How do you decide how much to accept your limitations and how much to push the envelope and see what you can do despite them? This is a question that Angelique constantly struggles with. Her anxiety has often prevented her from going to social gatherings, and she beats herself up about that. How does she decide when to give in to her anxiety and stay home and when to push herself to go out despite the anxiety?

I recently saw a photo of a Paralympics champion in action. She clearly does not allow the fact that she can't walk to stop her from racing. But does this mean that everyone should react that way?

And how do you decide what to do with your feelings about your illness? You need to acknowledge and feel them, but it's not helpful to get stuck in them. How do you balance feelings of grief, anger, and fear with striving for optimism and hope for the future?

Coping with Chronic Illness

Do you pretend to feel well when you don't because you're trying not to burden your family and friends? Or do you sometimes find yourself exaggerating how sick you feel so you can get more attention or take a break from life? Can you find a middle ground between the two?

Do you try to make sense of your illnesses and behaviors, accepting that you have genetic and/or learned predispositions to certain physical or psychological conditions or self-sabotaging behaviors? Do you accept treatment and the possibility that it might be a lifelong thing, or do you not? Do you explore a variety of treatments to find what is right for you?

Do you resent the fact that you are struggling with something that many others don't? Do you then feel guilty about those resentments, or do you chalk it up to being human and move on? Do you try to work through those resentments? If so, how?

Do you believe that you're worthy of being well? If you don't, do you try to change that? How can you be gentle with yourself even if you haven't found that sense of worth? Can you accept that the feeling may come and go but that, in time, you may be able to get to a place where you feel worthy more often than you feel unworthy?

If you experience depression or anxiety as the result of an illness or self-sabotaging behavior, remember that depression and anxiety affect your brain, which is what you use to make sense of the world. If your brain is not working properly, how will you know that? The reality you're experiencing at the time is the only one you know at that moment. That is a time that it's helpful to get feedback and observations from someone you trust. As they say in 12-step programs, "Your mind is a dangerous place. Don't go in there alone!"

It's also helpful to get reminders of what you've done in the past to make yourself feel better; these can be hard to remember when you're in the midst of depression or anxiety.

A Person With a Problem

If you criticize yourself for having an illness or a self-sabotaging behavior I invite you to take a different perspective. Think of yourself as a person *with* a problem as opposed to a person who *is* a problem.

What's the difference between the two? If you see yourself as a person who *is* a problem (a view that is encouraged by neglect and abuse in childhood and beyond) it is likely that you are trapped by shame. You do not believe that there is a "you" that can be separated from the problem and, therefore, you are not likely to believe that you can change or that it is worth trying.

On the other hand, identifying yourself as a person *with* a problem means that there is a "you" separate from the problem; the problem does not define you. For instance, if you are a person who has the disease of alcoholism you can identify yourself as a good person with many positive qualities who also happens to have a disease with which she needs to cope.

I Wouldn't Start From Here!

A friend of mine told me this joke:

A tourist in Ireland approaches a local person and asks how to get to Dublin, to which the local replies, "Well, I wouldn't start from here!"

The problem, of course, is that here is the only place you *can* start if you want to change. This implies acceptance of who you are right now. One of my graduate school professors told his counseling clients, "You're perfect just the way you are, and you need some work."

In other words you, as you are right now, are a valuable human being with many wonderful qualities. If you know that, or are at least willing to be open to the possibility that it might be true, it will make it easier for you to believe that you can accept aspects of yourself that are not so helpful or desirable. Only then can you begin to find a way not only to work around things you can't change, but also to change the things you can.

Unfortunately, it's not only hard to believe that we're OK despite whatever addictions or other issues we're struggling with; often the other people in our lives don't help. Annabelle, who takes antidepressants, has had her spouse say, "I think you need to take a pill!" when she's unhappy and the two of them are arguing. Charity, who's a recovering alcoholic, said, "I'm not allowed to have a bad day!"

Chapter 12 will introduce the Serenity Prayer, which can be extremely helpful when you are contemplating making changes in your life.

What Does It Mean to Heal?

Dr. Bernie Siegel, in his book *Peace, Love, and Healing*, gives many examples of patients with life-threatening illnesses who decide that healing, for them, is primarily about finding the greatest quality of life they can. Some, but not all, of those people also heal physically.

One example is a young woman named Evy who had ALS. She decided that she needed to learn to love herself and her body despite all the damage the disease had done. She began by making statements to herself about the parts of her body that she liked. Eventually she came to really love and accept her whole body as it was. And, over time, she actually reversed the physical damage the disease had done.

Many of the people whose serious illnesses eventually led them to live more fulfilling lives call those illnesses the best thing that ever happened to them. Even if you don't believe this is true of your own illness, it is worthwhile to try to find whatever gifts or growth it offers.

You can make a choice about how you react to the trials of life. You can become angry, isolated, and bitter, or you can try to find meaning and joy despite what you're suffering. As the Skin Horse says in *The Velveteen Rabbit*, "Generally, by the time you are Real, most of your hair has been loved off, and your eyes drop out and you get loose in the joints and very shabby. But these things don't matter at all, because once you are Real you can't be ugly, except to people who don't understand."

Illness might encourage you to slow down and take more time for yourself or to spend more time with family and friends. It might give you the chance to find out what's right about your "being" rather than your "doing" if you have always defined yourself by your accomplishments and outward identity. You don't have to be happy about the illness, but as long as it's there you might as well see whether it can give as well as take. And it offers an opportunity to work on balancing your needs with those of others.

And no matter what your illness or self-sabotaging behavior, remember that it does not have to define you.

Putting It Into Action

1. What did you learn from this chapter about your reactions to illness?

Vivian: I was the fourth of six children in my family and I usually felt lost in the shuffle at home, rarely noticed by my parents. I was diagnosed with leukemia when I was ten years old. My treatment included multiple hospital stays, one of which was for a bone marrow transplant. Because I was young I got extra care and attention from the medical staff. My parents spent days and weeks in the hospital with me. After the cancer went into remission my parents were always on the alert for possible signs that it was coming back.

In therapy I have realized that the only time I feel special and worthy of my family's attention is when I'm sick. But despite my desire to feel special I usually try to ignore symptoms of illness because I am a busy person and don't think I have time to take care of myself.

2. Are you comfortable with your feelings and actions related to illness? If not, how would you like them to change?

I'm used to being a successful, self-sufficient person. My need to be sick to feel special doesn't fit with that, nor does it fit with my habit of ignoring my own needs. I have realized that I want to find a middle ground between the two. I want to start taking care of myself mentally and physically; I also want to find a way to ask for and accept help from other people without having to be "broken" to feel worthy of that help.

3. What can you do to begin to shift your thinking and behaviors?

I have begun to have conversations with my inner 10-year-old. I reassure that part of me that she is worthy of attention whether or not she is sick and that the lack of attention she got before her illness was not her fault; it was the result of having overworked and overtired parents who didn't have the time or energy to give adequate attention to all of their children.

I have started yoga classes to strengthen myself physically and to become more aware of my body. I have improved my eating habits and am making a point of getting more sleep. When I get sick I don't ignore my symptoms.

My husband is not used to me taking care of myself, so he is a bit unsettled by my new behaviors. He is not used to being asked for help and he finds it challenging to take care of me when I'm sick.

On the other hand, he's also feeling freer to pay attention to his own needs. I had always made him feel guilty for babying himself when he was sick; now I do my best to recognize and accept his self-care. I am even learning to willingly take care of him when he's sick rather than resenting it when he stays home from work.

4. What self-sabotaging behaviors of yours would you like to change?

Patsy: I never exercise and I eat fast food daily, but I occasionally get on a health kick and start an extreme diet and exercise program. Because I try to make huge changes all at once I stop the diet and exercise routines within a couple of weeks, then beat myself up and call myself a failure.

Choose one of the self-sabotaging behaviors to be the first one you work on. What would be the hardest thing about changing it?

I have never eaten healthily and have never gotten regular exercise. I figure that I would feel better if I did things differently, but since I've never engaged in healthful behaviors it's hard for me to imagine doing them. I see all the ads and TV commercials that suggest that I should be much thinner and in better shape than I am and I feel like a failure. I hear and see suggestions for the way I "should" eat and the amount of exercise I "should" get and it doesn't appeal to me at all. Because of my history and my self-image I don't believe that it's possible for me to change my lifestyle and become healthier.

What might be a doable first step towards changing it?

I have a coworker, Frances, whose habits have always been similar to mine. Frances recently read an article that suggested finding a type of exercise that you enjoy and being more moderate in eating the foods you like rather than cutting them out entirely. The article also suggested ways to (gently) challenge negative thoughts so that it's more possible to change unhealthful habits.

Frances has been following the advice given in the article and is getting positive results. I decide that if Frances can do it I might be able to do it, too. I ask Frances for a copy of the article so I can begin to look at the possibility of following her example and getting healthier.

Chapter 9

Hope and Transformation

1. Before you started reading this book, how confident were you that you could achieve greater balance in your life? Rate it on a scale of 1-10 with 1 being not confident at all and 10 being completely confident.

2. How confident were you that you could sustain that balance over the long term? Again, rate it on a scale of 1-10 with 1 being not confident at all and 10 being completely confident.

3. Have you started making some of the changes suggested in this book?

4. If you have started making changes, how confident are you that you can achieve greater balance (1-10)?

5. Again, if you have started changing your thinking and behaviors, how confident are you that you can sustain those changes over the long term (1-10)?

Look at your answers to the quiz questions above. What do your numbers suggest about your hope for the possibility of long-term change? Are any of them higher than 5, suggesting that you are more hopeful than not? Have changed behaviors (if you've made changes) helped to boost your hope? If not, what might help?

The longer you work with new behaviors the better because, over time, they become more natural and automatic. If you're starting to feel like a changed person it's likely you'll be more hopeful than if you haven't noticed changes, and more hope will make it easier to continue changing.

I will suggest techniques in this chapter and the remaining three chapters of the book that are helpful in promoting change. So if your numbers don't reflect the amount of hope you'd like to have, hang in there. There's more help to come!

Claiming Hope

In Chapter 7 we looked at the wish for life to be fair and discussed ways to deal with the fact that it's not. This chapter will help you to find the balance between accepting reality and having hope for the future.

If you are to make lasting changes you need to maintain hope in the possibility of a future that is different from your current life. That hope will help you to keep going even if it seems as though change is not happening, if it is happening more slowly than you want, or if you're afraid you cannot maintain positive changes.

No matter how many bad things we've endured or how much we've suffered, human beings are hard-wired for hope. Neuroscientist Tali Sharot wrote a book called *The Optimism Bias: A Tour of the Irrationally Positive Brain*. Her premise is that because humans have the knowledge that we will die someday, a part of our brain has evolved that makes us feel optimistic in the face of all contrary evidence. Otherwise, she says, we wouldn't have the motivation to achieve things or to make and carry out plans. What's the point if we're only going to die anyway?

Do you remember the story of Pandora's box from Greek mythology? Pandora was given a beautiful container by the gods and told never to open it. Her curiosity got the best of her, though, and she opened it anyway. Out flew all the evils of the world. When she slammed the lid back down, the only thing remaining in the box was hope, which was later released, as well.

Hope helps us to believe that we can find something beyond the suffering and imperfections of our current lives. Human beings, especially those who have been abused or neglected, need the reminder that hope persists despite everything that might suggest otherwise. Hope can sustain us even in the most difficult times.

Hope is the basis for this book. I wrote it because I do believe, as imperfect as life is, that you can find more balance in your life, thus improving not only your life but also the lives of the people around you. I'm assuming you are reading the book because you believe the same thing, and I hope that it is giving you tools to help you make that belief a reality.

Balancing Anger, Sadness, and Hope

Lines from two songs from the Indigo Girls album *All That We Let In* express, for me, the need to balance anger and sadness with hope and finding meaning. The first, from the song "Come On Home," says, "I realize that some things never are made right." The other, from the title song, says, "I see those crosses by the side of the road/Or tied with ribbons in the median/They make me grateful I can go this mile/Lay me down at night and wake me up again."

There are things that never will be made right. It is not helpful to pretend those things didn't happen. It is important to feel and acknowledge anger and sadness about the past.

But it's also not helpful to be stuck in the past in a way that keeps us from having a positive present and future. We can try to transform our experiences into something positive by giving them meaning and purpose.

Think about MADD (Mothers Against Drunk Drivers). Rather than use their anger destructively, these mothers used it constructively, channeling it into a program intended to keep other mothers from losing their children. They didn't get stuck in anger and bitterness; they transformed their anger into hope that things could change.

Is It Worthwhile to Have Hope?

It's easy for us to roll our eyes when we hear or tell stories about triumphing over adversity. Cynicism suggests that these stories are too good to be true and are just made up to make people feel better. Even the greatest cynic, though, has a hopeful child inside; the cynic is just hiding that child so she won't be hurt.

No matter what has happened to us, the essence of who we are can never be destroyed. It may go into hiding, but it is always there somewhere.

Consider Viktor Frankl's book *Man's Search for Meaning*. In it, Frankl described his experience in a concentration camp. That experience helped him to realize that the one thing that can't be taken away from you is the power to choose your attitude. No matter what happens, you can choose to have hope and to find meaning in your life.

Hope for the Possibility of Change

The group *Cry, Cry, Cry* recorded a song called "By Way of Sorrow" that assures the listener that, despite the difficulties she has faced so far, she is destined for something much better. The chorus is, "You have come by way of sorrow/You have come by way of tears/But you'll reach your destiny/Meant to find you all these years/Meant to find you all these years." This can be a revelation to people who have a hard time imagining things getting better. After all, if they've never experienced it, it's hard to imagine what it would be like if they did.

Chrysalis House was named that because it is a place of hope and radical change. A Chrysalis House client is like a caterpillar that sequesters itself in a chrysalis (cocoon) to give it the protection it needs to allow its transformation. Chrysalis House is the cocoon, and the graduating client is the beautiful butterfly that emerges from the cocoon. The butterfly was always there inside each woman; she just needed to have enough safety to allow her to release that part of herself.

Even though you are probably not a client in a residential treatment center, you, too, need safety to allow yourself to become the person you want to be and are meant to be. And most importantly, you need the hope and belief that you can be transformed into a butterfly even if you haven't seen or imagined that part of yourself before.

Unfortunately, you probably don't have the luxury of going somewhere for six to twelve months to undergo transformation, so you need to find some other way to create an atmosphere in which it can happen.

It helps to take time every day to just be with yourself. You might choose to meditate or pray, take a walk, or do yoga. Whatever you choose, it should be something that helps you to be kind to yourself. It should also be something that you're reasonably sure you can (and will) fit into your day.

What Can Hope Do?

The hope for the possibility of change is powerful. Gail's mother went to therapy when Gail was a teenager, but she didn't tell the kids that she was doing it. Much later, when Gail was in therapy herself, her mother told her that she'd sought therapy to help her figure out what to do about Gail's father and their dysfunctional marriage. Gail told her mother that it would have helped her a lot to know that; it would have validated her perception that things were not as they should be, and it would have helped her to believe that it was possible for her family life to change.

I have many clients who are worried about how their issues have affected and continue to affect their kids. I encourage them to let their kids know that they are in therapy. It's a powerful thing for a child to know that not only is her parent acknowledging that she is not perfect, but that she's trying to change. Children really are resilient, and children who know their parents are trying to make things better can find it easier to endure any dysfunction that is still going on.

Getting Positives Out of Negatives

The bad things that have happened to us have obviously had negative effects upon us, but they can also affect us in positive ways. The negatives are obvious, while the positives often are not.

What can you gain from difficult circumstances? Each person's answers will vary, but here are a few examples.

Jillian is thankful that her childhood experiences have helped her to be a better parent, because she learned from the mistakes of her parents. She has a particular appreciation for her family because it's more cohesive than her family of origin.

Gail is grateful that the emotional crisis that brought her to counseling has led to healthier relationships with her parents and helped her to set and maintain healthy boundaries in her life, including at work. Not only does this benefit her; it also benefits her coworkers, her husband, and particularly her daughter, who is learning how to take care of herself while still respecting and caring for others.

Janet is grateful that her healing process has led her to realize that she's not alone. Participating in a counseling group for Adult Children has helped her to realize that many people struggle in the same way she does. She has learned that she doesn't have to go it alone and that it can be helpful to share vulnerable parts of herself with safe people.

Shana and others who are in twelve-step groups are grateful that their addictions have led to possibilities for healing that might not have been available to them otherwise.

Does this mean that these people are always happy, always grateful, and always aware of their blessings? Of course not! They all have times when they forget the lessons they've learned. They all have times when they're just plain angry or sad about the suffering they've endured.

They know that they haven't found shiny happy lives where everything is perfect. But at least they know they have some tools that they can use to deal with bad things that happen. And they know that it's the process, not the product (or the journey, not the destination) that's most important.

They don't need to focus on who they "should" be, how they "should" feel, or what they "should" have achieved by now, because they know (although they sometimes forget) that "shoulds" are about judgment and self-criticism, not about finding a better life.

Changing is Easy. Staying Changed is Hard.

Have you ever talked to someone who has quit smoking, only to go back to it in a few days, weeks, or months? She may tell you that it was easy to quit, but it was difficult to remain a nonsmoker long-term.

I'm hoping that you are excited about the things we've been discussing so far and that you are looking forward to trying some new behaviors. Maybe you've already started.

It's easy to get excited about something new. It can be difficult, though, to keep that enthusiasm going, especially if you don't get results right away. That instant gratification that your inner child is always looking for can get you in trouble. (When was the last time you met a five-year-old who was willing to wait for something she wanted?)

But we've already talked about the fact that these changes do not come quickly. How do you maintain hope when it would be so easy to give up and go back to your old ways of coping?

It's important not to give up when things don't work the first time...or the second...or even the third. As the fairy godmother said in the movie *Cinderella*, "Even miracles take a little time."

That's why it's helpful to have some support—for instance, from a friend, an accountability partner, a therapist, a religious/spiritual guide, a 12-step group, a support group, or a therapy group. Whoever you choose, she/he/they should feel safe and be gentle with you, but also hold you accountable for sticking to the changes you're trying to make.

It is also extremely important that you be gentle and patient with yourself. It does not help to put yourself down if you don't succeed immediately or if you have a relapse. Putting yourself down makes it more likely that you'll give up and go back to your old ways. I'm reminded of the saying, "The beatings will continue until morale improves!" Criticism is rarely an effective way to promote change.

But also be gentle with yourself if you put yourself down. Don't beat yourself up for beating yourself up!

Tools for Transformation

Remember that hope is not about things that have already happened. It is about believing that things can be different. Just because it has never happened to you doesn't mean it can't or won't happen. If you know of cases in which it has happened to someone else, it will make it easier to imagine it happening to you. After all, if it can happen for them, why couldn't it happen for you?

If your first response to "why couldn't it happen for you?" was "Yeah, right!" I invite you to try some of the approaches described in the rest of the book, particularly in Chapter 10.

In the meantime, here are a few things you can do to use hope to transform your life.

Verb Tenses

Pay attention to your verb tenses when you're talking about your behaviors. For instance, you may find yourself saying, "When I lose weight I always gain the weight back, plus more." Instead, try "When I've lost weight in the past, I've always gained it back, plus more."

What's the difference? The first version says that not only have you always done that in the past, you always do it in the present, and you'll always do it in the future. It is a basic, unchangeable part of who you are.

The second version, though, is more hopeful; it suggests that while in the past you always gained weight after losing it, you're open to the possibility that this time might be different. Sometimes having hope and being open to the possibility of change can allow it to happen.

Visualizations

You can use mental images to visualize the changes you're trying to make. When Jacqueline worked to heal damage to her right eye caused by the autoimmune disease called uveitis, she pictured what the healed parts of the eye would look like. She reminded herself that the blueprints of the healthy version of her eye were still in there somewhere and could be used to recreate the eye as it was meant to be.

She decided to reframe the way she looked at the damage. Perhaps instead of looking at it as an attack on her eye she could see it as an attempt to protect the eye from disease.

To support this new perspective she imagined a beautiful painting that was painted over with stick figures to protect it from thieves, or a beautiful chapel that was made to look like an ugly shack so it would be safe from invaders. Then she imagined the false painting being washed away to reveal the masterpiece underneath and the shack being removed to reveal the beautiful chapel.

Jacqueline knew that it was unlikely that her eye would be healed, but she chose to have hope that it would happen. That sort of hope, even if it doesn't lead to physical healing, can be empowering and promote emotional and spiritual healing.

Any image that works for you can be used to help you to change. Remember that anything is possible in your imagination. If you can visualize a possibility you are more likely to make it a reality.

Other Creative Approaches

I encourage you to keep a journal or a log of some sort in which you make note of what you're thinking, feeling, and saying. Not only will it clarify what you're doing and help you to make different choices as well as helping you to cement new behaviors, it will also allow you to see how much change is happening. Because the changes will be gradual it will be easy to forget where you started and not notice how much progress you've made. If you keep a record of thoughts, feelings, and behaviors, though, you can go back later and see just how much of a difference you're making.

Journaling is not the only creative way to facilitate and document change. Art and music can be used to express the way things are now, your hopes for the future, the process of transformation, and the results. For instance, Jacqueline uses clay sculptures to concretize her healing process. Kaitlyn writes poetry; Jeannine writes songs.

Remember that the process of creating is the most important thing here. If you have an idea of what you want the artwork, writing, or music to look or sound like, you may be disappointed if it doesn't turn out the way you planned. You may find yourself trapped by "shoulds"— it should have looked/sounded different, I should have done better, etc.

But while it is, of course, good for you to be pleased with how your creation looks or sounds, that's not really the goal in this case. The goals are healing and change. And anyway, just because the finished product doesn't match what you had in your head doesn't mean it isn't good!

You can maintain hope for a better future. You can use that hope in your search for life balance. The last section of the book offers more strategies and approaches that can help you make the changes you want.

Putting It Into Action

1. How can you create the safety that will enable your true self, your inner "butterfly," to emerge?

Jessica: I have joined a therapy group for Adult Children. Hearing others' stories that are similar to mine and having a group of people with whom I can share my experiences without worrying about being judged helps me to feel more comfortable in my own skin. I am relieved to know that there is a logical explanation for my low self-esteem, perfectionism, and inability to say no to others. I have the chance to practice new ways of thinking and behaving in the safety of the group. Other group members give me useful feedback that they deliver in a gentle and loving way.

2. Choose one of the "tools for transformation" described in the chapter (changing verb tenses, visualization, journaling, art, or music) and try it for a week.

If you work on changing your verb tenses, it can help to keep a log (on your cell phone, on a small notepad, or whatever works for you) of times that you had an opportunity to change your verb tenses and whether you did or didn't do it. Either way, try not to judge yourself!

If you use one of the other tools, try to set aside at least 15 minutes a day to devote to it. You can certainly go longer than that if you'd like. Don't beat yourself up if you don't meet the goal. It's meant to be a guideline to help you, not an obligation that drags you down.

Kirsten: I decided to do a clay sculpture to represent the transformation I was looking for. I used a dove to represent peace and the divine and, at the suggestion of my inner child, a rainbow to represent hope.

The sculpture took me longer than I expected and was sometimes frustrating, but overall I found it relaxing and meditative. I found that I looked forward to the end of the day when I could work on it.

I appreciated the fact that it was easy to redo things that didn't work out the way I'd intended. It didn't end up exactly the way I'd imagined it, which frustrated me at first. But I liked having something I could hold in my hands while I visualized changes I was trying to make.

3. At the beginning of the week, set an intention. The intention is meant to be something that helps you to care for yourself; it's not supposed to be a difficult task or a punishment. It helps to write the intention down somewhere (or record it) so that you can revisit it throughout the week.

Janelle: I set the intention to spend more time playing with and walking my dog. It's good for both of us; we're getting more exercise, spending more time outdoors, and having more fun.

The activities in #2 and #3 are things you can keep doing week after week. If one is not working for you, try another one. My hope is that whatever you're doing will help you to make the changes you're looking for.

Part IV

Chapter 10

Don't Believe
Everything You Think!

1. Are you more likely to criticize yourself (to yourself and/or others) than to compliment yourself (or accept compliments)?

2. Do you spend a lot of time trying to figure out what other people are thinking so you know how to talk or act around them?

3. Do you tend to notice the things you don't like about yourself more often than you notice the things you do like?

4. When you're undertaking a new project, do you worry that it will be a complete failure?

5. Do you feel like the things you don't like about yourself are more important to other people than the things you do like

> about yourself? For example, let's say you
> have a great sense of direction but have a
> lot of difficulty being on time for things.
> You might decide that nobody cares if you
> could find your way home even if you were
> randomly dropped somewhere you've
> never been, but that everyone looks down
> on you because you're always late.

This chapter presents five types of cognitive distortions, or Automatic Negative Thoughts (ANTs). These are patterns of negative thinking that we don't even notice most of the time because we've been thinking that way for so long. We're going to focus on the following ANTs: *mind reading; fortune telling or catastrophizing; mental filters; maximizing and minimizing; and black and white or all or nothing thinking.*

There are many ways in which ANTs detract from our ability to balance self-care with taking care of others. They lead us to devalue ourselves and our time, energy, and abilities. They interfere with setting and maintaining boundaries (like saying no to requests). They keep us stuck in the unhelpful ways of thinking and feeling that we learned when we were growing up.

Happily, though, you can learn to stomp on the ANTs and change the ways in which they influence you.

As you start to notice each type of ANT think about what you can do to challenge it. If you have a negative thought try replacing it with a more positive thought. Or ask yourself how likely it is that the negative thought is true. If you decide that it really is true, what might you be able to do to deal with it? Often when you have a negative thought you don't work through what you would do with the worst-case scenario. Many times that worst-case scenario is not as bad (or as insurmountable) as you think it is.

There is a lot of material here, so I've included specific questions and exercises for each of the five ANTs in addition to the "Putting It Into Action" section at the end. Take your time going through all of them.

It makes sense to address the ANTs one at a time and keep returning to this chapter. You don't need to try to deal with all five of them at once. After you've gotten familiar with challenging each individual ANT you'll be better prepared to challenge any of them as they come up.

Here are the two scenarios that I'll use throughout the chapter to illustrate each type of ANT.

1) You have left a voicemail for a friend suggesting that the two of you go to see a new movie that just came out. The movie is not the sort that the two of you usually go to see; it's shallow and mindless, which is just what you're in the mood for right now because you've had a very difficult week and you'd just like to escape for a couple of hours. A couple of days later you still haven't heard from your friend and you're wondering why; she usually returns calls the same day.

2) You are working from home and you email your boss a proposal for a new project first thing in the morning. You know that you are not the only one submitting a proposal, and only one proposal will be chosen. It's now the end of the workday and you haven't heard from him. You know that there's a tight deadline for this project and you're assuming that whichever proposal is chosen will be put into action soon, probably tomorrow.

Psych? Not!

Have you ever watched the TV show *Psych*? The lead character, Shawn Spencer, runs a "Psychic Detective Agency." When he was a kid his father taught him to fine-tune his observational skills; he uses those skills to convince people that he's psychic.

Psych is a funny show. It's not funny, though, when you feel (consciously or unconsciously) like you have to be psychic and read other people's minds so you can make them happy!

That's our first ANT (Automatic Negative Thought): *mind reading*.

You probably learned to read minds early in life. You found out that things went better for you if you could figure out what your parents, siblings, and others were thinking and feeling, then anticipate what they might want or need from you based on that.

But did you realize that you're still doing that today? And did you know that, as intuitive and perceptive as you are, your mind reading abilities are probably not as accurate as you think they are? That's partly because when you learned to read minds you were a child, and all children think the world revolves around them and that they're the cause of everything that happens. So if someone else is upset a child assumes it's her fault somehow.

Let's look at how mind reading might apply to the first scenario, with the movie invitation. You're making up all kinds of reasons for your friend's silence. You assume that she's appalled by your movie suggestion; you didn't explain your reason for suggesting it, so she has no way of knowing why you want to go see it. She is usually the one who suggests the movies you go to see and this is one of the few times you've had the courage to suggest one yourself.

Now she's seen the "real" you and doesn't like what she sees. She's probably rethinking your friendship entirely, which is why she's not calling you back. You assume she's reviewing the list of people she knows and choosing someone else to spend time with now that she knows who you really are.

Here's how mind reading might apply to the work scenario. You assume that your boss hates your proposal and is going with one of the other proposals; you know that the person who is chosen always hears from the boss first so they can get started implementing the proposal. The losers don't hear from the boss until later. And he's a nice guy who doesn't like to hurt people's feelings, so he's probably trying to figure out how to let you down easy.

Can you think of an example of mind reading that happened to you in the last few days? How did it affect you? What did you do about it?

In the future, make a point to notice the times that you find yourself trying to read someone else's mind. Answer the following questions for yourself:

Whose mind was I trying to read?

What prompted me to think I needed to read his or her mind?

What did I assume he or she was thinking?

How did I react to it? Did I feel a certain way? Did I say something? Did I change my behavior as a result?

Look for patterns in your mind reading. And when you find yourself doing it, ask, "How sure am I that this is what s/he is thinking? Is there another possible explanation? Do I really need to try to change this person's mind or feelings?"

The less you try to read other people's minds the happier all of you are likely to be.

Leigh: For the last couple of days my husband, Francis, has been unusually quiet at home. He hasn't been responding to questions or joining in conversations the way he usually would. He seems upset about something.

As always happens when Francis isn't acting like himself, I've been feeling anxious. I've been racking my brain trying to figure out what I might have done or said that has made him upset. And I've been doing my best to do everything around the house perfectly (cooking, cleaning, taking care of the kids) and to be positive around him. It hasn't been working very well.

For a while I don't say anything to him about his mood, but I feel like I'm about to go out of my mind. So I finally ask him what's going on. He says, "Nothing."

When I keep asking he finally decides to tell me what's going on. He says that work has been very stressful lately because a couple of people have been laid off, which makes more work for everyone else. And he got a phone call from his sister, who said that she thinks her marriage is falling apart. And he's also resentful because I used to go golfing with him all the time but now that we have kids I don't go anymore because I'm so busy with them, with work, and with keeping up with housework. He also wishes we had more physical intimacy, like we had before the kids.

So as it turns out, my mind reading was only partly accurate. But I'm still upset about the parts that do have something to do with me!

Please Put Down the Crystal Ball and Back Away Slowly!

The second ANT is related to the first one. *Fortune telling* or *catastrophizing* is assuming that you know what is going to happen in the future and that it's going to be bad; in fact, you predict the worst possible outcome of the situation.

You've seen the movies and TV shows with fortune tellers on them. Maybe you've had your own fortune told. Most of us, at one time or another, have wanted to know what was ahead of us, which is why fortune telling has been popular through the ages.

Professional fortune tellers sometimes predict bad things for the people who go to see them, but not always. When you're dealing with the fortune telling ANT, though, the ending is always a bad one.

If you find yourself predicting that something will go badly just because you are the one who is doing it, you have experience with fortune telling.

Sometimes catastrophizing is just a generalized feeling of doom; you don't have a specific negative outcome that you're expecting, but you have a feeling that disaster is going to occur anyway.

How might fortune telling or catastrophizing apply to our two scenarios?

In the personal scenario, you might conclude that your friendship was on the verge of collapse anyway and this was probably the final straw. She's going to find someone else to spend time with (and may already have been looking even before this happened). You won't be able to find another friend like her, especially since she'll probably tell everyone else you know what poor taste you have in movies. Soon no one will want to spend any time with you and you'll spend all of your non-work time alone and miserable.

In the work scenario, you might assume that your boss hated your proposal so much that he won't even give you a chance to submit a proposal the next time a new project comes up. He won't fire you, but you will no longer get opportunities to be noticed and show what you can do, so your career will eventually fade into obscurity and you'll end up doing your department's most menial, boring tasks from now on.

Your assignment for this ANT is to be alert for examples of fortune telling/ catastrophizing in your life. Think about the following questions:

What event triggered my fortune telling?

What was going on in my life that might have contributed to my feeling of doom (time of day, weather outside, presence of particular people, in a particular place or setting, etc.)?

What did I assume would happen?

Did I think of any possible actions I could take to forestall disaster?

Did I believe that it was possible for me to take those actions?

Did I take those actions?

What was the result?

Did the anticipated disaster (or events that might lead to that disaster in the future) happen?

What was the worst that could have happened, and could I have handled it?

As you take the time to examine your fortunetelling/catastrophizing thoughts and notice the patterns and the real-life endings of the stories it is likely that you will realize that the worst rarely happens and, if it does, you are able to do what you need to do to get through the situation. That's an empowering feeling!

Leigh: Of course, when Francis tells me that he's feeling resentful because I don't go golfing with him anymore and we don't have sex as often as we used to, I immediately jump to the worst-case scenario: Francis is going to leave me because he has decided that I'm no longer the woman he married. He's probably already found another woman who meets all of his sexual needs and who loves golf as much as he does. Pretty soon he'll end up marrying her, leaving me to raise the kids alone.

After I panic for a while I stop and take a deep breath. Despite the issues Francis brought up, our relationship is pretty stable. We do still find some time for each other, although not as much as we used to. And Francis really believes in marriage; he's more likely to try to work through problems than to divorce me.

If the worst happened, at least I have a career to support the kids and myself, and Francis would no doubt pay child support. I have family members in the area who could help with babysitting when I need it.

I decide that Francis has a valid point, though, so we talk about it and find some times that we can get a babysitter and go golfing together like we used to do. We also discuss our needs regarding emotional and physical intimacy and begin to explore ways that we might both be able to get our needs met.

I also catastrophize about the other things Francis mentioned that were bothering him; what if Francis gets laid off, too? What will we do then? And if Francis's sister, who seemed to be so happily married, is getting a divorce, what are the chances that our marriage can survive?

I also stomp on these ANTs. Francis is a valued employee who has skills none of the other employees in his division have, so he's unlikely to be laid off. If he is, his unique and in-demand skill set will likely get him another job quickly. And, yes, Francis's sister appeared to be happily married, but I don't know how good her marriage really was—we didn't see what went on behind closed doors. Anyway, each couple is different. Just because one couple gets a divorce doesn't mean another couple is likely to divorce.

Is It Time to Change Your Filter?

For the third ANT we'll look at the *mental filter* you use when you look at the world and at yourself.

You are exposed to all kinds of information all day long. Your brain uses filters to decide what information is useful and what will be ignored so that you don't get overwhelmed.

You've heard many times that a pessimist sees a glass as half empty while an optimist sees it as half full. This shows the differences between people's mental filters; some people are naturally inclined to notice the positive aspects of a situation while others are more likely to notice the negative ones.

Like mind reading, mental filters develop during childhood. If you had a parent who tended to see the negative aspects of a situation or person there's a good chance that you learned to see things the same way. If you had a parent who was frequently critical of himself or herself and/or others you probably learned to pay more attention to the things you don't like about yourself than the things you do like.

How might mental filters come into play in the personal scenario? You may think of all the times that you and your friend discussed movies and she pointed out things she didn't like about movies that you secretly wanted to see. You may forget all the times that you wanted to see a particular movie and, even though you hadn't said anything to your friend about it, that was the movie she suggested. You may also forget the times that you suggested a movie and she loved it. Because of your selective attention to past experiences you may conclude that you and your friend have completely different tastes in movies.

In the work example, your mental filter might lead you to remember all the times that your boss chose someone else's proposal over yours, or all the times that he criticized or changed your proposals. You would pay little, if any, attention to all the times he chose your proposals over others and highlighted specific things about them that he particularly liked.

Your assignment this time is to notice your mental filters and the information they let in and keep out. Consider the following questions:

Which do you tend to notice more: negative things or positive ones?

Do you discount and disbelieve compliments while taking all criticisms to heart?

In your work and personal life what do you tend to remember more, your successes or your failures?

If you frequently find yourself filtering out positives and paying attention to negatives, consider making a conscious choice to change that. Overall, you tend to get what you expect to get, so noticing positive things will most likely bring more positive things to you. And the more positive things come to you the more you'll notice them and the more you'll get.

The longer you practice noticing positives the easier it will be, so keep practicing!

Leigh: I definitely notice negatives more than positives, and I am much more likely to notice (and believe) criticisms than I am compliments. The negatives stay with me and make me feel depressed and anxious, while the positives are soon forgotten.

When someone compliments me I assume they're just making it up to be nice to me. But if they say something critical I'm likely to believe it, especially if it sounds like something I've always been told by my parents.

When Francis told me the reasons he was being so quiet I focused mainly on his comment about me. It just reinforced my idea that I was inadequate and couldn't meet everyone's needs sufficiently.

Later, I reviewed the situation and put it into perspective. As Francis said, I was not the only trigger for his bad mood. And there are things we can do to change the issues he has with our marriage.

What Happened to the Molehill?

You've known people who always seem to make mountains out of molehills. They're the ones who create drama wherever they go. But you may engage in your own version of mountain making without even knowing it.

This time our focus is on *maximizing and minimizing*. It's related to the mental filter. Just as you may tend to filter out positives and only pay attention to negatives, you may also tend to exaggerate negatives and understate positives, giving more weight to the negatives than you do to the positives.

One example of maximizing and minimizing that may have happened when you were growing up was your parents' reaction to your report card. For instance, if you got an A in every subject but math (where you got a B), your parents might have told you that math was the most important subject in school and that if you didn't pull your grade up you'd never get into college or make a success of your life. You might have gotten the idea that you couldn't possibly be intelligent if you didn't get an A in math. And you probably would have learned to maximize negatives.

Have you ever assumed that something must not be very difficult if you were able to do it easily? If you did, you were minimizing your abilities. It's not surprising that if something is easy for you it might not occur to you that it doesn't come naturally to everyone. And if you grew up in a family that discounted your strengths it would be even more natural for you to discount yourself.

Here's how maximizing and minimizing might apply to the two proposed scenarios.

In the personal scenario, you might maximize all the differences between yourself and your friend, including the way you dress, your choice of career, and your home decorating styles. You may remember all the times that you felt like an unsophisticated kid compared to what seemed to be her sophisticated, "having it all together" adulthood.

You may minimize all the things that have made your friendship strong, including your long history together, the variety of experiences you've shared, the times you've laughed together, the times you've supported each other during difficult experiences, and your mutual appreciation of your differences.

In the work scenario, you might remember that you studied something completely different in college than the field you're in right now, while everyone else majored in subjects that were much more closely related. You might exaggerate that fact to make it the most important criterion for success in the field while minimizing your natural ability to do the work, your years of experience in which you've continuously improved your skills, numerous awards you've won for your work, and your dedication to your work that leads you to excel.

You might also forget that these are the reasons your boss hired you for such an important position, choosing you over many others who might have seemed like more logical choices. And you may dismiss the times that you've had important insights into projects that you arrived at specifically because your educational background was different from those of your coworkers; you offered a different perspective that was immensely valuable to your company.

The exercises for the previous section are a good warm-up for this section. Now that you have practiced being aware of a tendency to notice negatives and dismiss positives, take some time to notice the times you exaggerate negatives and minimize positives. Think about the answers to the following questions:

Do I weigh my various personal characteristics equally, or do I consider my negatives to be more important or noticeable than my positives?

Am I noticing a pattern to my maximizing negatives and minimizing positives?

In what areas of my life do I tend to maximize and/or minimize?

What is leading me to do this?

What positives can I notice that will help to shift the balance between positives and negatives?

Let these questions guide the changes you want to make in your thinking.

> *Leigh: Just as I am more likely to notice negatives than positives, I am also likely to give more weight to the negatives than to the positives. When the situation happens with Francis I immediately jump to the conclusion that playing golf and being physically intimate with Francis are the most important parts of our marriage, overshadowing everything else. Why else would they be the only things he mentioned about me? I'm so*

focused on those issues that I don't think about all the things Francis loves about me.

When I think about it I realize that I maximize my mistakes and minimize my successes at work. When I make a mistake I blow it out of proportion, but when I succeed at something I assume that it's either not difficult or my success is a fluke.

My mother was the one who taught me to maximize and minimize. She was depressed for my entire childhood and she had an extremely negative view of life. I'm now making a deliberate effort to turn things around for myself, not to continue to follow in her footsteps.

Don't Listen to Those Hair Color Commercials: It's Time to Keep the Gray!

So, drum roll please....the last of our five ANTs! This one is extremely common. I saved it for last because this ANT can be harder to stomp on than the others. It's *black and white, all or nothing* thinking.

Did you ever read a list of tips on how to successfully take a multiple-choice test? One is that if one of the answer choices uses a word like "always" or "never," it is unlikely to be the correct answer. That's because people and things are rarely "always" or "never" anything.

Despite this we, as human beings, like to be able to put things at one extreme or another. It's a lot less complicated than trying to distinguish among all the possible shades of gray.

We've previously discussed thinking and behaviors learned in childhood. Black and white, all or nothing thinking is definitely in that category. Small children are black and white thinkers by nature. They believe that individual people are all good or all bad; they can't be both. Very often kids in dysfunctional families label one parent as good and the other as bad; it's not until much later that they realize the "bad" parent wasn't all bad and the "good" parent wasn't all good.

Kids haven't yet developed the ability to understand that everyone has a mixture of good and bad traits and characteristics.

As we grow up we develop the ability to distinguish among shades of gray. There are still times, though, when we go back to our old black and white thinking, often in challenging situations that remind us of our pasts.

It's easy to go to extremes in our lifestyles. For instance, you may spend years eating unhealthful food and not exercising, then suddenly decide that you're going to go on a healthful diet and train for a marathon. You go from one extreme to the other.

The problem is that you're more likely to be able to sustain something that's in the middle. For instance, you can try adding healthful food to your diet but not completely cutting out the less healthful stuff. Or you can get one or more exercise games for your gaming system and commit to using them at least three times a week.

Let's look at how all or nothing, black and white thinking applies to our two scenarios.

In the personal scenario, you may decide that this one movie suggestion is the final straw and that it will end your friendship forever. Your friend will not remember anything else about you other than your appalling taste in movies. You blew it forever; there's no redeeming yourself now. If you call her to explain your movie choice it will just feel like you're making something up to get back in her good graces.

In the work scenario, you may decide that you never should have tried to get into this field at all. You've wasted decades of your life on this when you should have been doing something for which you were actually qualified. In fact, you haven't just wasted decades; you've wasted your whole life, because you're too old to start fresh in a new field. You'll get to the end of your life, look back, and realize you are leaving nothing of value behind. You didn't even get married and have kids because you were so dedicated to work that ended up not mattering anyway, so your life is a complete failure.

For this ANT, notice the times that you take one extreme position or another, or when you suddenly flip from one thought to its extreme opposite.

Look at your life as a whole. What situations have you seen as all or nothing, black or white?

Why have you taken those extreme positions?

Who set examples for you?

How do you feel when you think about choosing the middle ground in one of those situations? Does it feel unfamiliar and uncomfortable? What do you think might happen?

As I mentioned earlier, this ANT is hard to squish. I recommend that you start with relatively harmless situations. A good first effort might be to look at your diet or exercise habits and choose one small change that you could make to move towards a healthier, more moderate and sustainable lifestyle. For instance, if you drink sodas or coffee at every meal try substituting water once a day. That's not a radical change, but success at that can give you the confidence to try some more changes.

> *Leigh: Any time Francis criticizes something about me I immediately jump to the conclusion that I'm a terrible wife. I compare myself to friends who are married and conclude that they are fabulous wives and that I'm not.*
>
> *I do the same thing at work. If my supervisor makes a suggestion about something I'm working on I assume I should already have known whatever it is she's showing me and that I'm failing at the project. It doesn't occur to me that she's my supervisor for a reason; she has more experience and knowledge than I do. It's OK for me not to know everything. It doesn't mean I'm a failure.*

Black and white thinking is a lot easier than trying to find the middle ground; again, this is something I learned from my mother.

How do I decide what's OK and what's not? If I'm either the best or the worst, I know what to do. But what if I'm good but have some flaws? How do I look at myself then? How do I decide whether I'm good enough?

Let's revisit the two scenarios we've been discussing throughout the chapter. You might find that your friend was on vacation for a week and left her cell phone at home. And maybe your boss was in meetings all day and didn't have time to read your proposal. You may have gotten the deadline wrong, so he might not even have to choose a winning proposal until next week.

So whatever your friend thought of the movie or your boss thought of your proposal, it's worth stepping back and considering possibilities other than the disastrous ones that came immediately to mind. Even if your friend didn't like your choice of movie or your boss didn't like your proposal, it's unlikely that either your friendship or your career has been ruined. And even if both of those things were true, chances are you'd find ways to deal with them. When you think something is a total disaster and you'll never survive, think of all the other times that you've survived seeming disasters and consider the possibility that you might survive this one, too.

And keep stomping those ANTs!

Putting It Into Action

1) What will you do to help yourself remember to pay attention to ANTs?

Joanne: Knowing that it's hard to remember to notice and change things I've been doing forever, there are a few things I've been doing to help myself continue to pay attention to ANTs.

I've set my phone to chime periodically throughout the day. The chime brings my mind back to the task of noticing ANTs.

I try to remember to think about ANTs when I have pauses in my day, like when I'm stopped at a red light.

I have post-it notes stuck in various places at home and around my desk at work to remind me.

But the most helpful thing, I think, is having accountability partners. I've shared this chapter of the book with most of my friends as well as trusted family members and coworkers. When one of us notices that an ANT has come up for the other person, he or she points it out. Then I (or whoever it is who needs to stomp on the ANT) come(s) up with a challenge to the negative thought, a way to reframe the situation. If we get stuck we help each other come up with ideas.

2) How will you keep track of situations in which ANTs come up so you can start to notice patterns?

When I notice an ANT I use the voice recorder on my phone to make a note of it; if I'm in a meeting or somewhere else I need to be quiet, I send myself a text or write myself a note. Using the voice memos, texts, and notes, I jot down reminders of the ANTs at the end of the day. I have a chart that I use to track the ANTs in context, including events, feelings, and types of ANT.

3) After you've had some practice noticing and challenging ANTs, think about your patterns regarding them. Do(es) one or more ANT(s) show up more often than the others? If so, which one(s)? Do you have any guesses about why this is true?

I've noticed that all the ANTs show up pretty frequently for me, but I think the two biggest ones for me are mind reading and maximizing/minimizing.

The reasons for the mind reading are pretty clear. I never felt safe at home when I was growing up. My parents' moods were very unpredictable. I kept trying to figure out what I could do to make them happy or at least keep them from being hostile. And I'm also very sensitive to other people's moods, so I pick up on their feelings easily. Then I feel like I have to try to figure out why they're feeling the way they are, whether it's my fault, and what I can do to change their mood.

From what others have told me, I minimize my personal and professional accomplishments and maximize others' accomplishments. For minimizing...I just do what makes sense to me as I go along. It usually doesn't occur to me that I might be doing things that interest and/or impress other people.

And maximizing...I'm more impressed with what others do than with what I do because they think differently and they do things I don't think I could.

When I was growing up my parents always praised my brother for his accomplishments but they rarely praised me for mine, so I learned to believe that other people do things that are worth noticing but I don't.

4) Are there any ANTs that you find relatively easy to challenge? If so, which one(s)? Why do you think they're easier to challenge than others?

Although I catastrophize sometimes, I find that ANT easier to stomp on than the others. I'm pretty good at thinking logically, so I can come up with plenty of arguments against the worst happening. Of course that doesn't immediately convince the feeling part of me, so it's still not easy, but with practice I've helped that part to be OK when I tell her that we'll get through the situation no matter what.

5) Are there any ANTs that you find particularly difficult to challenge? If so, which ones? Do you have any ideas about why they're harder for you?

The hardest ANTs for me to deal with are mind reading and black and white thinking. It's hard for me to stop mind reading because, as I mentioned before, I am very sensitive to others' feelings. It's hard for me to set a boundary so I don't take on their feelings as my responsibility. I'm working on being able to feel OK within myself no matter what others are feeling, but it's very hard.

Black and white thinking is also very hard for me to deal with. It's not difficult to recognize, but it's difficult for me to find the middle ground between the extremes. I can notice when I swing from one end to the other, but I have problems figuring out what a reasonable balance is.

One thing that I find particularly difficult is saying no. How do I decide how much I should agree to do for others and how much I should decline to do because I need to take care of myself? I'm still working on finding the right balance for me.

Chapter 11

Other Helpful Approaches

1. Do you do ever feel like you need to calm your mind because it feels like it's going a thousand miles an hour?

2. Do you spend a lot of time thinking about the past or worrying about your future?

3. Do you have a lot of body aches and/or physical tension?

4. Do you feel like you, at some point, lost track of your goals for your life or strayed from the path you wanted to take?

5. Does it seem like you have a lot of feelings that just get bottled up instead of being expressed?

The techniques I explained in the last chapter are part of a therapy approach called *cognitive behavioral therapy*, or *CBT*. I have found CBT useful, both personally and professionally, in changing unhelpful patterns of thinking and behavior.

But cognitive behavioral therapy is not the only approach I use with my clients, or that I have used for my own personal growth. I'd like to introduce you to some of the other approaches that I have found helpful; because I am drawing from my own personal and professional experience, though, keep in mind that this is not an exhaustive list of what's available.

You can use most of these approaches either with a therapist or on your own, but some of them do require that you work with a therapist or other professional.

I'm listing a variety of possibilities because one size does not fit all. As with anything else, if it isn't a good fit you're less likely to stick with it and benefit from it.

As you consider using some of these techniques, if the thought comes to you that you don't have the time (or money) for therapy or other ways of focusing on yourself, remember (again) that by helping yourself you're also helping the other people in your life. Making sure that you balance your own needs with those of others helps to insure that you will have the time, energy, and desire to help others when they need it.

And if you are struggling with depression, anxiety, or other results of abuse and/or neglect, remember that you are not the only one who is suffering. If you don't address these issues, they don't just affect you; they also hurt the people who love and care about you.

Note: You are responsible for your own well-being while working with these techniques. If anything traumatic or overwhelming comes up for you, please seek the help of a professional. And, as always, if you think you might harm yourself or someone else, please call 911 or go to the nearest emergency room.

Techniques That Don't (Necessarily) Require a Therapist

Narrative Therapy

The thoughts we think and the things we say have power. Narrative therapy is based on the idea that there is no fixed reality, but rather that we create our own realities with our thoughts, feelings, and words. If you said yes to question 4, you could benefit from narrative therapy.

Names Can Hurt You!

Our lives are based on stories that we tell ourselves, stories that we most likely learned long ago and of which we are probably unaware. Remember that in Chapter 5 I mentioned that dysfunctional families tend to categorize and label children. You may have been the smart one, the pretty one, the funny one, the athletic one, the artistic one, the good one, or the bad one.

But whichever label you were given, you were shaped by it. Whether you conformed to it or rebelled against it[2], it affected who you believed you were, and who you believe you are today.

Many parents have told their children that they will never amount to anything, that they won't find their ideal partner, and that they are destined for a life of menial, meaningless work. That's a very hard label to shake.

If one or both of your parents told you this, how has that prediction shaped you? Have you managed to succeed despite it, or have you fallen into its trap? What is it like if your parents predict success for your siblings but not for you?

---

[2] Many people believe that if they have rebelled against their families of origin by doing the opposite of what was expected, they have escaped their influence. This is not true. Just as the opposite of love is not hate but indifference, reacting against someone means that you are still being defined by him or her. You are still enmeshed. Instead of rebelling, it makes sense to find out what lifestyle works for you, then take the necessary steps to move towards achieving that lifestyle.

Take a moment to think about the labels you were given as a child, and labels that you are given today. How do they fit you? How do they limit you?

Roxanne feels like a misfit in her family, like the only one who didn't get it. When she was growing up her parents encouraged that by telling her that all of her siblings were smarter and more talented than she was.

While it seems that her siblings have all managed to find the American dream of financial success, the house with the white picket fence, and the 2.3 children, Roxanne doesn't have that.

What's more, she doesn't think she wants it. She constantly questions herself because of this, and remembers that it's been this way all of her life. Does that mean it's OK for her to be different and unsuccessful by our society's standards, does it mean she has not lived up to her potential, or is it somewhere in between?

Is it wrong that, at age 45, she still doesn't know what she wants to be when she grows up? She is attending college in hopes that she will be able to get a better job than the one she has now. Every semester she struggles to decide what classes to take; does she take the practical ones that can lead to a job, or does she take the classes she enjoys, like sculpture and photography? She thinks of a line from the Billy Joel song "James": "Do what's good for you or you're not good for anybody." But what is good for her, anyway?

How Do Life Stories Change?

Consider Honey, a 13-year-old girl who lived in a poor neighborhood but who was bused to a school where most of the children were wealthy. One day, because her mother had no money to give her, Honey stole five dollars from another student so she could buy lunch. She was caught and punished by being suspended from school for a week.

Many of the teachers and other students had already, of course, made assumptions about Honey because she was poor. Now they had more fuel for the fire.

If no one had intervened for Honey those assumptions might have defined her high school career and, possibly, the rest of her life. But Honey's creative writing teacher, Mrs. Mason, knew a different side of her: the sensitive girl who wrote wonderful stories and poems.

Mrs. Mason, with Honey's permission, took some of her writing to the next faculty meeting and passed it around. The other teachers were quite impressed by what they read and came to understand Honey better. They realized that she didn't deserve the reputation she had gotten.

Then one of Honey's short stories and one of her poems were selected for the school literary magazine. Many of the students who read them also got to know Honey in a different way than they had before.

By the time Honey graduated her reputation had changed considerably. Now most people no longer saw her as a thief; they saw her as a talented writer who had a great future ahead of her. Honey eventually learned to see herself the same way.

She got a full scholarship to college and majored in English. After college, with a lot of work and struggling (and a lot of minimum wage jobs to support herself), she managed to become a published author. She was eventually able to earn a living as a writer.

It's quite possible that none of that would have happened if Mrs. Mason had not helped to change Honey's personal story for the better.

Can I Do That?

In Chapter 8 I talked about "I wouldn't start from here" and the fact that here is the only place you *can* start, whether you want to accept that or not.

But what if you decided to look at "here" differently? What if, in the tapestry of your life, you could find a thread of the life that you would love to be living? What if you focused on that one thread, made it the central part of the tapestry, and incorporated other threads that fit in with it?

That is the core of narrative therapy.

In previous chapters I've talked about the dangers of the word *should*. To me, thinking you *should* do or be something is a sign of someone else trying to dictate your story. It's not something that you chose and it's probably not something that fits who you are. It is something that is being imposed from outside, the internalization of someone else's voice.

Changing Your Perspective

If you feel like you are living someone else's negative prediction, look back over your life. Was there a time when your life was different, even in a small way, or for a short time? What are the details of that experience? Maybe you successfully edited the school yearbook when you were in high school. Or maybe you successfully completed a difficult project at work that you hadn't expected would go well.

If you find one of those threads of success in your past story, you have evidence that you can experience success. If you were successful once, you can succeed again.

Maybe you were frequently called fat when you were growing up and have always struggled with your weight. You probably believe that you are destined to be overweight all of your life. But was there a time in your life when you succeeded in losing weight and keeping it off for some time?

If so, you know that it's possible for you to lose weight, and maybe you have (or can find) new knowledge or resources now that can help you to keep the weight off permanently.

Maybe you have never lost a significant amount of weight and/or kept it off but you know someone who has. Who's to say that you can't do the same thing? No, you haven't done it in the past, but that doesn't mean you can't do it now.

How Long Is This Going to Take?

It takes time for a new story to take hold. New ways of thinking or behaving are not established immediately; it's likely that the old story will keep coming back and trying to take over. You can be alert to that, though, and be prepared to defend the new story.

Think about the expression "the straw that broke the camel's back." Each individual piece of straw is nearly weightless. But pile thousands of them together, and all it takes is one more seemingly insignificant piece of straw to make the weight too much for the camel to handle.

And think about the power of water. Who would think that a small trickle of water could influence anything? But when the water flows over the same piece of rock long enough, it breaks the rock down.

Consider a stream flowing down a mountain. It follows a path that has been worn into the stone over a period of many years. But what happens if you divert the stream? Over time it will wear a new path in the rock and a new course will be established. But there needs to be something that persists in diverting the water until that new path is deep enough, or the water will probably return to the path it took originally.

Researchers have shown that the same thing can happen in the human brain. Our habitual ways of thinking create paths in our brains. But just as the water can be diverted in a new direction, your thoughts, if aimed in a different direction for a long enough time, will create new paths and a new default way of thinking will be established. That doesn't mean that the occasional thought might not go down the original path, but if so, it will be much easier than it once was to direct your thinking back to the preferred path.

Can I Get Rid of All That Other Stuff?

Going back to the image of the life tapestry for a moment, think about all of those other threads in your tapestry, the ones that represent parts of yourself you don't like. Should you cut them out entirely? No. Those experiences and parts of you are also important to who you are now, even though you are trying to emphasize new aspects of yourself. As Captain Jean-Luc Picard said in the episode of *Star Trek: The Next Generation* called "Tapestry":

"There are many parts of my youth that I'm not proud of. There were loose threads - untidy parts of me that I would like to remove. But when I pulled on one of those threads, it unraveled the tapestry of my life."

He realized that those untidy parts of him had been helpful; every negative quality has the potential to be a positive one if channeled in the right direction. And it can complement the qualities that you like and want to encourage.

So the idea of balance comes back again. Although you are creating a new version of yourself you will not completely erase the person you have been, and that's not a bad thing.

If you'd like to know more about how to use this approach, try Jim Loehr's book *The Power of Story: Change Your Story, Change Your Destiny in Business and in Life*. It can help you to identify the story you have been living and begin to make the changes you want.

Mindfulness and Meditation

Mindfulness and meditation have many physical and mental health benefits. You can learn and practice them with a therapist, but you can also try them on your own.

Mindfulness

If you said yes to question 2, I suggest that you try mindfulness. Mindfulness means being fully present physically, mentally, and emotionally where you are right now. Many of us spend a lot of time thinking about the past or wondering about the future. It's OK to do that, but it's also important to be completely in the "now" sometimes.

Have you ever been in the middle of some significant event and found yourself mentally rehearsing how you would tell someone about it later? Doing that distracts you from fully participating in the experience because you're so busy thinking about how you will reflect on it in the future.

When is the last time you ate a meal without doing something else (like reading, watching TV, or having a conversation) at the same time? Eating is one activity during which most of us are anything but mindful.

There is a practice called *mindful eating* that invites you to experience food in a whole new way. When you practice mindful eating you shut everything else out and focus entirely on experiencing the food with all of your senses, including vision, touch, hearing, smell and, finally, taste.

Mindfulness includes the idea of *beginner's mind*, which means approaching an experience as if for the first time. Having a beginner's mind is helpful in mindful eating, for instance. Can you experience and eat a raisin as if you'd never seen, felt, smelled, or tasted one before?

Mindfulness also helps us to develop what is called an *observing ego*. The observing ego is like another person watching us (and our thoughts and feelings) from outside. The observing ego just watches;

it does not judge. That's helpful when we're dealing with emotions that feel overwhelming, or when we are attacked by our inner critical voices.

When we're feeling emotionally overwhelmed the observing ego can help us detach and see ourselves as separate from the feelings rather than identifying completely with them. If we're feeling depressed, despairing, or anxious and think things will never get better, the observing ego can help us to remember times that we have escaped depression and anxiety and felt better.

When your critical voice is taking over, the observing ego can help you take a mental step back and see that voice for what it is: a part of you that is trying to be helpful but that is actually holding you back.

Practicing mindfulness has other benefits, as well. In 1979 Dr. Jon Kabat-Zinn of the University of Massachusetts Medical School founded a program in *mindfulness-based stress reduction (MBSR)*. MBSR can be used to relieve diverse issues, both physical and mental, including, among others, fatigue, stress, sleep problems, depression, and anxiety. You can learn more about MBSR at http://www.umassmed.edu/cfm/stress/index.aspx.

Meditation

If you said yes to question #1 you could benefit from meditation, although it will probably be challenging at first.

People who meditate regularly tend to be calmer and happier than people who don't. Meditation can have physical benefits, as well; it can improve cardiovascular health, lessen chronic pain, and strengthen your immune system.

There are a number of types of meditation, including breathing meditations and walking meditations, among others. You can use guided meditations or music to help you achieve a meditative state. There are also many books that can guide you.

It's important to find a type of meditation that works for you, or you're likely to give it up quickly. And remember that there's no such thing as perfect meditation. No matter how experienced you are, you will get distracted at times. That's fine—just return to the meditation as many times as you need to.

Here's an example of a breathing meditation:

Wear loose, comfortable clothing. Find somewhere that you can sit or lie down comfortably. If you are going to try to make a regular practice of meditation you may want to set aside a room or area of your house to be your meditation place. You may also decide to have candles or other things to help you center yourself and more easily achieve a meditative state.

Turn your phone off and, if necessary, put a "do not disturb" sign on the door. You may also want to turn the lights down.

Then turn your focus inward, to your breathing. Track your breaths, mentally saying "In" and "Out" as you breathe in and out. Or you can choose to count, or to repeat a short phrase or mantra that has meaning for you.

Don't worry when thoughts intrude on your meditation. That happens to everyone, even people who have been meditating for years. Just notice the thought, perhaps saying "thought" to yourself, then let the thought slip away like a leaf floating down a stream, and return your attention to your breath.

I would suggest that you start with a short period of meditation time, maybe only a minute or even 30 seconds. As you get more and more used to the practice of meditation you can gradually increase the time.

As always, be aware of your experience. If meditation is just a chore that you're impatient to get through it probably won't be helpful. In that case, consider exploring other options.

Jon Kabat-Zinn's *Mindfulness for Beginners: Reclaiming the Present Moment--and Your Life* provides an introduction to mindfulness and meditation.

EFT

EFT (Emotional Freedom Technique), like acupuncture, deals with channels of energy *(meridians)* in the body. The goal is to balance the body's energy and to free up energy that might be "stuck" so that emotional, psychological, and even physical issues can be resolved.

EFT consists of tapping on a series of points on the body while making statements relating to the issue that is being addressed. The more specific the statements are, the better it will work. It is most helpful to tap on specific experiences that relate to the problem.

EFT has been used to address a variety of issues, including anxiety, phobias, post-traumatic stress disorder (PTSD), physical problems, and more. Gary Craig, who developed EFT, suggests that you "try it on everything."

EFT is a useful tool because the sequence is easy to learn,[3] it takes very little time, and you don't need any special materials to do it. Over time you will become better and better at using EFT effectively.

It can be helpful to have an experienced EFT practitioner (some psychotherapists, for instance, use EFT with their clients) work with you, especially when you're first starting out, but you don't have to do that. You can also find videos of EFT practitioners that will guide you through EFT sequences aimed at specific issues.

Children can learn to use EFT, too. A good book to introduce EFT to kids is *The Wizard's Wish: Or, How He Made the Yuckies Go Away – A Story About the Magic in You*, written by Brad Yates.

Gary Craig's *EFT Manual* offers guidance on using EFT to address a wide range of issues. You can also find EFT information at http://www. eftuniverse.com/.

---

[3] See Appendix for a version of the EFT sequence.

Yoga

As with any form of exercise, you should check with your doctor before doing yoga. I recommend starting with a yoga class even if you eventually intend to practice alone, because there are aspects of yoga postures that can only be learned by being physically present with the teacher.

You know that exercise is good for you. You may also know that exercising triggers "feel good" chemicals called *endorphins*, and therefore can help relieve anxiety and depression.

Yoga is one of the most beneficial forms of exercise that I have found. Hatha yoga (the physical practice, which is only one aspect of yoga) increases physical strength and flexibility. It can also provide great cardiovascular benefits. And it can be a physical method of meditation.

If you answered yes to question 3, consider trying yoga. No matter how out of shape you are, you can learn yoga. And modifications (including the use of yoga props) can be made to accommodate just about any physical condition. Some people do "chair yoga." And there are prenatal and postnatal yoga classes that can help a woman have an easier and more comfortable experience before, during, and after childbirth.

If you have trouble turning off your brain, yoga can help. When Piper was first learning yoga there were so many different things to focus on that her mind couldn't wander if it tried; she was too busy trying to make her various body parts do what they were supposed to do. Then the teacher said, "Breathe," and she thought, "Are you kidding me? I'm supposed to focus on all of these things *and* breathe at the same time?"

Eventually, the poses became familiar and she was able to relax and enjoy the meditative quality of her practice.

Yoga can slow racing thoughts and calm anxiety; it can also lift your spirits if you are depressed and help release emotions if you feel stuck.

During a yoga class, doing a hip opening pose, Piper suddenly experienced deep sadness and found tears running down her face. After class the teacher explained that this made sense because hip openers release emotions. Piper found that she was also able to release other emotions, including anger, through her practice of yoga.

While many yoga books are aimed mainly at the philosophy behind yoga, Georg Feuerstein and Larry Payne's *Yoga for Dummies* offers a guide to the practice of hatha yoga.

If you find that you enjoy the physical practice of yoga you might also want to explore yoga's other aspects. A good introduction is Rolf Gates and Katrina Kenison's *Meditations from the Mat: Daily Reflections on the Path of Yoga.*

Journaling

Have you kept a diary or journal at some point in your life? While writing in a diary is useful for remembering events, writing in a journal is a great way to express and work through thoughts and feelings. If you said yes to question 5, journaling may be something you'd like to try.

A journal can be a place to record your dreams. You can work through problems in your journal; seeing an issue written in black and white can often trigger insights that you might not get otherwise. You can use your journal to have a dialogue with another person or even an object or a place. You can write letters to family, to acquaintances, or to people you admire or would like to meet. Or you could write short stories and/or poetry.

Your journal can include art (drawing, painting, etc.). You can put anything in your journal—it's up to you. The important part is to be free to be yourself in a way that you can only be if you know you're not going to be observed or criticized. And that includes doing your best to keep self-criticism at a minimum!

If you are worried about someone else finding your journal and reading it, find a way to secure it so you can feel free to express yourself. You can put it in a locked drawer, for instance, or you can journal on your computer and password protect it.

For further ideas and suggestions for journaling try Sandy Grason's *Journalution: Journaling to Awaken Your Inner Voice, Heal Your Life and Manifest Your Dreams.*

Other Forms of Self-expression

As I've mentioned before, it's important to find things that work for you. If you hate to write, journaling may not be helpful for you; at the very least it will be hard to motivate yourself to do it.

If you don't want to journal, what else can you do to express yourself—draw, paint, sculpt, sing, play an instrument, dance, run, kick a soccer ball? Everyone can find something to use for emotional release. It may just take time and experimentation to find one that works for you.

Dream Work

While you can certainly do dream work on your own, it can be useful to work with a therapist or other professional experienced in dream interpretation so you will have someone who can give you guidance and feedback to help you to begin. Even though I have been doing dream work for years, I still find it helpful to discuss dream interpretation with others; outside perspectives are very helpful.

Recording dreams is a great way to get in touch with what's going on in your unconscious mind. Keeping a dream journal can help you to see the patterns in your dreams and get more insight into their meanings.

If you don't usually remember your dreams it may help to think, as you start to fall asleep, about your intention to remember them.

Keep paper and a pen or pencil next to your bed so that you can write dreams down as soon as you wake up; the longer you wait, the less you are likely to remember. It's best to do as little moving as possible between waking up and recording dreams, as even movement can chase away the memories. Turning on the lights is also likely to make you forget your dreams, so you may want to have a small flashlight so you can see well enough to write dreams down.

When you first start recording them it's likely that your dreams won't make much sense to you. As you record more of them, though, you will probably see patterns emerging.

As you get familiar with the content of your dreams you may find that certain images keep coming up and have consistent meanings for you. For instance, in Nikki's dreams, a house represents her mind. The basement symbolizes her unconscious mind. She knows that if she dreams about the house she grew up in, it's related to childhood thoughts and feelings. If she dreams of a house that is a combination of her childhood house and her current one, it probably refers to current thoughts or feelings that are similar to thoughts or feelings from her childhood.

Water, to Michaela, represents feelings. When she was first in therapy she had a lot of dreams about tidal waves sweeping over her because she was feeling overwhelmed by emotions.

For Mallory, driving a car refers to progressing towards the achievement of her goals. If she dreams that she's in the back seat and unable to control the car, she knows that something is interfering with that process.

And when Trudy dreams about a clogged toilet she knows that she has a lot of "stuff" to deal with. If she dreams that she's in a public place and the restroom is full or otherwise unavailable, it means she's feeling unable to release some of that "stuff."

This last example can show just how literal dream symbols can be. Our dreaming minds can't tell us directly, through words, what they're trying to communicate. So they represent thoughts using symbols.

You may see something in a dream that is a literal example of an expression common in our language. For instance, if you dream that you're looking for a needle in a haystack it may mean that you're searching for something in your life that is hard to find.

Dreams often use objects and symbols in ways that are particular to the person dreaming them. So it helps to think of any associations, past or present, that you have with each symbol.

Be careful about taking dreams too literally. For instance, the people who appear in your dreams may or may not be representing those actual people. Many dream people represent parts of you. So, again, think of the associations you have with those people, then think about how those characteristics might apply to you. This can also happen with objects in your dreams.

For help with doing your own dream interpretations, try Robert A. Johnson's *Inner Work: Using Dreams and Active Imagination for Personal Growth.*

Here's a sample dream interpretation:

Mallory's dream:

I am in my car. It is pitch black outside. I am approaching an extremely steep hill (paved) with other cars driving on both sides of me and behind me. There is no marked road, so cars are scattered around with no discernible pattern. I don't see any scenery or landmarks, just the expanse of pavement on the steep hill.

I start up the hill, hoping that my speed and momentum will enable me to get to the top. It soon becomes clear that my car does not have enough power to make it. Other cars are doing better, though, and I feel like I need to get out of their way.

It seems that I have no choice but to roll backwards down the hill, which terrifies me, particularly because I know that I might run into another car. (In real life I really do hate when I have to stop on a hill that is steep enough that my car drifts backwards when I take my foot off the brake—there's no way I would ever choose to drive a car with a manual transmission!)

I suddenly notice that there is a flat place off to the right where I can stop and be out of others' way. I wake up before I get a chance to try to get there.

Possible interpretation:

To me, a car represents my self-will, the goal-oriented part of me—the part that is "driven." So by trying to get to the top of this extremely steep hill I am trying to use sheer strength of will to accomplish what may be an impossible task.

When I first started to work with this dream I was discouraged by the failure that was implied by my having to give up on my goal and roll back down the hill. Then there's my fear of rolling down a hill backwards in my car; this fits with my fear of not being able to use strength of will to achieve the difficult goals I set for myself. It also fits with my Adult Child belief that I am the only one who can or will help me to survive.

Then I remembered the idea that everything in a dream represents part of me. If that's true, the other cars represent parts of me. And if that's true, then going back down the hill and finding a way to get to the flat area to the right of the hill could be seen as getting out of my own way! So maybe the dream was trying to tell me that I don't need to try so hard, that if I allow myself to let go I may get to where I need to be.

It's also interesting that the flat area is to the right of the hill. I wonder if that represents my right brain, which is the less concrete, less linear, more creative, dreaming part of me?

Law of Attraction

The idea behind the Law of Attraction (popularized by the movies *The Secret* and *What the Bleep Do We Know?*) is that like attracts like. Each one of us emits energy, and the universe gives back to us in kind. If we put out positive energy we will get positive results; if we put out negative energy we will get negative results.

According to the theory behind the Law of Attraction, the universe can't tell the difference between your thoughts and reality. So if you are able to picture yourself having or being something and truly believe it, it will happen.

If you are starting a new business, picture yourself in your office, getting call after call from new clients. Picture your appointment calendar being completely full. Picture your satisfied clients referring all of their friends to you. If you can believe it, it can happen.

If you believe that you are successful, you will find success. If you feel like a failure, you will fail. Many people expect the "same old same old" or predict that bad things will happen, and often they get exactly that.

Did you know that many people who win the lottery or come into large amounts of money in some other way end up with no more money than they had before? Some people refer to this as having a financial set point. That is, you have in your mind that you are someone who has a certain amount of money (generally very little), and you find a way (without realizing it) to get back to that set point.

If this sounds a bit too "woo woo" for you, look at it in terms of cognitive therapy. Changing the way you think can change the way you feel as well as leading to improved life outcomes.

For instance, let's say you believe you are successful. You will give off successful energy and you will speak and act confidently. Other people will react to your energy, your words, and your actions and treat you as if you are successful. This positive feedback will increase your positive feelings and, most likely, will lead to success.

If, however, you believe that everything you try is doomed to fail, you will give off that hopeless energy and you will speak and act in ways that communicate your lack of self-confidence. Again, other people will respond to the energy you are giving off, but this time they will treat you like the failure you believe yourself to be. This will strengthen your idea that you will fail, which becomes a self-fulfilling prophecy and a vicious cycle.

So how can you use this principle to achieve success even if you don't really believe it? Try "acting as if." Even if you have doubts about your ability to be successful, acting like you believe it can still lead others to believe it. Remember that they can't read your mind. So acting like you believe it will tend to lead others to react to you in more positive ways. That, in turn, will make it easier for you to believe.

I do not take the Law of Attraction as far as some people do (we attract physical illnesses, personal disasters, etc.), but I do believe that it works. And depending upon how you look at it, even cognitive therapists believe in it, to some extent.

For more information and practical exercises, I recommend Michael Losier's *Law of Attraction: The Science of Attracting More of What You Want and Less of What You Don't*.

The MBTI® and the Enneagram

I often recommend the MBTI® (Myers-Briggs Type Indicator®) and the Enneagram to my clients. Both are used to help people understand their personality types, which in turn can help them to accept themselves and others.

The MBTI®

If you are interested in using the MBTI®, it is best to have a certified MBTI® practitioner administer the MBTI® and help you to process the results. You can find an MBTI® practitioner in your area by visiting www.aptinternational.org.

If no MBTI® practitioner is available where you live you can take another test designed to help you find your type in David Keirsey's book *Please Understand Me II: Temperament, Character, Intelligence.*

The MBTI® was created by a mother and daughter, Katherine Briggs and Elizabeth Briggs Myers. They based it upon Carl Jung's personality type theory.

The MBTI® is designed to show your *preferences* between members of each of four pairs of opposite characteristics: Introversion/Extraversion, Sensing/Intuition, Thinking/Feeling, and Judging/Perceiving. Your four preferred characteristics are put together to indicate your *type*, i.e. "ESTP" or "INFJ." This creates a total of 16 different types, all equally valid and valuable.

Introversion and Extraversion have to do with the way you recharge your energy (by being alone or with other people). Introversion means something different in this case than it generally does in our society; introverts are not necessarily shy (although some are), and not all extraverts would classify themselves as outgoing.

Sensing and iNtuition (the letter N is used to represent intuition because the I is used for Introversion), which are the *perceiving* functions, deal with the ways people take in information and the types of information they're likely to pay attention to. Someone with a preference for Sensing tends to be a "Just the facts, ma'am" sort of person, seeing what is actually there. Someone with a preference for iNtuition looks instead for possibilities and/or the big picture. To put it another way, someone who prefers Sensing sees individual trees whereas someone who prefers iNtuition sees the forest.

Thinking and Feeling, the *judging* functions, deal with the ways we use the information that we take in; in other words, what criteria do we use to make decisions? Both are logical ways to make decisions, but someone with a preference for Thinking is likely to make decisions based upon objective, impersonal criteria, whereas someone with a preference for Feeling is more likely to make decisions based upon their effect on people. This does not mean that people with a preference for Thinking don't have feelings or that people with a preference for Feeling don't think, though.

The final pair, Judging and Perceiving, relates to whether you like things settled, planned, and decided (Judging) or whether you prefer to keep things open-ended (Perceiving). For instance, someone with a Judging preference might plan exactly what she will do on her day off while someone with a Perceiving preference is more likely to wing it and see what she feels like doing when the time comes. Again, the names can be deceptive: someone with a Judging preference is not necessarily judgmental, and someone with a Perceiving preference is not necessarily more perceptive than others.

I find the MBTI® very useful in gaining understanding of yourself and others. You may find that the reason you never felt like you fit in was because you have an uncommon personality type, or because everyone in your family except you had certain personality characteristics in common. You may realize that you have spent much of your life trying to adapt to others by becoming something you're not, when being yourself would be much better for all concerned.

For a simple, but useful, introduction to the MBTI® I recommend Renee Baron's *What Type Am I?* David Keirsey's book *Please Understand Me II* also introduces the idea of four *temperaments*, a useful addition to MBTI® theory.

Paul D. Tieger and Barbara Barron-Tieger's *Nurture By Nature: Understand Your Child's Personality Type—And Become a Better Parent* can help you parent your kids by working with their personality types.

And it can help you understand who you were as a child and how that affected your life.

If you're struggling with career issues I'd recommend that you get a copy of the latest edition of Tieger and Barron-Tieger's *Do What You Are: Discover the Perfect Career for You Through the Secrets of Personality Type*, which uses the MBTI® to help people understand what careers might work for their personality type and why.

The Enneagram

There are therapists and other professionals who are experienced at working with the Enneagram. If you can find one of these professionals, you will get a fuller understanding of how the Enneagram works and how it applies to you. If you are working on your own, you can find Enneagram tests in Don Richard Riso and Ross Hudson's *Discovering Your Personality Type* and in David N. Daniels and Virginia A. Price's *The Essential Enneagram*.

A good basic introduction to the Enneagram is Renee Baron and Elizabeth Wagele's *The Enneagram Made Easy*. Pat Wyman's *Three Keys to Self-Understanding* integrates the MBTI®, the Enneagram, and inner child work.

The Enneagram is less commonly known than the MBTI®, but the two complement each other well. While the MBTI® is designed to show your essential personality type, the Enneagram helps you to understand the ways in which you make yourself safe in the world. Each Enneagram type has a whole range of possible expressions, from the most defensive and unhealthy to the most enlightened and healthy.

There are nine Enneagram types, numbered One through Nine; as with the MBTI®, no type is considered better than another. Depending upon the version of Enneagram theory you use, you also have a *wing* that is one of the two types adjacent to your type on the Enneagram diagram (for instance, One with a Nine wing or One with a Two wing).

The names I use to describe the nine types are:

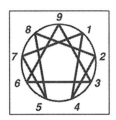

1- The Perfectionist; 2-The Helper;
3-The Performer; 4-The Dreamer;
5-The Thinker; 6-The Loyalist/Skeptic;
7-The Free Spirit; 8-The Advocate; and
9-The Peacemaker.

Both the MBTI® and the Enneagram can help you to recognize the strengths and the challenges that come with your personality type. Knowing that, you can work to maximize your strengths and work around (or through) your challenges.

Techniques that Require a Therapist or Other Professional

Imago Relationship Therapy

I talked about *imago therapy* in Chapter 3. Created by Dr. Harville Hendrix, PhD and his wife, Helen LaKelly Hunt, M.A., M.L.A., it is a type of therapy that is designed to help couples to learn to nurture and support each other.

The idea is that we, without intending to do so, find romantic partners who trigger our childhood wounds. This generally leads to conflict when the partners feel attacked by each other and become insecure.

The purpose of the therapy is to teach partners how to help each other to heal from childhood wounds. It is too late for our parents to heal those wounds for us, but our romantic partners can help us if they choose to do so and we choose to let them.

One of the core pieces of imago therapy is the *couple's dialogue.* When you have a conversation with another person, or particularly if you're having an argument, it is likely that you are not fully listening to what the other person is saying because you are preparing your response while he is talking.

The couple's dialogue changes this. When a couple is engaged in this type of conversation each gets a turn to express something important to him or her. Let's say your partner starts. He tells you something that he wants you to know. After he tells you, you paraphrase what he said, ask "Did I get it right?" and "Is there more?" This continues until he says that there is nothing more that he wants to say on that topic. At that point, you express to him that you can understand why he might hold this position, and then venture a guess as to the feelings he has about it. You don't have to agree with his point; you just have to make it clear that you understand it.

Then it's your turn to be listened to, reflected, and understood.

If you're interested in learning more about imago therapy or experiencing it for yourself, you can read Dr. Hendrix's books, including *Getting the Love You Want: A Guide for Couples*. You can visit the imago therapy website (gettingtheloveyouwant.com) to find imago therapy couples' retreats and/or imago therapists in your area.

Psychodrama

Another therapeutic approach that I find valuable, but which may be harder to find, is psychodrama. It is usually done in a group setting, although psychodrama techniques can also be used in individual or couples' therapy.

Psychodrama is a therapeutic approach developed by Jacob Moreno that uses drama as a healing tool. A psychodrama has a director (the therapist), a protagonist (the person whose issue is being worked on), and supporting roles. The psychodrama consists of the enactment of one or more scenes, after which the drama is processed and participants can reflect upon what happened, how they are feeling, etc.

This is a very powerful approach that can be used to work through emotional issues, to practice new behaviors, and more.

If you would like to learn more about using acting to work through emotional issues, I recommend Stephanie Auerback Stolinsky's *Act It Out: 25 Expressive Ways to Heal from Childhood Abuse.*

Sandtray Therapy

Despite how it might sound, sandtray therapy is not just for kids. It is quite effective for adults, too. I have experienced sandtray therapy in a workshop and found it very emotionally powerful.

The office of a sandtray therapist is usually lined with shelves that are full of objects representing characters and symbols. The client chooses objects and characters and places them in a tray of sand. Afterwards, the therapist works with the client to interpret the meaning of the tray. Using the sandtray in therapy can help a client bypass defenses and go much deeper into her issues than she might otherwise be able to do.

To read one person's account of the experience of sandtray therapy, see Bob Livingstone's *Redemption of the Shattered: A Teenager's Healing Journey Through Sandtray Therapy.*

Acupuncture

Acupuncture can be used to address a variety of issues including anxiety, depression, fatigue, stress, physical pain, menstrual issues, and much more. Even if there is no specific issue that you are working on, acupuncture supports wellness by balancing the body's energy.

The basic idea is that there are channels of energy in the body called *meridians.* This energy, or life force, is called *qi*, which is pronounced "chee." If one or more of the meridians is blocked, or if the energy is out of balance, physical, psychological, and emotional problems result.

The acupuncture model with which I am familiar is the Chinese "Five Elements" approach, which is an aspect of Traditional Chinese Medicine (TCM). The five elements are air, fire, water, earth, and wood. Each element is associated with certain emotions and body organs, among other things; the meridians are named according to the organs with which they are associated (such as the Lung Meridian, the Heart Meridian, or the Kidney Meridian).

During your first visit with an acupuncturist she will take a medical history and ask you some questions about your reasons for coming. Before each treatment the acupuncturist will spend some time talking to you, then check your pulses (yes, pulses—there are six pulses in each wrist, not just one, that acupuncturists check). She will also, at some visits, check your tongue, which is an important diagnostic tool in Chinese medicine.

The main part of an acupuncture treatment consists of placing very thin, flexible needles in various points on your body. Your acupuncturist may check your pulses periodically during the treatment. You will probably notice some benefits even after the first treatment, but even more as treatment progresses.

A good introduction to traditional Chinese medicine, including acupuncture, is Alex Holland's *Voices of Qi: An Introductory Guide to Traditional Chinese Medicine.*

Putting It Into Action

1. Have you ever used or experienced any of the approaches in this chapter? If you have, are you still doing it/them? If one of them has been helpful to you but you're no longer using it, what might you do to restart it and stick with it?

Myrna: I've tried meditation many times, but never stuck with it for more than a week. It was hard to find time to fit it in, and I got frustrated because I couldn't keep thoughts from intruding.

I've also journaled at different times in my life and found it helpful when I did it. Just like meditation, I had trouble finding time to do it, especially after my twins were born!

I took yoga classes for a couple of years, sometimes three times a week, and loved it. Then my work schedule changed and, just like the other stuff, I let my yoga practice go by the wayside.

Now I'm trying again. I realize that I tend to get really enthusiastic about something at first, then have a hard time keeping up. So I'm trying to be more realistic about it.

Instead of writing in a journal, which never seems to happen, I'm recording my "entries" on my phone, which is easier for me. When I get a chance I listen to them, and sometimes even transcribe parts of them. Getting feelings out and allowing myself to be "heard" is helpful even if I don't do anything else with it.

I'm not trying meditation right now, but I have managed to clear time in my schedule for a yoga class. The class is on Sunday mornings when everyone's home, so I've asked my husband to watch the kids while I'm in class. I find the yoga to be meditative, and I manage to find a few minutes here and there during the week to at least do a sun salutation or two. It's definitely helping me to feel better physically, mentally, and emotionally.

2. What story are you living? If you woke up tomorrow morning and you were exactly who you wanted to be, how would you be different than you are now?

Nicole: I feel sad when I think about these questions. When I was a little kid I was confident and proud of myself. Then my parents got divorced and my mother remarried. My stepfather had kids, too, and he treated them much better than he treated me. He questioned me all the time and never praised me. My mom was afraid to make him angry, so she didn't do anything to protect or support me.

The older I got, the more withdrawn and self-critical I became. I took in all the messages I heard from my stepfather all of those years, and I started telling myself those things.

Now I don't believe I can do anything right. I only have a few friends, and I don't go out with them much. I don't tell them what I'm thinking and feeling because I'm afraid they'll think I'm a loser and they'll leave. I'm really lonely.

If I could be exactly who I wanted to be, I'd be the adult version (although a bit wiser and more realistic) of the confident little girl I was before my stepfather came into my life. I'd have more friends, I'd have the courage to date, and I would be trusting enough to share myself with others.

3. Which approaches from the last chapter and this one might help you to move towards that ideal life?

My stepfather died recently, which helps a bit because I'm at least no longer getting those negative messages from outside myself. Reading Chapter 10, I realized just how many ANTs come up for me all the time. So I'm going to use some of the CBT techniques from that chapter to start to challenge those thoughts.

I'm trying to find the thread of that person I was as a little girl so I can reclaim that story.

I'm interested in using the MBTI® to figure out why my childhood affected me the way it did and to better understand the real me.

4. Using one or more of the approaches you listed in the previous question, what will be your first step(s) towards change?

I've found a therapist who uses the MBTI®, so I'm going to go to her to take the MBTI® and to learn what that means for me. I'm hoping it will help me to be more self-accepting.

Meanwhile, I'm keeping track of the ANTs that come up for me and am working on challenging them so I can get a more realistic picture of myself.

Chapter 12

The Serenity Prayer

1. Do you spend a lot of time and energy trying to get other people to change?

2. Do you seem to gravitate towards situations in which it's difficult or impossible to achieve the goals you've set for yourself?

3. Do you get frustrated when other people don't do what you think they should do?

4. Have you ever been annoyed by the way a group or project was going, then quit without saying anything to anyone about it?

5. Have you ever had issues in a romantic relationship and assumed the problem was completely the other person's fault?

The Serenity Prayer[4] is a fabulous tool to use when you're trying to achieve balance, including the balance between taking care of self and others. Whether or not you are a member of a 12-step group such as Alcoholics Anonymous, Al-Anon, or Adult Children of Alcoholics, you can benefit from this staple of 12-step philosophy.

> *God grant me the serenity*
> *to accept the things I cannot change;*
> *courage to change the things I can;*
> *and wisdom to know the difference.*

These four simple lines provide a valuable guide to life, but they are not at all easy to apply. How do you figure out what you can change and what you can't change? How can that help you to find the balance you're looking for?

God, grant me the serenity to accept the things I cannot change...

Acceptance and powerlessness are important themes in 12-step groups. An alcoholic, to recover, has to accept that she is an alcoholic and that she is powerless over alcohol. So if you're not an alcoholic, what does this have to do with you? A lot. You, too, have things over which you are powerless and which can make your life miserable if you insist on trying to control them.

Letting go of the need to control things and people is extremely difficult for those who grew up in alcoholic or otherwise dysfunctional households. If you answered yes to questions 1, 2, and/or 3, you probably have trouble accepting the things you cannot change.

---

[4] One of the biggest problems many people have with 12-step programs is the reference to a "Higher Power," which is most often interpreted as the Christian idea of God. I do not believe it is necessary to believe in God to benefit from 12-step programs, and it is certainly not necessary to believe in God to make good use of the Serenity Prayer. Feel free to call it the "Serenity Poem" or whatever you're comfortable with, and to take the word "God" out if you wish.

There are certain things you can't control or change no matter how much you want to. Of course there are global issues that are not easily influenced by one person. But you can't force another person to change, either, which can be hard to accept. If others realize that you're trying to get them to change they're likely to dig in their heels and resist you. Then you'll probably end up with the opposite of the result you were going for.

Polly has a workaholic spouse, Allan. In the past Polly made frequent comments about wanting/needing Allan to come home sooner, spend more time with the family, etc. Unfortunately Allan saw this as nagging, which often made him dread coming home in the evenings. Therefore, Polly's comments had the opposite effect of the one intended. This became a vicious cycle, with more comments from Polly leading to longer work hours for Allan, which led to more comments, and on and on.

Is this a problem you deal with too? If so, don't throw up your hands and give up; remember that there is more to the Serenity Prayer than acceptance.

…The courage to change the things I can…

While there are many things you can't change, there are also many things that you *can* change. Yes answers to questions 4 and 5 suggest that you may get so caught up in the things you can't change that you forget to try to change the things you can.

The main things you *can* change are your own thoughts, words, and actions. For example: Polly *can't* force Allan to cut back his work hours. She can, however, change the way she talks about it. It's easy for her to go to the door shouting, "Where have you been? I've been waiting for you ever since I got home from work three hours ago! You're NEVER home when you say you will be! I'm always worried sick, wondering if you got into a car accident or something! And I'll bet you brought work home, too!"

It's not so easy for Polly to step back a bit, calm herself down, and explain her position using non-hostile "I" statements. "I" statements take ownership of your feelings. It is hard for someone to refute a statement about what you're feeling.

For instance, Polly might say something like, "So, did the management meeting go overtime again? I know you hate that! Could you give me a call next time that happens so I know you won't be home at the usual time? I got frustrated and worried when you didn't come home because I didn't know where you were."

Shouting at Allan about what he's done wrong is unlikely to work because he's likely to feel like he has to defend himself, which may lead to him attacking Polly. And, again, it's not likely to make him change.

If Polly uses the "I" statements approach consistently, and for a long enough time, Allan may start to keep a more regular schedule or at least be more considerate of her position. Ironically, often the best way to get people to change is to accept them as they are!

But remember what we discussed in earlier chapters. You know that even when you're fully committed to making a positive change in your life it takes time for that change to stick. So it makes sense that it might take even longer than that for your changed behaviors to lead to someone else changing his behavior.

If you're patient and hang in there it's likely that change will come. And if it doesn't, it may be time to reevaluate the relationship; maybe it's time to think about whether it needs to change significantly or even end.

…And the wisdom to know the difference.

I think this is the hardest part of the Serenity Prayer, but it is also the most important. It's the part of the prayer that offers the balance we've talked about throughout the book. It invites you to try to find the balance between taking responsibility for things and letting go of things for which you cannot, or should not, hold yourself responsible.

How do you know when you can (or should) try to change something? And, having decided that it's a good idea to try to make a change, how do you go about it?

In any given situation it's likely that there are aspects you can change and ones you can't. In that case it helps to take a step back and break things down. OK, you're frustrated about not being able to change a person or situation. Is there something you *can* change about it?

Further Examples

Here are some examples of ways some people have used the principles behind the Serenity Prayer to guide them through difficult situations.

Samantha's husband, Rick, was what some people call a "functional alcoholic." He had a good job and didn't usually let his drinking interfere with his work, although there were times that Samantha called Rick's boss and said that he had the flu and wouldn't be in that day when he was actually hung over. She was pretty sure Rick's boss knew what was going on, but Rick was a good worker so his boss didn't say anything about his drinking.

There were occasionally some iffy situations when Rick took a client out to lunch or dinner, had too much to drink, and embarrassed himself, so his boss learned that it was best for someone other than Rick to do the wining and dining.

Rick was the family's main source of income. Samantha sold real estate on commission, so she never knew what her paycheck would be. Unfortunately, when Rick drank on weekends he also gambled. So he often lost a large chunk of his paycheck as soon as he got it; Samantha did her best to run the household on what was left.

To make matters more difficult, Samantha was afraid to let Rick drive their twelve-year-old son, Blake, anywhere because she didn't know if Rick would be drunk and have an accident. So she was the only one taking their son to sports practices and band rehearsals.

Samantha tried, over and over again, to make Rick stop drinking. She tried reasoning with him. She tried nagging him. She tried threatening to leave and take their son with her. She found all of Rick's secret stashes of alcohol and poured them down the sink. But no matter what she did he continued to get drunk and risk his family's future.

One night Samantha woke up at 3:00 in the morning, having just had a nightmare that Rick had been drunk and had run the car into the front of their house, very nearly injuring himself, Samantha, and Blake.

She realized that she was recreating the situation she had known growing up; her mother tried unsuccessfully to get her father to stop drinking and continually told the kids and their father that she couldn't take it any more and she was leaving. But her mother didn't have a job and didn't know how to support her kids, so she never left. Samantha had been using the excuse that her unstable income prevented her from leaving, but she realized that this was not a good enough reason to just let things continue the way they were.

Samantha started attending Al-Anon meetings and learned how her family history had affected her. She learned how to "detach with love" and to let Rick be responsible for himself, which included facing the consequences of his actions. She decided what she could and could not tolerate from him, and she began to make plans to leave him if necessary.

She took some courses so that she could advance her real estate career and she began to work full time. With her increased income she knew that she would be able to support herself and Blake.

She and Blake did an intervention with Rick. They told him that they loved him and that they wanted to have the family life they had before Rick started drinking heavily. They talked about the things they used to do together, like taking weekend bike rides and hiking in the mountains. They talked about the things they missed about spending time with him when he was sober. They asked him to stop drinking and to start going to Alcoholics Anonymous meetings. They acknowledged that it was his choice whether to do these things, but they told him that if he did not do them they would leave.

Rick said that he would change, and he did stop drinking and attended AA meetings for a couple of months. But when he lost a major account at work the stress led him back to drinking. Samantha and Blake gave him another chance, and he straightened up again for a few months.

This pattern continued for two years, after which Samantha decided that she was done. She filed separation papers and moved out, taking Blake with her. She was awarded full custody in the divorce but wanted Blake to have his father, so she let him visit Rick with the condition that Rick not be drinking before or during the time when Blake was with him.

When Samantha started attending Al-Anon meetings she also began to apply the Serenity Prayer to her life. She identified what she could change (herself, her thoughts, and her actions) and realized that she could not force her husband to change. She learned in the meetings that spouses of alcoholics are often addicted to being married to an alcoholic. She began to look more closely at her own issues and stopped focusing on making her husband deal with his.

But even though she no longer tried to change her husband's drinking, she did set some boundaries. She let him know what she would and would not accept, and she told him the consequences if he crossed those boundaries.

Because she loved Rick and wanted her son to grow up with both a mother and a father she did relax the boundaries somewhat, staying several times when he started drinking again. But she did what she needed to do to earn enough money to support herself and Blake so that she could leave if she decided it was the best choice. She made sure that their living situation was something that she could change, and then she made that change. She continued to try to treat Rick fairly, but still maintained boundaries regarding his behavior around Blake.

Francine and her three siblings lived within 15 miles of their aging father, Burt. Burt wanted to continue to live in his home, not go to a nursing home. He was no longer able to drive, though, and he had a lot of doctor's appointments to treat his rheumatoid arthritis, his heart condition, and other health issues. There were times that he was able to make use of a free shuttle service, but the hours were limited and he often forgot to call ahead so the shuttle would come pick him up.

Francine and her siblings all agreed that they wanted to honor their father's wish to stay in his home. They all agreed to pitch in and help take care of what needed to be done around his house and for him.

This went well for a month or so, but then Francine started noticing that the others weren't doing the things they'd agreed to do. Her younger brother Mike had said he would mow the lawn once a week, but it was starting to look like a jungle.

Her younger sister Georgia, who was self-employed and worked from home, said that she would take Burt to some of his doctor's appointments, but then several times in a row she called at the last minute and said she was tied up so she couldn't take him.

Francine's youngest brother, Devon, who was an accountant, said he would take over the management of Burt's finances, but he rarely seemed to find the time to go to Burt's house and do it, and bills were piling up.

Francine found herself doing (or asking her husband to do) the things that the others had promised to take care of. She began to feel like the others were taking advantage of her overdeveloped sense of responsibility. And her husband and kids were beginning to resent all the time she was away from home because she was taking care of Burt.

She was also worried that all the time she was away from work taking her father to appointments might jeopardize her job.

This was a familiar pattern for the family. Francine, the family hero, was usually the one to make sure things got done and to clean up the family's messes. She was responsible for herself, her siblings, and often her parents, as well. She had always accepted this as her role, but now that she was in her early 40s it occurred to her that she needed to take care of herself, too, and not take responsibility for people who could be responsible for themselves.

The "don't take responsibility for others, let them face the consequences of their actions" approach, though, was complicated in this situation. Their father genuinely needed help, and she didn't want him to suffer just because her siblings were being irresponsible. How could she take care of herself and yet make sure that the innocent party (Burt) wasn't harmed?

Francine arranged for her siblings (who all said they were too busy to take the time to get together) to "meet" her on a conference call to discuss the situation. She thanked them for agreeing that Burt should be allowed to stay in his house, and she thanked them for volunteering to help. She then said that it seemed life had gotten in the way of their being able to help, though, because Burt wasn't getting all the help he needed. Did they have any ideas about what to do?

At first all of her siblings defended themselves, explaining their reasons for not being able to follow through on their promises. Francine listened to all of their protests, then told them that her goal was not to blame or to criticize, but to find workable solutions to the problems. Eventually they were able to agree on some new approaches.

All four of them agreed to chip in some money each month to hire someone to mow the lawn in the summer and shovel snow in the winter, as well as to have Burt's house cleaned every two weeks.

Francine told Georgia that she would call her at the beginning of each week to check in and see if Georgia was available to take Burt to his appointments. Georgia, in turn, agreed to plan better and call the shuttle to pick Burt up if she knew she wasn't going to be available to take Burt. Only as a last resort would she ask Francine to take on that responsibility.

Devon agreed to buy a financial software program to manage Burt's finances. He also agreed to sit down with Francine to show her how to use the program and to set up automatic payments where possible, thus greatly cutting down on the time required to do the finances. He said that he would meet with Francine once a quarter to make sure that everything was going smoothly.

Francine agreed to coordinate all of these things and deal with and/ or delegate other daily tasks that needed to be done for Burt. She wasn't completely happy with this solution, because she was still putting in much more time than Devon, Georgia, and Mike. She managed to make up for some of this by not volunteering for so many jobs at church and her kids' school, and by deciding that this year would be her last year of chairing the school PTA.

She found that setting firmer boundaries and taking a stand with her siblings began to create subtle changes in the way they treated her. It wasn't night and day, but she noticed that the three of them didn't lean on her quite as much as they had in the past.

At times when she felt resentful of the extra time she devoted to her father's care, she reminded herself that at least this time she had made a conscious choice based upon her feelings for her father; she had not just fallen into the caregiver role by default.

Ursula grew up in a poor family and did not have the opportunity to participate in sports or other extracurricular activities. She was jealous of her friends whose parents bought them anything they wanted, including nice clothes and cars. Her father worked long hours to make ends meet and her mother was an alcoholic who was drunk much of the time, so Ursula didn't get much attention from them. She didn't have any siblings and few friends, so she was often lonely.

Ursula decided early in life that she would be different from her parents. When she was old enough she got a job so she could buy the things she wanted, including clothes and a car. She always worked hard and never complained about it. She got student loans and worked during college so she could pay for it. She rarely attended campus parties and limited her drinking so she wouldn't follow in her mother's footsteps.

Ursula met Zachary, whose family background was similar to hers, in college. Ursula had an internship during her senior year that turned into a full-time job after graduation. Zachary's supervisor at the part-time job he had during college recommended him to a friend who owned a software company, so he, too, was employed full-time after graduation.

Ursula and Zachary got married soon after they graduated. Five years later they had a son, Carter. Both were making good money, and they were determined that Carter would have the childhood they had never had. So they signed him up for sports and got him music lessons. They helped him with his homework. Zachary coached Carter's soccer team and Ursula, who had taken some piano lessons in college, helped him practice music.

Any time Carter expressed an interest in trying something new Ursula and Zachary found a way to help him do it. They spent a lot of time driving him from one activity to another. When he turned 16 they bought him a car. They saved money from the time he was born so that they could pay for his college education without him having to work; Ursula, in particular, believed it was important for him to be able to concentrate on his studies without outside distractions. Sometimes Zachary expressed concerns about the possibility that they were spoiling Carter, but they continued to do what they had been doing.

Carter dated a lot in college but never had a long-term relationship. He also partied a lot, and almost got kicked out of school more than once. He had a hard time deciding on a college major, so he tried several different ones, including music, education, and marine biology, before graduating; this extended his time in college to six years. He eventually got a degree in business administration.

Ursula and Zachary remembered the excitement they had felt when they graduated and started new lives on their own. They were a bit puzzled when Carter didn't really seem to look hard for a job during his last year of college.

He came back to live with them after he graduated; they decided that he didn't have a job yet because the economy was difficult and there were not many jobs to be had. They joked that they had been too nice to him when he was growing up, so he had less incentive to find a place of his own right after college. Secretly, though, each worried about what Carter was going to do.

Carter said that he was applying for jobs, but he still didn't seem very committed to it. They asked him to do household chores in lieu of paying rent, but he didn't do them. It seemed he had no incentive to do what they asked him to do; after all, he was living in their house for free and doing anything he wanted! Two years later nothing had changed, and Ursula and Zachary were beside themselves trying to figure out what to do.

Ursula and Zachary realized that while their childhoods had not been good, there had been value in them, too, because they had learned to work hard for what they needed and wanted. They realized they had gone too far in the opposite direction with Carter by doing everything for him. Based upon his childhood experience he had developed a sense of entitlement and believed that the things he wanted should just be given to him without any effort on his part.

Ursula and Zachary had threatened many times to kick Carter out of the house during the two years he had been living with them after college, but they had never done it. Ursula worried that, with a history of alcoholism on both sides of his family, Carter might turn to alcohol if he felt like he couldn't make it on his own. And Ursula felt responsible for the way Carter had turned out because of the way they had raised him.

Ursula and Zachary also realized, though, that they weren't doing Carter any favors by continuing to allow him to live the life he was living. Carter needed to learn to take care of himself. The question was, what could they do about that?

They knew that if they again threatened to kick Carter out, he wouldn't believe them because of the times they had not followed through in the past. So they decided to make things official. They drew up an agreement that Carter would have to sign if he were to continue to live with them. If he refused to sign it, they would give him notice that he had 30 days to move out or they were going to call the police.

The agreement specified that he needed to really commit to finding a job, filling out at least five serious applications every week and having at least one interview per month. Within six months he would be required to begin paying rent, and within a year after that he would have to move out. They specified the penalties for violating any of the terms of the agreement, starting with being banned from the house for certain periods of time, and, finally, giving him 30 days notice if he was still in violation of the agreement.

Carter agreed to sign the document, and Ursula and Zachary had it notarized to make it completely official. Carter still didn't really believe they'd enforce it, though, so he continued to make no effort whatsoever to get a job. They kicked him out of the house for a week, then allowed him to come back and try again. This happened twice before he finally got serious about applying for jobs.

At the six-month mark he still didn't have a job; he again challenged them by refusing to pay rent, and was given consequences as he had before. He finally got serious, got a job, and paid rent as agreed. One year after that he got his own apartment and moved out.

Carter was angry with Ursula and Zachary for doing what they did. He refused to speak to them or see them after he moved out. Ursula and Zachary both worried about him and wondered where he was and what he was doing. It was not until ten years later that he contacted them, having finally realized that they had done what was best for him as well as for them.

Ursula and Zachary did well at setting boundaries and sticking to them. The initial results were not what they had hoped for, and they worried a lot about Carter when he wasn't communicating with them. There were times that they questioned their actions and wished that they hadn't done what they did.

But when they really thought about it they knew that they had done the right thing. Carter did need to learn to be responsible for himself, and he wasn't going to do it on his own. They couldn't make him become responsible, but they could refuse to enable his unhealthy behaviors.

They knew it had been a risk to make him leave the house, and they had no way of knowing if he would ever speak to them again. They were greatly relieved and very grateful when he got back in touch with them because they knew that it could have gone much differently.

Doreen was a chemist who worked for a pharmaceutical company. She loved her work, and she was happy to be contributing to the development of medications that could help people to live longer and more comfortably. She did not, however, enjoy the high-pressure environment. The company she worked for wanted quick results because they were trying to develop as many new medications as they could to boost business when their existing medications went out of patent.

To this end, the company had several chemists working on the same project at the same time, with the hope that faster results would be obtained. A recent statistical analysis suggested that there was a limit to the added benefits obtained from adding new chemists to a project, though, so they were considering downsizing Doreen's division.

Doreen was both a hard worker and a perfectionist, so she worked overtime most days to get her assigned work done to her satisfaction. Her coworkers, on the other hand, were not so dedicated. They didn't do any overtime and sometimes, if they thought they could get away with it, left early.

Because everyone in the group was working on the same project it was not always obvious who had done what part of the work. So Doreen's coworkers, who were much more likely to speak up than Doreen was, usually got more credit than they deserved for the work that was done.

Doreen knew that her job might be on the line, so she started to work even harder than she had before; meanwhile, her coworkers worked less and less. She felt increasingly pressured to get things done to make up for her coworkers' laziness.

Finally Doreen realized that something had to change. She was getting increasingly exhausted by the workload but was also finding it harder and harder to sleep because of work-related anxiety. What could she do to keep her job and still lower her stress level? How could she reduce her workload to a reasonable level and get the appropriate recognition for her efforts?

The first conclusion she came to was that she had to speak up for herself more. Her coworkers, who appeared to think very highly of themselves, did not hesitate to speak up in meetings and take credit for things that Doreen had done.

Doreen was not inclined towards self-promotion, and she didn't want to be a "tattle tale" and accuse her team members of lying about their work. That might backfire on her, too, if her supervisor thought she was the one who was lying to get ahead.

Still, she resolved to speak up more in meetings. She often had ideas to contribute, but second-guessed herself enough that someone else often made the point before she did. So she decided to prepare for meetings by looking at the agenda ahead of time and writing down some points she wanted to make. That way she might be less hesitant to speak up.

She knew that, for all of their talk, her coworkers had less experience and knowledge than she did, so she decided to create opportunities, where possible, to steer meeting discussions towards relevant topics that she understood better than the rest did. She was determined to make sure that her expertise was recognized.

As Doreen had expected, this was easier said than done. Despite her extra preparation for meetings she was still nervous about speaking up, so the first couple of meetings went much as all the others had; she hesitated just long enough before speaking that someone else got to the point before her.

After a while, though, she managed to find the courage to speak up more. She started with relatively safe comments that were unlikely to be challenged. She became increasingly comfortable with this over time and began to speak even more.

Then she began proposing new ideas and new approaches to projects. The first time she did this someone else challenged her and she immediately backed down. The next time she was more prepared for possible opposition, so she defended herself for a little while before giving up.

She started to notice that many of the ideas she'd proposed that were rejected later ended up being the ideas the group went with. This gave her more courage to stick to her guns and not back down when challenged.

She hit another setback, though, when one of her ideas was accepted by the group but later turned out not to work. Being the perfectionist that she was, this really hit her hard. But she stepped back and looked at the results of that failed suggestion. Yes, it caused her team to get behind on the project, but that wasn't the first time that had ever happened, and the project was still done on time. And her supervisor did not, as she feared, reprimand her for making a mistake.

She suddenly remembered her high school orchestra director's demand that the orchestra members "make their mistakes with authority." It was better to have the courage to put herself forward and risk being wrong than it was to meekly hold back and not contribute potentially valuable ideas in meetings.

After a while Doreen became much more comfortable speaking up in meetings. She began to get more recognition from her supervisor for her work. Her expertise spoke for itself, so she didn't have to "tattle" on the other team members; it became clear that she was a strong contributor to the work being done. This led to less anxiety, better sleep, and fewer overtime hours for Doreen as she realized that her job was not teetering on the brink.

Doreen used the principles of the Serenity Prayer when she changed her approach at work. She realized that she couldn't change her coworkers' work habits. She knew that, no matter what she did, they would continue their pattern of self-promotion. Rather than retreating and accepting that she might lose her job, she made positive changes in her behaviors at work. She didn't do anything that felt like it was wrong, as "tattling" would have done. And in the end, she became a more valuable employee even though she was putting in fewer work hours than she had before.

None of the people in these examples knew how things were going to turn out. They couldn't control the future or other people, so they took risks when they changed their behaviors. The results were not always what they wanted; as happens in many areas of life, some things went better than others. But even when things didn't go as they'd hoped, they believed that their decisions were sound, no matter what the results.

A Final Note about the Serenity Prayer

Changing the way you look at things is often a good approach, but if you find yourself letting someone take advantage of you, it's time to consider other changes. As discussed earlier, if your spouse is a workaholic, nagging isn't likely to make him change. Does this mean, though, that you should just accept what you consider to be unacceptable behavior? No, you shouldn't.

Taking responsibility for your own actions and feelings is a good start. Try to open a dialogue about the issue and see if there's some sort of common ground that can be found. One way or another, though, it's important to decide what you can and cannot accept, then choose words and actions that support your decision. It's also important to decide what is and is not your responsibility; how do you know when to let go of something or someone?

The Serenity Prayer, while offering wisdom and encouragement, is another tool for your toolbox, not a magic wand that will instantly fix everything. If you use it on a regular basis, though, it will help you to find more of the life balance that has been the focus of this book.

Putting It Into Action

1. Choose a situation in your life that is not working well. What are the issues as you see them?

Olivia: I have been having a lot of trouble with my alcoholic mother. She's what is called a "dry drunk," which means that even though she hasn't had any alcohol for three years, she hasn't changed any of her other alcoholic behaviors. She goes to AA meetings but says she doesn't get much out of them. The only other thing that has changed is that she's become more self-righteous because she thinks she's in recovery.

When I was growing up my mother was verbally abusive to me. She told me at least once a day that I was thoughtless and inconsiderate. Any time I did something she didn't like she made me write down exactly what I had done wrong and apologize for it. I had to read what I'd written to my father, who then beat me.

Often, though, my "crime" was just an innocent mistake, like knocking over my glass of milk. Sometimes I hadn't even done what my mother said I had. That didn't matter, though; I still had to give a written apology. I hated having to apologize (and be beaten) for things I didn't even do!

My mother criticized everything I did; in her eyes, I could never do anything right. And any time I found something I liked and was good at (playing the cello and running track, for instance) she told me it was a waste of time and made me quit.

Meanwhile, she signed me up for volleyball and softball, neither of which I could play very well. I hated every minute of those practices and games.

Anyway, back to the present...

After my father died my mother moved into a house across the street from mine. One day she sat in her front yard and watched my kids playing. Then she called me and yelled at me for letting them play outside unsupervised, even though I was in the kitchen and could clearly see them out the window.

After she did this a couple of times I got tired of it, so I took the kids into the back yard to play. My mother then called and told me I shouldn't let the kids play too close to the woods. They might get ticks or be snatched by dangerous men lurking among the trees.

There were many more things she criticized about my parenting, too many to list.

She also talked a lot about everything she'd done for me, calling me ungrateful. She told me that she had only the best motives for the things she did and that I was the problem. She said I was making assumptions about what she was thinking and that she was thinking no such thing. All she wanted was to have a good relationship with her daughter, and she couldn't understand why I didn't like her and said bad things about her.

It was bad enough that she said those things to me, but she often did it in front of my kids, and I was afraid that they weren't going to respect or listen to me because of it. It was so tempting to bad mouth her to them!

When she moved into my neighborhood she started going to a nearby church. She talked a lot about how much she liked the church, the pastor, and the congregation.

Then all of a sudden she started coming to my church and made friends with a lot of the women there. She talked to them a lot about my kids. When I asked her about it, she said she was just making conversation. From what I heard, though, it sounded to me like she was implying that I was a bad mother.

I wondered why she had suddenly switched churches. She told me it was because she wanted to have more quality time with me, but given the past, I assumed she was looking for more ways to criticize me.

Every Saturday night my family and I go to her house for dinner. Again, she presents it as a good thing because we're spending more time together. She makes sure we know how much work she puts into the meals, but she won't let us bring any food or do the dishes.

We hate having to go over there every Saturday, especially since there are other things we'd like to do with our Saturday evenings. My husband gets mad at me because I don't stand up to my mom and tell her we're not going over there any more, or at least that we're not going every week.

2. What aspects of the situation can you not change?

I can't make my mother behave differently, or to see that she's not really in recovery. As they say in 12-step programs, it's not my job to "take her inventory."

I can't make her change the way she thinks about me, including her assumptions about what I'm thinking.

I can't change my childhood, and I can't change the things we've done and said to each other. I can't make her move so that she doesn't live across the street any more.

While I could theoretically try to keep her from seeing my kids, I still want them to know their grandmother, so I won't do that. That means that I can't control how she acts or speaks around them.

I can't keep her from going to our church.

3. What aspects of the situation can you change?

I can set boundaries with my mother.

Even though I can't force her to do so, I can ask her to return to her other church. Then I can work on dealing with whatever decision she makes. If she chooses not to honor my request I can find a way to accept that.

I can be careful about what I say to my kids about her. No, she doesn't act appropriately towards me, but it doesn't help to pull my kids into the conflict. I can do my best to teach them a different way of being, despite her influence.

I can speak up for myself and for my family. I can limit conversations with her and refuse to engage in all the old battles we've always fought.

I can work on letting go of believing some of the things that she has always told me, including that I'm ungrateful.

I can listen to her suggestions about my parenting and think about them objectively. There are things I can learn from her, but that doesn't mean I have to take in everything she says.

I can tell her that we will no longer be coming over to her house for Saturday dinner every week. We will go sometimes, but we will choose the times that work for us. I can talk myself through dealing with her responses and her attempts to make me feel guilty.

I think the hardest thing, but one of the most important, that I can change is the assumptions I make about her and what she's thinking. It's possible that she really is trying to be a better mother to me. I've been unwilling to consider that possibility because I'm used to the adversarial relationship we've always had. Just as she blames me for everything that's wrong in our relationship, I tend to do the same to her.

I'm now starting to look at my own thinking and behaviors and trying to take what she says at face value, while still not naïvely believing everything she tells me.

4. How are things different now that you have begun to accept what you can't change and to change what you can?

The changes are empowering. I'm getting better and better at choosing my reactions to my mother. I'm also getting better at accepting her as she is, which is improving our relationship.

I'm really happy that I'm showing my kids a better way of dealing with people than the ones I learned from my parents. I'm showing them that they can respect both themselves and other people.

It is definitely difficult to do these things, but it's getting a bit easier the more I do it.

Conclusion

Take a moment to give yourself credit for all the hard work you've done as you've gone through this book.

Think about the realizations you've had about yourself. How do you see yourself differently than you did before? How are you treating yourself differently? How have your relationships changed?

Finding balance in your life is not easy, but it is worth it. By reading this book and taking its message to heart, you've taken a very important step towards achieving and maintaining that balance.

I hope that you will find people who will support you in your new, healthier approach to life. One place to find support is with my online community at www.FindYourMeTime.socialgo.com. The others in the community will understand what you're trying to do and will encourage you and give you feedback and accountability.

And who knows, you may inspire others to look for this type of balance in their own lives. That would be a great way to help others by helping yourself.

Appendix

Emotional Freedom Technique (EFT) Sequence

This version of the EFT sequence is a shortened version of the original that was developed by Gary Craig; it also adds the tapping point on the top of the head.

Before you begin the EFT sequence think of the most detailed description of the problem that you can, preferably a specific incident, and notice your feelings about it. If you notice multiple feelings, work on one at a time. Once you've identified a feeling you want to work on, mentally rate the intensity of that feeling on a scale of zero to ten, with zero meaning you don't notice the feeling at all and ten meaning that you're experiencing the most extreme version of that feeling you've ever had.

Step One: The Setup

Repeat an affirmation three times while you tap the "Karate Chop" point (this will be explained shortly).

The Affirmation

Even though I have this _____, I love and accept myself.

(As an alternative, you can make up a second half of the affirmation that relates to the first half.)

The blank is filled in with a brief description of the problem you want to address. Here are some examples.

**Even though I have this fear of elevators, I love and accept myself.* OR Even though I have this fear of elevators, I believe I can ride in this elevator.*

**Even though I have this digestive problem, I love and accept myself.* OR Even though I have this digestive problem, I believe that I can heal.*

**Even though I have this sadness about my childhood, I love and accept myself.* OR Even though I have this sadness about my childhood, I am willing to let myself have my feelings.*

**Even though I have this craving for cigarettes, I love and accept myself.* OR Even though I have this craving for cigarettes, I believe that I can resist it.*

**Even though I have this anxiety, I love and accept myself.* OR Even though I have this anxiety, I believe that it is possible for me to feel better.*

The Karate Chop Point

The Karate Chop point (abbreviated **KC**) is located at the center of the fleshy part of the outside of your hand (either hand) between the top of the wrist and the base of the little finger, the part of your hand you would use to deliver a karate chop. You vigorously *tap* the Karate Chop point with the fingertips of the index finger and middle finger of the other hand.

Step Two: The Sequence
The Reminder Phrase

The Reminder Phrase is a word or short phrase that describes the problem and that you repeat out loud each time you tap one of the points in The Sequence. In this way you continually "remind" your system about the problem you are working on.

The best Reminder Phrase to use is usually related to what you choose for the affirmation you use in The Setup. For example, if you were working on a fear of elevators, The Setup affirmation would go like this....

Even though I have this fear of elevators, I love and accept myself.

Within this affirmation, it makes sense to use the words "fear of elevators" as the Reminder Phrase.

Or as an alternative, you can use multiple statements that relate to the problem while tapping the points. For instance, you might say "fear of elevators" while tapping on the first point, then "fears about being trapped" while tapping on the second point, then "remembering how scared I was when I got stuck in an elevator at age 4" while tapping on the third point, etc.

Repeat the "Reminder Phrase" while you tap each of the following points (in order) 5-7 times.

At the beginning of the eyebrow, just above and to one side of the nose. This point is abbreviated **EB for beginning of the **EyeBrow**.

On the bone bordering the outside corner of the eye. This point is abbreviated **SE for **S**ide of the **E**ye.

On the bone under an eye about 1 inch below your pupil. This point is abbreviated **UE for **U**nder the **E**ye.

On the small area between the bottom of your nose and the top of your upper lip. This point is abbreviated **UN for **U**nder the **N**ose.

Midway between the point of your chin and the bottom of your lower lip. This point is abbreviated **Ch for **Ch**in.

The junction where the sternum (breastbone), collarbone and the first rib meet. To find it, first put your first finger on the U-shaped notch at the top of the breastbone (about where a man would knot his tie). From the bottom of the U, move your finger down toward the navel 1 inch and then go to the left (or right) 1 inch. This point is abbreviated **CB for **C**ollar**B**one.

On the side of the body, at a point even with the nipple (for men) or in the middle of the bra strap (for women). It is about 4 inches below the armpit. This point is abbreviated **UA for **U**nder the **A**rm.

On the outside edge of your thumb at a point even with the base of the thumbnail. This point is abbreviated **T for **T**humb.

On the side of your index finger (the side facing your thumb) at a point even with the base of the fingernail. This point is abbreviated **IF for **I**ndex **F**inger.

On the side of your middle finger (the side closest to your thumb) at a point even with the base of the fingernail. This point is abbreviated **MF for **M**iddle **F**inger.

On the inside of your little finger (the side closest to your thumb) at a point even with the base of the fingernail. This point is abbreviated **LF for **L**ittle **F**inger.

The last point is the karate chop point, which has been previously described under the section on The Setup. It is located in the middle of the fleshy part on the outside of the hand between the top of the wrist bone and the base of the little finger. It is abbreviated **KC for **K**arate **C**hop.

** On the top of the head. This is abbreviated **TH** for **T**op of **H**ead.

The abbreviations for these points are listed below in the same order as given above.

EB = Beginning of the EyeBrow

SE = Side of the Eye

UE = Under the Eye

UN = Under the Nose

Ch = Chin

CB = Beginning of the CollarBone

UA = Under the Arm

T = Thumb

IF = Index Finger

MF = Middle Finger

LF = Little Finger

KC = Karate Chop

TH = Top of Head

When you've gone through the sequence, take a moment to check in with yourself. Are you still experiencing the feeling you were trying to address? If so, use the zero to ten scale to rate the intensity of the feeling. If it's low enough that you're satisfied and if there are no other emotions you need to address regarding the situation, you're done. If the intensity of the feeling is higher than you'd like and/or there are other feelings to be addressed, repeat the sequence. You can repeat it as many times as necessary.

If you have done the sequence multiple times and have not achieved your goal, you may need to be more specific in stating the problem, or there may be another feeling or incident that needs to be addressed.

Resources

Codependency

Beattie, Melody. *Beyond Codependency: And Getting Better All the Time.* Center City, MN: Hazelden Foundation, 1989.

_____. *Codependent No More: How to Stop Controlling Others and Start Caring for Yourself.* Center City, MN: Hazelden Foundation, 1992.

_____ . *Codependents' Guide to the Twelve Steps: How to Find the Right Program for You and Apply Each of the Twelve Steps to Your Own Issues.* New York: Fireside, 1992.

_____ . *The Language of Letting Go.* Center City, MN: Hazelden Foundation, 1990.

Mellody, Pia, Andrea Wells Miller, and J. Keith Miller. *Facing Codependence: What It Is, Where It Comes From, How It Sabotages Our Lives.* New York: HarperCollins Publishers, 1989.

Pfister, Marcus. *The Rainbow Fish.* New York: NorthSouth Books, Inc., 2001.

Silverstein, Shel. *The Giving Tree.* New York: HarperCollins, 2004.

_____ . *The Missing Piece.* New York: HarperCollins, 1976.

_____ . *The Missing Piece Meets the Big O.* New York: HarperCollins, 1981.

Relationships

Dayton, Tian, Ph.D. *Emotional Sobriety: From Relationship Trauma to Resilience and Balance.* Deerfield Beach, FL: Health Communications, Inc., 2007.

Iverson, Rachel. *Don't Help a Man Be a Man: How to Avoid 12 Dating Time Bombs.* Venice, CA: Rebel Girl Publishing, 2005.

McBride, Karyl, Ph.D. *Will I Ever Be Good Enough?: Healing the Daughters of Narcissistic Mothers.* New York: Free Press, 2008.

Payson, Eleanor D., M.S.W. *The Wizard of Oz and Other Narcissists: Coping with the One-Way Relationship in Work, Love, and Family.* Royal Oak, MI: Julian Day Publications, 2002.

Adult Children

Ackerman, Robert J. *Perfect Daughters: Adult Daughters of Alcoholics, rev. ed.* Deerfield Beach, FL: Health Communications, Inc., 2002.

Black, Claudia, PhD. *It Will Never Happen to Me: Growing Up With Addiction As Youngsters, Adolescents, Adults, 2nd ed.* Center City, MN: Hazelden Foundation, 2002.

Farmer, Steven, M.A., M.F.C.C. *Adult Children of Abusive Parents: A Healing Program for Those Who Have Been Physically, Sexually, or Emotionally Abused.* New York: Ballantine Books, 1990.

Kritsberg, Wayne. *The Adult Children of Alcoholics Syndrome: A Step-By-Step Guide to Discovery and Recovery.* New York: Bantam Books, 1988.

Oliver-Diaz, Philip and Patricia A. O'Gorman. *12 Steps to Self-Parenting for Adult Children.* Deerfield Beach, FL: Health Communications, Inc., 1988.

Woititz, Janet Geringer. *Adult Children of Alcoholics, Expanded Edition.* Deerfield Beach, FL: Health Communications, Inc., 1990.

Twelve-Step Programs

Adult Children of Alcoholics (ACoA or ACA)

www.adultchildren.org

Adult Children: Alcoholic/Dysfunctional Families. Torrance, CA: Adult Children of Alcoholics World Service Organization, 2006.

Alcoholics Anonymous (AA)

www.aa.org

Alcoholics Anonymous: The Big Book, 4th edition. New York: Alcoholics Anonymous World Services, Inc., 2001.

Twelve Steps and Twelve Traditions. New York: Alcoholics Anonymous World Services, Inc., 2002.

Al-Anon/Alateen

(for people who have been affected by someone's problem drinking)

www.alanon-alateen.org

How Al-Anon Works for Families and Friends of Alcoholics. Al-Anon Family Groups, 2008.

Chemically Dependent Anonymous (CDA)

www.cdaweb.org

Chemically Dependent Anonymous. Severna Park, MD: C.D.A. Communications, Inc. General Service Office, 1990.

Narcotics Anonymous (NA)

www.na.org

Narcotics Anonymous, 6th ed. Chatsworth, CA: Narcotics Anonymous World Services, Inc., 2008.

Nar-Anon

(for people who have been affected by someone's chemical addiction)

www.nar-anon.org

Conyers, Beverly. *Everything Changes: Help for Families of Newly Recovering Addicts*. Center City, MN: The Hazelden Foundation, 2009.

Sex and Love Addicts Anonymous (SLAA)

www.slaafws.org

Sex and Love Addicts Anonymous: The Basic Text for the Augustine Fellowship. The Augustine Fellowship, 1986.

Inner Child Work

Bradshaw, John. *Healing the Shame That Binds You*. Deerfield Beach, FL: Health Communications, Inc., 2005.

_____ . *Homecoming: Reclaiming and Championing Your Inner Child*. New York: Bantam Books, 1992.

Miller, Alice. *The Drama of the Gifted Child: The Search for the True Self*. New York: Basic Books, 2008.

Taylor, Cathryn L. *The Inner Child Workbook: What to Do With Your Past When It Just Won't Go Away*. New York: Penguin Putnam Inc., 1991.

Whitfield, Charles L., M.D. *Healing the Child Within: Discovery and Recovery for Adult Children of Dysfunctional Families*. Deerfield Beach, FL: Health Communications, Inc., 1987.

_____ . *A Gift to Myself: A Personal Workbook and Guide to "Healing the Child Within."* Deerfield Beach, FL: Health Communications, Inc., 1990.

Wyman, Pat. *Three Keys to Self-Understanding: An Innovative and Effective Combination of the Myers-Briggs Type Indicator Assessment Tool, the Enneagram, and Inner-Child Healing*. Gainesville, FL: Center for Application of Psychological Type, Inc., 2001.

Life Should Be Fair/Hope

Frankl, Viktor E. *Man's Search for Meaning, rev.* New York: Pocket Books, 2006.

Hay, Louise L. *You Can Heal Your Life*. Carlsbad, CA: Hay House, Inc., 1999.

Kushner, Harold S. *When Bad Things Happen to Good People*. New York: Anchor Books, 2004.

Pelzer, Dave. *Help Yourself: A 3-Step Plan for Turning Adversity into Triumph*. New York: Penguin Group, 2000.

Sharot, Tali. *The Optimism Bias: A Tour of the Irrationally Positive Brain*. Vintage, 2012.

Stephens, Deborah Collins, Jackie Speier, Michealine Cristini Risley, and Jan Yanehiro. *This Is Not the Life I Ordered: 50 Ways to Keep Your Head Above Water When Life Keeps Dragging You Down*. San Francisco: Conari Press, 2007.

Viorst, Judith. *Necessary Losses: The Loves, Illusions, Dependencies, and Impossible Expectations That All of Us Have to Give Up in Order to Grow*. New York: Free Press, 1998.

Depression

Larson, Joan Matthews, Ph.D. *Depression-Free, Naturally: 7 Weeks to Eliminating Anxiety, Despair, Fatigue, and Anger from Your Life*. New York: The Ballantine Publishing Group, 1999.

Bloomfield, Howard H., M.D. and Peter McWilliams. *How to Heal Depression*. Del Mar, CA: Prelude Press, 2001.

Huber, Cheryl and June Shiver. *The Depression Book: Depression as an Opportunity for Spiritual Growth*, rev. ed. Chicago: Keep It Simple Books, 2004.

O'Brien, Sharon. *The Family Silver: A Memoir of Depression and Inheritance*. Chicago: University of Chicago Press, 2004.

Weintraub, Amy. *Yoga for Depression: A Compassionate Guide to Relieve Suffering Through Yoga*. New York: Broadway Books, 2004.

Williams, Mark, John Teasdale, Zindel Segal, and Jon Kabat-Zinn. *The Mindful Way Through Depression: Freeing Yourself from Chronic Unhappiness.* New York: The Guilford Press, 2007.

Bipolar Disorder

Jamison, Kay Redfield. *An Unquiet Mind: A Memoir of Moods and Madness.* New York: Vintage Books, 1995.

Miklowitz, David J. *The Bipolar Disorder Survival Guide: What You and Your Family Need to Know, 2nd ed.* New York: The Guildford Press, 2011.

Suicide

Jamison, Kay Redfield. *Night Falls Fast: Understanding Suicide.* New York: Vintage Books, 2000.

Anxiety

Bourne, Edmund J. *The Anxiety and Phobia Workbook.* Oakland, CA: New Harbinger Publications, 2010.

Davis, Martha, Ph.D., Elizabeth Robbins Eshelman, M.S.W., and Matthew McKay, Ph.D. *The Relaxation and Stress Reduction Workbook, 6th ed.* Oakland, CA: New Harbinger Publications, 2008.

Nicholson, L.A. *What Doesn't Kill Us: My Battle with Anxiety.* CreateSpace, 2011.

Alcoholism/Addiction

Carnes, Patrick, Ph.D. *A Gentle Path through the Twelve Steps: The Classic Guide for All People in the Process of Recovery, 3rd ed.* Center City, MN: The Hazelden Foundation, 2012.

Iliff, Brenda. *A Woman's Guide to Recovery.* Center City, MN: The Hazelden Foundation, 2008.

Cognitive Behavioral Therapy

Greenberger, Dennis, PhD and Christine A. Padesky, PhD. *Mind Over Mood: Change How You Feel by Changing the Way You Think.* New York: Guilford Press, 1995.

McKay, Matthew, Ph.D. and Patrick Fanning. *Self-Esteem: A Proven Program of Cognitive Techniques for Assessing, Improving, and Maintaining Your Self-Esteem. 3rd ed.* Oakland, CA: New Harbinger Publications, 2000.

Schiraldi, Glenn R., Ph.D. *The Self-Esteem Workbook.* Oakland, CA: New Harbinger Publications, 2001.

Narrative Therapy

Loehr, Jim. *The Power of Story: Change Your Story, Change Your Destiny in Business and in Life.* New York: Free Press, 2008.

Mindfulness/Meditation

Kabat-Zinn, Jon. *Mindfulness for Beginners: Reclaiming the Present Moment--and Your Life.* Boulder, CO: Sounds True, 2012.

Levine, Stephen. *Guided Meditations, Explorations and Healings.* New York: Anchor Books, 1991.

Nepo, Mark. *The Book of Awakening: Having the Life You Want By Being Present to the Life You Have.* York Beach, ME: Conari Press, 2000.

Salzberg, Sharon. *Loving-Kindness: The Revolutionary Art of Happiness.* Boston: Shambhala, 1995.

EFT

Craig, Gary. *The EFT Manual, 2nd ed.* Santa Rosa, CA: Energy Psychology Press, 2011.

Yates, Brad. *The Wizard's Wish: Or, How He Made the Yuckies Go Away – A Story About the Magic in You.* CreateSpace, 2010.

Acupuncture/Chinese Medicine

Beinfield, Harriet, L. Ac. and Efrem Korngold, L.Ac., O.M.D. *Between Heaven and Earth: A Guide to Chinese Medicine.* New York: Ballantine Wellspring, 1991.

Holland, Alex, M.Ac., L.Ac. *Voices of Qi: An Introductory Guide to Traditional Chinese Medicine.* Berkeley, CA: North Atlantic Books, 2000.

Yoga

Chopra, Deepak, MD and David Simon, MD. *The Seven Spiritual Laws of Yoga: A Practical Guide to Healing Body, Mind, and Spirit.* Hoboken, NJ: John Wiley & Sons, Inc., 2004.

Feuerstein, Georg, Ph.D. and Larry Payne, Ph.D. *Yoga for Dummies, 2nd ed.* Hoboken, NJ: Wiley Publishing, 2010.

Gates, Rolf and Katrina Kenison. *Meditations from the Mat: Daily Reflections on the Path of Yoga.* New York: Anchor Books, 2002.

Willis, Jennifer Schwamm (ed.), *The Joy of Yoga: How Yoga Can Revitalize Your Body and Spirit and Change the Way You Live.* New York: Marlowe & Company, 2002.

Journaling

Grason, Sandy. *Journalution: Journaling to Awaken Your Inner Voice, Heal Your Life and Manifest Your Dreams.* Novato, CA: New World Library, 2005.

Dream work

Johnson, Robert A. *Inner Work: Using Dreams and Active Imagination for Personal Growth.* New York: Harper & Row, 1989.

Law of Attraction

Losier, Michael. *The Law of Attraction: The Science of Attracting More of What You Want and Less of What You Don't.* New York: Wellness Central, 2006.

MBTI ® (Myers-Briggs Type Indicator®)

Baron, Renee. *What Type Am I?: Discover Who You Really Are.* New York: Penguin Books, 1998.

Delunas, Eve, PhD. *Survival Games Personalities Play.* Carmel, CA: Sunink Publications, 1992.

Keirsey, David. *Please Understand Me II: Temperament, Character, Intelligence.* San Diego, CA: Prometheus Nemesis Book Company, 1998.

Myers, Isabel Briggs with Peter B. Myers. *Gifts Differing: Understanding Personality Type*. Palo Alto, CA: Davies-Black Publishing, 1995.

Pearman, Roger R. and Sarah C. Albritton. *I'm Not Crazy, I'm Just Not You: The Real Meaning of the Sixteen Personality Types*. Palo Alto, CA: Davies-Black Publishing, 1997.

Quenk, Naomi L. *Beside Ourselves: Our Hidden Personality in Everyday Life*. Palo Alto, CA: Davies-Black Publishing, 1993.

Thomson, Lenore. *Personality Type: An Owner's Manual*. Boston: Shambhala Publications, 1998.

Tieger, Paul D. and Barbara Barron-Tieger. *Do What You Are: Discover the Perfect Career for You Through the Secrets of Personality Type 4th ed.* New York: Little, Brown and Company, 2007.

_____. *Nurture By Nature: Understand Your Child's Personality Type—And Become a Better Parent*. Boston: Little, Brown and Company, 1997.

Enneagram

Baron, Renee and Elizabeth Wagele. *The Enneagram Made Easy: Discover the 9 Types of People*. New York: HarperCollins Publishers, 1994.

Daniels, David and Virginia Price. *The Essential Enneagram: The Definitive Personality Test and Self-Discovery Guide—Revised and Updated*. New York: HarperOne, 2009.

Palmer, Helen. *The Enneagram: Understanding Yourself and the Others in Your Life*. New York: HarperCollins, 1998.

Riso, Don Richard and Russ Hudson. *The Wisdom of the Enneagram: The Complete Guide to Psychological and Spiritual Growth for the Nine Personality Types*. New York: Bantam Books, 1999.

Imago Relationship Therapy

Hendrix, Harville, Ph.D. *Getting the Love You Want: A Guide for Couples, 20th Anniversary Edition.* New York: Henry Hold and Company, LLC, 2008.

Psychodrama

Stolinsky, Stefanie Auerbach, Ph.D. *Act It Out: 25 Expressive Ways to Heal from Childhood Abuse.* Oakland, CA: New Harbinger Publications, Inc., 2002.

Sandtray Therapy

Livingstone, Bob. *Redemption of the Shattered: A Teenager's Healing Journey Through Sandtray Therapy.* San Mateo, CA: Bob Livingstone LCSW, 2002.

The Serenity Prayer

Flanagan, Eileen. *The Wisdom to Know the Difference: When to Make a Change—And When to Let Go.* New York: Penguin Publishing, 2009.

Made in the USA
Middletown, DE
24 December 2016